Blessings
Deborah Newman

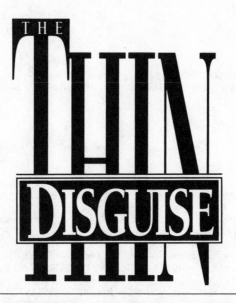

THE THIN DISGUISE

OVERCOMING AND UNDERSTANDING ANOREXIA AND BULIMIA

Pam Vredevelt,
Dr. Deborah Newman,
Harry Beverly,
Dr. Frank Minirth

A
JANET
THOMA
BOOK

THOMAS NELSON PUBLISHERS
NASHVILLE

For general information about other Minirth-Meier Clinic branch offices, counseling services, educational resources and hospital programs, call toll-free 1-800-545-1819.

National Headquarters:
(214) 669-1733   (800) 229-3000

Published in Nashville, Tennessee, by Thomas Nelson, Inc., and distributed in Canada by Lawson Falle, Ltd., Cambridge, Ontario.

Unless otherwise noted, Scripture quotations are from the NEW KING JAMES VERSION of the Bible. Copyright © 1979, 1980, 1982, Thomas Nelson, Inc., Publishers.
Scripture quotations noted NIV are from The Holy Bible: NEW INTERNATIONAL VERSION. Copyright © 1978 by the New York International Bible Society. Used by permission of Zondervan Bible Publishers.
Scripture quotations noted AMPLIFIED are from THE AMPLIFIED BIBLE: Old Testament. Copyright © 1962, 1964 by Zondervan Publishing House (used by permission); and from THE AMPLIFIED NEW TESTAMENT. Copyright © 1958 by the Lockman Foundation (used by permission).
Scripture quotations noted NASB are from THE NEW AMERICAN STANDARD BIBLE. Copyright © 1960, 1962, 1963, 1968, 1971, 1972, 1973, 1975, 1977 by The Lockman Foundation and are used by permission.

Library of Congress Cataloging-in-Publication Data

The Thin disguise : understanding and overcoming anorexia and bulimia
/ Pam Vredevelt . . . [et al.].
    p.   cm.
    Includes bibliographical references.
    ISBN 0-8407-7715-9
    1. Anorexia nervosa. 2. Bulimia. 3. Eating disorders—Religious aspects—Christianity. I. Vredevelt, Pam W., 1955–
RC552.E18T45 1992
616.85 ′26—dc20   92–15471
                                            CIP

Printed in the United States of America

1 2 3 4 5 — 96 95 94 93 92

ACKNOWLEDGMENTS

Together, the authors wish to thank Kathi Mills, a gifted writer, who skillfully combined the ideas and illustrations of four different authors into a readable, enjoyable form.

We are also grateful for our editor, Janet Thoma. Janet doesn't have her name on a book she hasn't labored over. She has been our inspiration and guide along a journey she has taken hundreds of times, but somehow she has remained fresh and patient with the new kids on the block.

We thank Susan Salmon, Laurie Clark, and all the other folks at Thomas Nelson for their commitment to excellence. Susan and Laurie are wonderful at finalizing details and keeping everyone on their deadlines.

Many thanks to Laura Bertzyk, for the expertise and professionalism she brings to our ED unit as an RDLD and for her guidance through the chapters in this book on healthy eating.

To Adair, Bess, Craig, Donna, Dora, Elizabeth, Frank, Jerry, Julie, Kevan, Kima, Linda, Louise, Marie, Marilyn, and Pauline—the nurses and MHT's at NTMC Westpark Hospital—thank you for enriching our program and making possible what we do on the Eating Disorder Unit. And to Marty Whitsell (LVN), thank you for your enduring work and commitment to those suffering with eating disorders on our unit and for your assistance in group therapy.

We'd each like to thank our families:

To John, for your loving support and encouragement.

Pam

To Brian, Rachel, and Benjamin, for your love and support.

Debi

To Laura, Kristen, and Kyle, for sacrificing to allow me the opportunity to be a part of this book. I love you.

Harry

To Mary Alice, Rachel, Renee, Carrie, and Alicia, for your patience and graciousness.

Frank

Finally, we extend a special thanks to all those on the road of recovery at the ED clinic and at Christian Counseling Services who have been willing to share their lives with others and who have graciously allowed us to be a part of their healing process as they have stepped out from behind the thin disguise.

CONTENTS

PART ONE: **BEGINNING THE SEARCH FOR ANSWERS**

1. What Is an Eating Disorder?   3
2. What Are the Symptoms?   16
3. What Happens to My Body?   33
4. What Keeps the Cycle Going?   48

PART TWO: **THE PATHWAY TO RECOVERY**

5. Breaking the Cycle of Secrecy   69
6. A Family Affair   81
7. Unveiling the Masks   99
8. The Pain of Perfectionism   121
9. Feeling Free   135
10. Sexuality and Shame   151
11. Saying Good-Bye to the Losses   166
12. Establishing Healthy Eating Patterns   173
13. I Like the Way I Look   189
14. Setting Up a Support System   201
15. Healthy Eating for Life   209
16. A Word to Loved Ones   227
17. One Final Word   242

APPENDICES

1. Food Exchange Lists   249
2. Seven-Day Meal Plan   262
3. Exchange Lists for Meal Planning   269
4. Thought Records   272
5. Daily Food Planners   273
6. Organizations   275
   Notes   277

PART ONE

BEGINNING THE SEARCH FOR ANSWERS

1

WHAT IS AN EATING DISORDER?

The emaciated sixteen-year-old girl stood between her mother and father, nervously twisting a long strand of dull, coarse brown hair between her thin fingers. The fear in her dark eyes was evident. It was obvious that Cindy Briscoe's parents were much more in favor of the upcoming session with Harry Beverly, director of the eating disorder unit of the Minirth-Meier Clinic in Dallas, than was Cindy. Harry introduced himself to her parents, Jack and Christine Briscoe, and then to Cindy, who nodded briefly but did not answer. Harry couldn't help noticing her jaws twitch as he spoke to her.

"Will you excuse us for a moment?" asked Cindy's mother. "Cindy and I need to discuss something privately." With her hand firmly on her daughter's elbow, Christine Briscoe steered Cindy to the far corner of the lobby. Harry couldn't hear what they were saying, but he observed that Christine was doing most of the talking. They were back within minutes.

"Cindy's ready to see you now," Christine announced. "Aren't you, dear?"

Cindy's eyes widened with panic, and she turned from her mother to look pleadingly at her father. Jack Briscoe smiled but said nothing. Defeat replaced the panic on Cindy's face as her gaze dropped to the floor. Her bony shoulders sagged under her oversized turtleneck sweater.

"I guess so," she mumbled.

Once inside his office, Harry and Cindy began to talk.

"Why are you here, Cindy?" Harry asked.

"My parents think I have a problem with . . . they think I'm too thin," she answered.

"Do you think you're too thin?"

Cindy shook her head. "No," she said. "I'm not."

Harry went on. "What would you think about gaining fifteen pounds?"

Cindy's face froze. "Oh no," she declared. "I could never do that."

"What do you suppose a girl your age and height should weigh?" Harry probed gently.

Cindy shrugged. "Oh, I don't know. Maybe 115, 120."

"And how much do you weigh, Cindy?"

"Eighty-four pounds."

"That's quite a bit of difference," Harry remarked. "Why do you suppose that is?"

"I don't know," said Cindy. "I'm just comfortable this way, that's all. Pretty much, anyway."

"Pretty much?" said Harry. "You mean eighty-four pounds is not what you consider the ideal weight for you?"

Cindy shook her head again. "No," she said. "I would like very much to get down below eighty pounds. That would be ideal for me."

Harry knew Cindy would never be happy with her weight. Cindy was anorexic. Her parents wanted her to step out from the thin disguise, the eating disorder that caused her to see herself through distorted eyes. That's also why Marian Grier came to the clinic, although her eating disorder was different from Cindy's.

Marian, a stunning blonde with bright blue eyes, first approached Pam Vredevelt, who is director of Christian Counseling

Services in Portland, Oregon, at the close of a seminar Pam had given at a local athletic club. Immaculately dressed, the woman looked as if she modeled for *Vogue* magazine. She asked Pam if she had a minute to listen.

The checkered history of her life seemed to focus on one complaint: "I want so much to be the best at everything I do. I need to feel like I'm really excelling or else life isn't worth living. Everyone is drawn to winners, but it's hard to win all the time and to always be the best."

Marian Grier, a thirty-seven-year-old wife and mother of four, was a Vanderbilt graduate with a 4.0 GPA. A part-time legal secretary at a prestigious law firm in downtown Portland, Marian had all the appearances of a happy, successful life. Pam, however, sensed something more.

"Have you been struggling with an eating disorder?" Pam asked.

Marian flinched, looked down at the floor, and nodded hesitantly.

Pam continued. "Can you tell me about it?"

Marian lifted her head slightly. "I never intended for it to go this far," she said, her voice barely above a whisper. "It started in college, maybe once a week or so. I'd binge on chocolates and sweets, then vomit to get rid of the extra calories. But it got worse—so much worse!"

Her shoulders heaved as tears spilled over onto her cheeks. "I feel so trapped! I can't quit, and I'm scared it's going to end up killing me. I don't know what to do. I've done everything I know to stop, but I'm hooked."

Marian was tired of wearing the thin disguise. Pam sensed that Marian wanted to talk further so she suggested that they sit down together in an empty conference room. At first Pam led the conversation toward Marian's job and family to put her at ease and learn more about her. Then she addressed Marian's bulimia. "You said your bulimia started in college," Pam said as she looked directly into Marian's eyes. "How?"

Marian's eyes darted nervously around the empty room, as if checking to be sure she wouldn't be overheard.

"I was about twenty," she confessed. "I wore a size twelve then. One evening I was sitting around the dinner table with some friends in the college cafeteria, and somehow we got on to the subject of dress size. We were comparing facts and figures when it dawned on me that I wore the largest size. I remember swallowing that last bite of dessert with tremendous guilt and thinking, *I've got to find a way to shrink.*

"The next day I found my escape. It was a sorority tradition to go out for pizza at ten every Thursday night. Six of us devoured three giant pizzas in less than thirty minutes. A sorority sister who was sitting across from me stood up to go to the women's room and mumbled, 'I've got to get rid of this.' I was confused by her statement but passed it off. Then I decided to use the restroom before leaving. As I pushed open the swinging door, I heard someone heaving in the first stall. I was just about to knock and ask if I could do anything to help when my sorority sister walked out. With a sigh of relief she said, 'I feel so much better now.'

"I had always wondered how she could eat like a horse and keep her petite figure. Now I knew. I can't tell you how excited I got thinking about this great solution! I could eat whatever I wanted and leave my size twelves in the past."

"And so you started bingeing and purging," Pam interjected.

Marian shook her head yes. Then she lowered her eyes and stared at the floor.

Marian Grier was bulimic. Both she and Cindy suffered from eating disorders.

WHAT IS AN EATING DISORDER?

To the uninformed, an eating disorder is something that people should just "snap out of."

To the curious, an eating disorder afflicts only people who are neurotic.

To some Christians, an eating disorder is something that happens to non-Christians.

To most people, an eating disorder is confusing—and we'd rather not think about it.

But to those with anorexia nervosa or bulimia, an eating disorder is a life-threatening problem. The sight of food assaults the senses and unleashes a flood of memories of failure, pain, and conflict. It is a reminder of shattering defeats and triggers doubts about the person's competency to gain control of life. Sometimes this compulsive behavior can lead to death.

Both anorexia nervosa and bulimia are characterized by a compulsive urge to control weight. Very simply, *anorexia nervosa is self-induced starvation resulting in extreme weight loss. Bulimia is a pattern of bingeing (eating large amounts of food) followed by self-induced vomiting and/or laxative abuse—with or without weight loss.*

HOW BAD IS THE PROBLEM?

Some years ago a television documentary focused on a teenager named Carrie who was hooked into a destructive lifestyle of self-starvation. The final scene showed Carrie's parents standing arm in arm over her grave site. They were stunned. Their fifteen-year-old daughter had gone from 120 pounds to 70 pounds in just five months. Her energetic body had been reduced to bone and organs functioning solely by life-support systems . . . and now she was dead—all for the sake of thinness.

Another highly publicized case of anorexia was that of musician Karen Carpenter. On February 4, 1983, while searching her closet for something to wear for the day, Karen collapsed to the floor. Paramedics anxiously administered help, but she went into cardiac arrest. Despite the continuous efforts of professionals to resuscitate her, Karen was pronounced dead at the hospital. Dead at thirty-two! Another victim of anorexia nervosa.

Carrie and Karen are not the only people who have been entangled in the chains of this disease. Experts now estimate that one of every one hundred women between the ages of twelve and twenty-five suffers from anorexia, while one of every seven women in the same age group develops bulimia. Although men can also fall victim to these eating disorders, the occurrence is much less frequent; only about 10 percent of all anorexics or bulimics are men.[1]

These findings are based on documented cases. Medical professionals feel safe in assuming that there are at least as many more "in the closet" victims as there are those who are seeking professional help.

Consider these additional facts:

- Today more than 50 percent of American girls have been on a reducing diet before completing adolescence.[2]
- Sixty percent of all models and ballerinas have eating disorders.[3]
- Experts predict that 1 to 3 percent of the female population will have anorexia or bulimia at one time in their lives.
- A high incidence of eating disorders is found among serious athletes. Dr. Charles Tipton, professor in the Department of Physical Education, Physiology, and Biophysics at the University of Iowa, says that in a study of 582 wrestlers who were certified for competition, he found that on the average seven to eight pounds were lost the day prior to a match: "The weight slash came as a result of rigid exercise, strict food deprivation, fluid restriction, and exercising in a hot environment. Dehydration is by far the quickest and probably the most frequently used method of weight loss. Food deprivation is second."[4] Gymnasts also represent a large number of young people with eating disorders. When she was only sixteen years old, Olympic medalist Cathy Rigby began bingeing and purging to keep her weight down for gymnastic competition. The habit lasted for the next twelve years.[5]

As you can see, eating disorders are common, especially among young people.

[handwritten margin note: how are these facts changed?]

WHEN DOES AN EATING DISORDER BEGIN?

Although eating disorders can begin later in life, most often the problem begins to manifest itself in the adolescent or teen years. Cindy was twelve when she first acted out her anorexic tendencies. Yet the underlying problems began in her childhood. As a toddler, Cindy seemed to have a relatively happy home life. But the older she got, the more her mother's resentment built toward her. Throughout her adolescence, the pressures from her mother's anger, her father's emotional absence, and her many unmet needs built to an intolerable level.

At the same time, she was aware that her body was changing. She was beginning to develop a woman's body, with hips and breasts—like her mother's. Cindy thought that her mother was fat, that her hips were definitely too large. She feared that she would end up looking just like her. And so she began to restrict her food intake. Marian Grier's bulimia began in college when she saw her sorority sister binge, then purge.

Anorexia nervosa and bulimia are life-threatening compulsions. If you or someone you love is anorexic or bulimic, you need to get help as soon as possible. To gain further insight, you may wish to fill out the Dying to Be Thin Questionnaire. It is not intended to be a diagnostic assessment, but it can help you identify the severity of your anorexic or bulimic tendencies or those of someone you love.

DYING TO BE THIN QUESTIONNAIRE

Answer the following questions honestly. Write the number of your answer in the space at the left. (If you are taking this quiz for someone you love, obviously that person will become the "I" in the statements.)

_____ 1. I have eating habits that are different from those of my family and friends.
1) Often   2) Sometimes   3) Rarely   4) Never

_____ 2. I find myself panicking for fear of gaining weight if I cannot exercise as I planned.
1) Almost always   2) Sometimes   3) Rarely
4) Never

_____ 3. My friends tell me I am thin, but I don't believe them because I feel fat.
1) Often   2) Sometimes   3) Rarely   4) Never

_____ 4. My menstrual period has ceased or become irregular due to no known medical reasons.
1) True   2) False

_____ 5. I have become obsessed with food to the point that I cannot go through a day without worrying about what I will or will not eat.
1) Almost always   2) Sometimes   3) Rarely
4) Never

_____ 6. I have lost more than 25 percent of the normal weight for my height. (For example, you weigh 120 lbs. and lose 30 lbs.)
1) True   2) False

_____ 7. I would panic if I got on the scale and found I had gained two pounds.
1) Almost always   2) Sometimes   3) Rarely
4) Never

_____ 8. I find that I prefer to eat alone or when I am sure no one will see me. Then I can make excuses so I can eat less with friends and family.
1) Often   2) Sometimes   3) Rarely   4) Never

_____ 9. I find myself going on uncontrollable eating binges during which I consume large amounts of food to the point that I feel sick and make myself vomit.
1) 3 or more times per day   2) 1–2 times per day
3) 1–2 times per week   4) Rarely   5) Never

_____ 10. I use laxatives as a means of weight control.
   1) On a regular basis   2) Sometimes   3) Rarely
   4) Never

_____ 11. I find myself playing games with food.
   (Example: cutting it up into tiny pieces, hiding food so
   people will think I ate it, chewing it and spitting it out
   without swallowing, or telling myself certain foods are
   bad.)
   1) Often   2) Sometimes   3) Rarely   4) Never

_____ 12. People around me have become very interested in what
   I eat, and I find myself getting angry at them for pushing food on me.
   1) Often   2) Sometimes   3) Rarely   4) Never

_____ 13. I have felt more depressed and irritable than I used to,
   and/or have been spending increasing amounts of time
   alone.
   1) True   2) False

_____ 14. I keep a lot of my fears about food and eating to myself
   because I am afraid no one would understand.
   1) Often   2) Sometimes   3) Rarely   4) Never

_____ 15. I enjoy making gourmet, high-calorie meals or treats
   for others as long as I don't have to eat any myself.
   1) Often   2) Sometimes   3) Rarely   4) Never

_____ 16. The most powerful fear in my life is the fear of gaining
   weight or becoming fat.
   1) Often   2) Sometimes   3) Rarely   4) Never

_____ 17. I find myself totally absorbed when reading books
   about dieting, exercising, and calorie counting to the
   point that I spend hours studying them.
   1) Often   2) Sometimes   3) Rarely   4) Never

_____ 18. I tend to be a perfectionist and am not satisfied with
   myself unless I do things perfectly.
   1) Almost always   2) Sometimes   3) Rarely
   4) Never

_____ 19. I go through long periods of time without eating anything (fasting) as a means of weight control.
1) Often   2) Sometimes   3) Rarely   4) Never
_____ 20. It is important to me to try to be thinner than all of my friends.
1) Almost always   2) Sometimes   3) Rarely
4) Never

Add your score together and compare with the table below:
Under 30—Strong tendencies toward anorexia nervosa
30–45—Strong tendencies toward bulimia
45–55—Weight conscious, not necessarily with anorexic or bulimic tendencies
Over 55—No need for concern[6]

If you or someone you love scored below 45, seek more information about anorexia and bulimia and also contact a counselor or physician to determine what kind of assistance would be most helpful. Anorexia nervosa and bulimia can be overcome with the proper support and counsel. The earlier you seek help, the better, although it is never too late to start on the road to recovery.

THE ROAD TO RECOVERY

Our book attempts to extend a lifeline to persons with eating disorders. It is not intended to be a substitute for professional help. Instead, it is intended to offer tools to those who are suffering. It is designed to turn on a light for those who are "in the closet" and to give assurance that the battle can be won. It is written to give information and support to the family and friends of those who struggle. They, too, encounter difficult challenges. And finally, it is written for the professional counselor as a resource for clients who desire to use both psychological and biblical tools in the process of restoration.

This book is the unique collaboration of two different clinics, the Minirth-Meier Clinic, a nationally known clinic with nineteen offices in various cities in the United States, and the Christian Counseling Services in Portland, Oregon. Each author specializes in the treatment of eating disorders. Harry Beverly is director of the Minirth-Meier inpatient eating disorder unit at Westpark Hospital in Dallas, Texas. Dr. Deborah Newman is a licensed professional counselor who specializes in eating disorders with the inpatient and outpatient units of the Minirth-Meier Clinic in Dallas. Pam Vredevelt is also a licensed professional counselor who specializes in the treatment of eating disorders, codependency, and sexual abuse; she is director of Christian Counseling Services in Portland, Oregon. Most of her work with patients is done on an outpatient basis, so our combined counseling experiences include extensive work with patients who have serious eating disorders and those whose problems are less severe. Finally, Dr. Frank Minirth, cofounder of the Minirth-Meier Clinics and a diplomate of the American Board of Psychiatry and Neurology, provides the medical information necessary to recover from an eating disorder.

In Part One you will read about some factors that contribute to anorexic and bulimic behavior. In Chapter 2 we will look at the type of emotional and behavioral symptoms we diagnosed in Cindy and Marian. As we do so, you will want to think about your own symptoms or those of someone you love. In Chapter 3 we will tell you about the physical effects of these eating disorders, which, as we have said, may be life-threatening. Then in Chapter 4 we will examine the addiction cycle, which keeps persons locked into their eating disorders.

In Part Two we will walk you through the process of recovery we use with our patients. We will begin by helping you overcome your tendency to deny your eating disorder. Then we will investigate your other areas of denial. In most cases, anorexics and bulimics come from dysfunctional families; yet they deny problems in the family of origin. We will help you to identify these problems in Chapter 6 and to see the masks you wear in your relationships with people in Chapter 7. Persons with eating disorders also have a deep need to appear perfect to others; Chapter 8 will discuss the pain of perfectionism. And, for years, they have denied themselves the right to "feel." Feelings have been suppressed so long that those with eating disorders have extreme difficulty identifying or expressing their feelings. We will help you to do so in Chapter 9. Unfortunately, sexuality is often confused with shame by people with eating disorders; we will help you to see your sexuality as an essential part of your femininity in Chapter 10 and then say good-bye to all the losses resulting from your eating disorder in Chapter 11.

We will look at some nutritional changes to reverse the physical deterioration from starving and bingeing in Chapter 12. Our guest expert in this area is Laura Bertzyk, who is a registered dietitian at the Westpark Hospital and counsels with patients, like Cindy Briscoe, who are admitted to the Minirth-Meier unit there. You will read stories that have evolved in sessions with some of our other clients; they have graciously permitted you a peek into the private areas of their lives. Although details have been changed to provide anonymity, you will sense their pain. You will see that they are individuals much like you . . . with jobs, families, and church and social involvements. You will also feel their joy and wonder in new beginnings and sense their newfound freedom. Finally, in Chapter 16 we will talk directly to the family and friends of those who have eating disorders. They can help their loved ones and themselves by understanding the part they play in the patient's recovery.

Perhaps you will find stories similar to your own experiences as you read this book. Be encouraged to face head-on whatever surfaces. One way to do that is to record your thoughts, feelings, and insights concerning your disorder in a notebook. You may want to call it your Personal Growth Notebook. As you read, keep your notebook handy so that you can use it to answer questions, take notes, or express your innermost thoughts. Seeing your thoughts and feelings on paper can be enlightening. Your perspectives will become clearer, and you will also have a concrete point of reference from which to evaluate your growth.

Cindy Briscoe overcame the emotional and physical bondage of the thin disguise. She is no longer an emaciated sixteen-year-old but a lovely high school graduate looking forward to a career and marriage. Marian Grier also shed her thin disguise. She no longer binges and purges to cope with pain. Today, marriage brings her joy, and a sense of peace resides within. We know that you, too, can free yourself (or someone you love) from this bondage. Let's make the journey to recovery together.

2

WHAT ARE
THE SYMPTOMS?

Friend. Adviser. Sympathetic listener. Clients often describe their counselors in one of these ways. Counselors are also diagnosticians, since counseling is partly a fact-finding process. When we first interview those with eating disorders, we ask them certain questions. The answers tell us if the individual is anorexic or bulimic and if inpatient hospitalization or outpatient counseling is needed. That's the process Harry Beverly followed as he met with Cindy Briscoe the day she came to the clinic.

As we reinact some of that session, think about yourself or someone you love. Are these common symptoms characteristic of you or a loved one? After we consider Harry's interview with Cindy, who is anorexic, we will listen in as Debi Newman talks with Tina Morgan, who is bulimic. Both are eating disorders, but the symptoms are usually different.

WHAT ARE THE SYMPTOMS OF ANOREXIA NERVOSA?

After Harry's initial comments, he asked Cindy, "You told me that you are hoping to get your weight to less than 80 pounds. Yet you also said that you thought an ideal weight for someone of your age and approximate height was 115 to 120 pounds. Why do you suppose there is so much difference between what you would like to weigh and what you think of as the ideal weight?"

Cindy looked down at her arms. "I'm small boned, I guess. Look at how fat I am at eighty-four pounds!" She pulled the sleeve of her sweater up so Harry could see her forearm, which was so thin her wrist bone stuck out like a rock on a sandy beach.

The first symptom of anorexia nervosa is that the person thinks, *I'm much too fat,* even when emaciated. Most anorexics want to stay under one hundred pounds; we say they don't like three-digit numbers. We often ask them, "How much weight do you want to lose?" Most of them will reply, "I don't know."

"Well, just dream with us for a while," we'll say. "Tell us, if you could get down to an ideal weight, what would that be?"

People will often cite a goal weight, but that ideal weight will continually shift downward. When the person reaches 85 pounds, the ideal weight becomes 80. Once the magic 80 is obtained, it's lowered to 75. We believe that any weight lower than 75 percent of the ideal body weight for that person's height is symptomatic of anorexic nervosa (see the weight chart on page 18 to determine if you or someone you love is below that level).

Somehow when Cindy looked at her extended forearm that day in Harry's office, she didn't see the protruded wrist bone or the way her hand seemed to overpower her arm. So Harry pressed her a little further. "When I look at your hand there, it seems to be much too big for your arm. Don't you really think your arms are very thin?"

Cindy didn't answer. She just stared at her outstretched arm.

Anorexics' heads, hands, and feet appear too big for their bodies. They can restrict food enough to lose dramatic amounts of body weight, but it is impossible to change the size of their head, hands, and feet. Often they admit that their friends have told them that. In fact, many wear big sweaters, as Cindy Briscoe did, and other bulky clothes to make themselves look bigger than they actually are—and to keep themselves warm.

DESIRABLE WEIGHTS FOR ADULTS

Men

HEIGHT		SMALL FRAME	MEDIUM FRAME	LARGE FRAME
Feet	Inches			
5	2	128–134	131–141	135–150
5	3	130–136	133–143	140–153
5	4	132–138	135–145	142–158
5	5	134–140	137–148	144–160
5	6	136–142	139–151	146–164
5	7	138–145	142–154	149–168
5	8	140–148	145–157	152–172
5	9	142–151	148–160	155–178
5	10	144–154	151–163	158–180
5	11	146–157	154–166	161–184
6	0	149–160	157–170	164–188
6	1	152–164	160–174	168–192
6	2	155–168	164–178	172–197
6	3	158–172	167–182	176–202
6	4	162–178	171–187	181–207

Weights at ages 25–59 based on lowest mortality. Weight in pounds according to frame (in indoor clothing weighing five lbs., shoes with one-inch heels).

Women

HEIGHT		SMALL FRAME	MEDIUM FRAME	LARGE FRAME
Feet	Inches			
4	10	102–111	109–121	118–131
4	11	103–113	111–123	120–134
5	0	104–115	113–126	122–137
5	1	106–118	115–129	125–140
5	2	108–121	118–132	128–143
5	3	111–124	121–135	131–147
5	4	114–127	124–138	134–151
5	5	117–130	127–141	137–155
5	6	120–133	130–144	140–159
5	7	123–136	133–147	143–163
5	8	126–139	138–150	146–167
5	9	129–142	139–153	149–170
5	10	132–145	142–156	152–173
5	11	135–148	145–159	155–176
6	0	138–151	148–162	158–179

Weights at ages 25–59 based on lowest mortality. Weight in pounds according to frame (in indoor clothing weighing three lbs., shoes with one-inch heels).

Source: The Metropolitan Life Insurance Co.

Cindy never answered Harry's inquiry about her pencil-thin arms so he rephrased it. "Why do you want to look so thin?"

"Well, I like that thin look," she began. "And I like the feeling of my stomach being empty. When I eat too much, I feel bloated and sick at my stomach. I feel good when my stomach is empty."

"How do you keep your stomach empty so you will feel that way?"

"Most of the time I don't eat at all, and when I do eat, I try to get rid of the food."

Voluntary starvation, which often leads to emaciation and sometimes death, is another symptom of anorexia nervosa. Rigid dieting is the sole means of dramatic weight loss. There are no underlying medical reasons, although Cindy would receive a full physical after she was admitted to the hospital to make sure. Anorexics occasionally binge, however, and then they rely on laxatives or self-induced starvation to lose the two or three pounds they have gained.

Often the extent of laxative abuse reveals to us the severity of the patient's illness. At first Cindy told Harry that she took a couple of laxatives a day. Finally, she admitted to sometimes taking fifteen or so.

"Do you use anything else, Cindy?" Harry asked. "Like Dexatrim®?"

"Yes, Dexatrim® keeps me from feeling hungry. Then I don't have to eat for the rest of the day. Most of the time I take Dexatrim® just in case I might feel hungry."

Even though Cindy, as most anorexics, regarded food as an enemy, she had an obsessive interest in recipes and cooking; she was also involved in rituals concerning food, exercise, and other aspects of her life. Cindy told Harry she enjoyed making dinners for her family—trying out new recipes—but she never ate the food. "I'm very careful about calories," she admitted. "In fact, I eat only a muffin or crackers for breakfast." Later in the conversation she also admitted that during the day she would hide M & M's in her purse and pop one or two every so often. It was kind of a ritual for her. If she had to eat a meal with her family or if they all went out to dinner together, she'd starve herself the next day or take laxatives. Another ritual. A lot of anorexics drink fluids to get a sense of being full when they're really not.

Cindy told Harry, "I have a set routine that I stick to every day. Coffee at 7:30 A.M., an orange at noon, and celery and carrots at 6:00 P.M. It really feels good to be able to set my eating goals each morning and then go to bed at night knowing I've accomplished those goals."

She was right. It felt good to set and accomplish goals. But Harry would show her that her goals were destructive, and in the next weeks he would help her reassess them. Healthy goals and routines could be substituted for her unhealthy ones—and the sooner, the better.

Most anorexics have poor self-esteem. They often come from families with high standards; they feel, "If I can perform, if I can take a pound off, I'll feel good about myself." They also are driven by perfectionistic standards.

Excessive exercise is another symptom but usually in the early part of the disease. At first the anorexic (especially a college girl) does a lot of sit-ups, jumping jacks, fast-walking or anything to burn calories. Yet as the disease progresses, the person becomes so weak she cannot exercise.

Finally, Harry Beverly asked Cindy, "Tell me about your best friend."

"Well, Suzy used to be my best friend. But I don't see her much anymore," she replied.

"Why not? Don't you like her anymore?" Harry knew the answer, but he wanted Cindy to say it aloud. Suzy probably hadn't discarded Cindy. Cindy had become so depressed and irritable that she hadn't wanted to be with her friends. Most anorexics talk about their past friends.

Cindy's parents suspected that she needed to be hospitalized. Her answers to the questions verified that. She was obviously depressed. She was taking fifteen laxatives a day, as do most se-

COMMON SYMPTOMS OF
ANOREXIA NERVOSA

1. The person thinks, *I'm much too fat,* even when emaciated.

2. The person voluntarily starves, which often leads to emaciation and sometimes death.

3. The person goes on occasional binges followed by fasting, laxative abuse, or self-induced starvation.

4. The person has an obsessive interest in recipes and cooking.

5. The person observes rituals involving food, exercise, and other aspects of life.

6. The person is perfectionistic.

7. The person has low self-esteem.

8. The person exercises excessively.

9. The person is introverted and withdrawn; she avoids people.

10. The person maintains rigid control.

11. The person is characterized by depression, irritability, deceitfulness, guilt, and self-loathing.

12. Period stops.

verely ill anorexics. They also go through periods in which they faint from abusing these over-the-counter drugs. That's another symptom of concern to us. Cindy admitted to feeling dizzy at times; her parents later told Harry that she fainted several times.

In the next days Harry began talking to Cindy about her reasons—we call them rationalizations—for starving herself.

COMMON REASONS FOR STARVING

When we ask patients, "Why do you starve yourself?" we receive an assortment of answers. If you cannot pinpoint some of the reasons you starve yourself (or if you are concerned about someone you love), you might like to look at what others have noted. As you do, it will become apparent that you are not alone; others feel and think in similar ways.

Today I have to starve. "I ate too much yesterday. I have to starve myself today, or I'll end up looking like a blimp."

Each morning when Cindy got up, she took inventory of the day before. And regardless of what she had eaten, the tape— "Today I have to starve"—played in her head. Yet she would not have looked like a blimp if she had eaten properly that day. Harry challenged her, "Look around you at all the people you know who do not look like blimps. They eat every day. So can you."

Her next reason was an illogical extension of this one.

I deserve to be punished. "I need to beat my body for performing so poorly. I ate so much last night that I have to run twenty miles today and skip meals. It was terrible of me to behave in such a childish way."

Cindy did not need to be punished. She needed to get help and learn how to be kind to herself. Beating her body today for what she saw as her failure yesterday would only compound the problem.

Food is my source of power. "I'm in charge of this area of my life. No one can make me eat. The harder others try to make me eat, the more powerful I feel because I can win."

When Harry first saw Cindy and her mother together, he could see the seesaw for control. This statement, which is typical of most anorexics, did not surprise him. In the days ahead Harry would help Cindy recognize that food is not a source of power. Although she thought she was in charge of this area of her life, in reality her obsession with food was controlling her. She was correct in believing that no one could make her eat. But rather than gaining power by starving, she was handing over her power to her obsession.

They deserve to be punished. "They haven't been fair to me lately. They look at me like I'm not important and like they don't care. If they want to treat me like that, then fine. I can play the game too—I won't eat. That will show them I don't care how they treat me and punish them for being so mean to me."

Cindy's mother tried to dominate her, so it was natural for Cindy to want to separate from her mother and make decisions for herself. But punishing her mother by starving herself would not hurt Mom. It would just hurt Cindy!

That's the pattern we see in the anorexic. The bulimic has different symptoms, which are unique to that eating disorder.

WHAT ARE THE SYMPTOMS OF BULIMIA?

Debi Newman first met Tina Morgan when the attractive twenty-one-year-old college junior came to the emergency room at Westpark Hospital. She looked every bit the part of the healthy, wholesome college girl. From her outward appearance, no one would guess that she had wrestled for years with a potentially deadly eating disorder. Her long black hair was lustrous, and her green eyes sparkled. Her size five figure was the envy of many of her friends.

"I don't know that I should be in the hospital," she said immediately. "I just got scared when I threw up and saw blood in the toilet."

This physical symptom scared Tina into coming to the hospital. Debi suspected that the blood Tina saw in the toilet was a result of the stress on the lining of her stomach or an inflammation of her esophagus from the constant vomiting. (The physical effects of bulimia and anorexia are so extensive that we will look at them in the next chapter.)

"I understand you attend TCU," Debi observed as she began the interview with Tina.

Tina's smile was dazzling. "Yes," she answered, tossing her head slightly as her long black hair cascaded down her back and shoulders. "I love it there. It's my third year. I'm a history major, you know."

Debi smiled. "No, I didn't know that," she said. "How wonderful for you. It must be fascinating."

"It is," Tina agreed. "So far, I have a straight *A* average. I'm just here between sessions."

"I see," said Debi. "Well, we're certainly glad you were able to come."

Tina's smile disappeared as her green eyes clouded over. "I had to," she said. "It . . . was really starting to get to me."

"'It', meaning the bulimia," said Debi.

Tina nodded.

"Tell me about your eating disorder. Tell me what a typical day is like."

Tina shifted in her seat. She drew her hands through her hair, then flipped it back, away from her eyes. "Oh, well," she hesitated for a moment, then began again. "I get up early in the morning. If I eat anything, it's very light—orange juice and a piece of toast, for instance. Then I go to work and school. By the end of the day I feel so tense and anxious about my grades and work, all I can think about is going home and bingeing."

Bulimia can be quickly defined as the binge-purge syndrome.

COMMON SYMPTOMS
OF BULIMIA

1. The person is caught up in the binge-purge syndrome.

2. The person is usually within ten to fifteen pounds of ideal body weight.

3. The person is a secretive binge eater. Binges may occur regularly and may follow a pattern. Caloric intake per binge may range from 1,000 to 20,000 calories.

4. The person binges; these are followed by fasting, laxative abuse, self-induced vomiting, or other forms of purging. The person may chew food but spit it out before swallowing.

5. The person may often experience fluctuations in weight because of alternating periods of bingeing and fasting.

6. The person observes rituals involving food, exercise, and other aspects of life.

7. The person is perfectionistic.

8. The person wants relationships and approval of others.

9. The person loses control and fears she cannot stop once she begins eating.

The bulimic regards food as a soothing agent, whereas food is an enemy to the anorexic. Tina used her secretive binges as tranquilizers; they occurred regularly and followed a pattern.

Yet after bulimics have enjoyed a binge, they feel guilty: "Oh, I shouldn't have done that. I'm going to get fat." Their binges are followed by fasting, laxative abuse, self-induced vomiting, or other forms of purging. Some bulimics may chew food but spit it out before swallowing. Tina Morgan used vomiting to control her weight.

Unlike anorexics, who are bone thin, bulimics are usually within ten to fifteen pounds of their ideal body weight. Yet their weight may often fluctuate because of alternating periods of bingeing and purging. Tina Morgan had recently gained five pounds, even though she had usually been able to maintain a certain weight. She had been unhappy about her weight all along, however, and felt she should be ten pounds lighter.

The bulimic and the anorexic are alike in that they develop rituals involving food, exercise, and other aspects of daily life. Tina went to different grocery stores to buy junk foods—donuts, cookies, chocolate candy, potato chips, all high in caloric content—after she finished school or work. Then she would hurry home to the apartment she shared with other girls who attended her college. She immediately went into her own bedroom, closed the door, and locked it so she could gorge on the sweets. Then she would purge all those added calories. (A bulimic's caloric intake per binge may range from 1,000 to 20,000 calories.)[1] The time of the day was also a part of Tina's ritual: always in the evening. She purposely kept herself busy during the day so she could overcome her desire to binge, but in the back of her mind she was looking forward to the evening when the routine would begin.

Perfectionism is typical of the bulimic as well as the anorexic. Tina's early comments about her grades made Debi Newman immediately aware of her perfectionistic tendencies. So did her immaculate appearance. The fourth child in a blue-collar family of six children, Tina had found herself competing—and usually achieving—in almost every aspect of her life from the time she was a very little girl. Like so many bulimics, Tina had an air of success about her. Debi was sure that, underneath her "together" exterior, Tina was a young woman with a very low sense of self-esteem.

As Debi talked further with Tina, she admitted, "The first thing I do in the morning is to look in the mirror. I particularly look at my stomach. If it's at all bloated, I don't feel good about myself for the rest of the morning." That, she said, was the reason she ate only a light breakfast. But as the day went by and that reflection in the mirror became dimmer, so did the connection between looking good and not eating. By lunch Tina was able to eat normally.

Socially, Tina Morgan and Cindy Briscoe were opposites, as most bulimics and anorexics are. Tina was outgoing and gregarious (Cindy was typically withdrawn). Most bulimics want relationships and the approval of others. Tina had lots of friends at school and at work. Yet none of her roommates or her other friends at school and at work knew about her eating disorder. Everyone thought of her as "a fun, nice person" who had everything all together. In reality Tina was as lonely as Cindy Briscoe.

Anorexics starve or restrict, as we mentioned earlier. They are proud of their control over food. Bulimics know they have no control over their relationship with food; they fear they cannot stop eating once they start. Tina Morgan felt shame and self-hate because she couldn't control her binges.

Before Tina went to the hospital, she denied her problem by thinking, *Well, I only do this once a week, and I need this. I'm under so much pressure with school. Some people drink, and I don't drink. Some are drug addicts, and I don't do drugs. (Look at my roommate and what she's doing.) This is my one little vice if you call it one.* Tina always felt she could stop bingeing and purging if she wanted to. Now she knew she couldn't stop.

"Are you bingeing and purging on a regular basis?" Debi asked her.

Tina pushed her long black hair back out of her eyes again. Then she nodded. "Every day," she admitted. "Sometimes more than once. It didn't start out that way, but now . . . now I don't know what to do."

Tina did not seem suicidal, but some bulimics are. Their lives become so out of control that they think, *It's not worth it. I can't stop it, and I can't make the pain go away with my bulimia anymore so I just want to die.* A statement like that is a red flag. Hospitalization is essential.

As Debi went through these questions with Tina, she was checking off an invisible list in her head that would determine if Tina needed hospitalization or could be treated on an outpatient basis. Debi heard Tina saying that much of her day was spent concentrating on food—so much so that she was beginning to get *B*'s and *C*'s on a few tests. She was becoming less functional, Debi could tell. Another red flag was the daily bingeing and purging. If a bulimic is involved in this cycle only once a week, she may be seen on an outpatient basis. Tina's constant use of laxatives was also a red flag—as was the blood she had seen in the toilet. Debi decided to admit Tina to the hospital that day.

"You've taken the first step by coming here," said Debi. "Now we can all work on your bulimia together."

And they began the process just as Harry and Cindy did, by looking at the reasons Tina thought she needed to continue her behavior.

COMMON REASONS FOR BINGEING AND PURGING

If you have had difficulty pinpointing some of the reasons you are caught by the cycle of bingeing and purging (or if you are concerned about someone you love), you might note how these statements reflect your attitudes and reasoning.

Food acts as my friend. "When I'm lonely and have no one else to be with, I can always submerge myself in ice cream and cookies."

Tina Morgan could name fifteen friends, yet as they talked, Debi knew that Tina felt no one was there for her as food was. At first Debi agreed with Tina. "No one is there for you like food. . . . But is that others' fault or yours?" she asked. "Remember you told me that you never admitted your bingeing and purging to anyone else. You sound like a pretty private person. Are you?"

"Well, about important things, I guess. I talk a lot," Tina admitted, "but not about my problems . . . or how I'm feeling."

Debi waited awhile for Tina to think about what she was saying. Then Debi asked, "Then how can anyone be there for you when you have a need?"

Often food is the bulimic's only friend because she won't allow anyone to get close to her. Yet food can never be a real friend. Although food is necessary for nutrition and is meant to be enjoyed, it is an inanimate object. It cannot love you or care for you or support you in a crisis. Taken to extremes, it can even become the source of your destruction.

Food reduces my anxiety and frustration. "The pressures of life overwhelm me sometimes so that all I want to do is find an escape from my constant worries. I can ignore the worries if I stuff them down with a box of Twinkies or cupcakes."

This was true for Tina. All the pressure she felt to be perfect—to get straight *A*'s, to look perfect, to perform perfectly at her internship—was relieved to some extent by her bingeing. For a moment she could let down, be totally out of control and imperfect. Until the binge was over! Then the anxiety came back, surrounded by a black cloud of guilt and self-shame. And shame begets more shame.

Food did not reduce Tina's anxiety and frustration. It simply dulled her pain temporarily because the food did not solve the underlying problems causing her to binge. In the long run, her eating disorder only increased and magnified the everyday anxieties and frustrations of her life.

It's their fault. "I binged because they set me off. I'm angry with my boyfriend or my roommate (or my parents or my husband), and so I go and binge and purge. But they set me off. They made me angry."

Marian Grier, the thirty-seven-year-old woman who looked like a *Vogue* model, used this as an excuse for her bingeing and purging. She told Pam Vredevelt, "I get angry with my husband, and we sometimes fight before he leaves for work. I get so upset that I take the kids to school and then hurry home and eat a whole pie, for instance. Then I throw it up. But I don't really feel much better," she admitted. "If he hadn't made me angry, I wouldn't have done it, though."

Bingeing is not someone else's "fault." Marian's husband did not hold her mouth open and force her to eat. She made a choice, and in the coming weeks Pam would help Marian understand the reasons behind that choice.

I deserve to binge. "I've gone all day without food. The diet cola and coffee kept me going, and since I was successful all day, I deserve to binge. I owe it to myself."

Tina Morgan was playing those tapes over and over again through the day. She thought, *I've had a salad for lunch and a diet cola, and at work I had only coffee—with Sweet 'N Low®—so I deserve all the chocolate in the world I want.* (Chocolate was her favorite binge food.)

"Do you deserve a healthy body?" Debi asked Tina. "You owe yourself a chance for a happy, healthy life. You won't achieve it through bingeing and purging."

I already blew it, so why fight it? "I've been on a rigid diet lately that allows only certain prescribed foods. My friend baked some fresh chocolate chip cookies, and I ate two of them before leaving her house. On the way home I figured, 'Oh, well, I've blown my diet already. I might as well really do it good.' So I stopped at a grocery store, spent twenty dollars on candy and junk food, and went on an all-out binge."

We tell our patients, "Just because you ate two cookies doesn't mean that you're a bad person or that you've blown your entire program. If you feel shame about eating the cookies, try to forgive yourself and get right back to healthy eating. Being hard on yourself will lead to more compulsions. Don't punish yourself for eating one or two unhealthy things by getting into a full-blown binge and purge."

THE BULIMAREXIC

You or the person you love may seem to be a combination of the anorexic and the bulimic. Some people are. We call them bulimarexic. Some days this person fits the characteristics of a bulimic and some days an anorexic. Or these alternating cycles may occur monthly or yearly. Other times a preteen may start as an anorexic, and then as she grows older, she becomes a bulimarexic. This condition was first diagnosed by Dr. Marlene Boskind-White and Dr. William C. White, Jr., in their book *Bulimarexia,* but it is not in the Diagnostic and Statistical Manual of Mental Disorders-III-Revised (DSM-III-R), which is the psychiatric reference to emotional disorders.

All of us see patients in our practice who fall in this category. Bulimarexics often understand themselves better if they can identify their symptoms. If not, they tend to tell us, "I'm not an anorexic because I binge and purge, and I'm not a bulimic because I often starve myself." We want them to know that they do have an eating disorder, even though they don't fall specifically into one category.

THE PROCESS OF HEALING

"How . . . how long is this going to take?" Cindy Briscoe's voice was hesitant, almost apologetic, as she asked the much-expected question at the end of her first session with Harry Beverly. From the little he had learned about his new anorexic patient so far, combined with what he had seen in similar cases in the past, he sensed Cindy's would be a lengthy recovery period. He also sensed that this answer was not the one she wanted to hear.

"How long is this going to take?" is not a question easily answered, although it is without a doubt the question foremost on the mind of every person seeking help for an eating disorder. Yet just as each individual is different, so is the time necessary for recovery.

In the more severe cases of anorexia and bulimia, such as Cindy Briscoe's and Tina Morgan's, hospitalization is strongly recommended. An initial four- to six-week period of closely supervised, concentrated treatment in a hospital, followed by at least one to two years of outpatient treatment, is the most likely method to bring lasting success.

Some cases, however, are treatable on a strictly outpatient program, usually consisting of weekly individual and group counseling sessions, which was Pam Vredevelt's recommendation for Marian Grier. Research and experience have proven the combination of individual and group counseling to be the most effective treatment for those working to overcome eating disorders.

All this may sound a bit intimidating for anyone considering seeking help for anorexia or bulimia, particularly if you're hoping for a "quick fix" solution. Unfortunately, there is no "quick fix," no magical formula for an instant cure. The road to recovery may seem long; it may seem hard; it may get worse before it gets better. But you can get better.

3

WHAT HAPPENS TO MY BODY?

The ravages of Cindy Briscoe's anorexia were readily visible to Harry Beverly when he admitted her to the hospital unit. She was severely underweight, with hands, feet, and a head that appeared entirely too large for her body; her long brown hair hung in limp, brittle strands. Her hands were cold to the touch. An almost visible "fog of depression" seemed to hover over her. But what about the other physical effects of Cindy's eating disorder that were not visible?

"It's really not that bad," Cindy explained to Harry as they talked during that first meeting. She anxiously wrapped and unwrapped her hair around her fingers; her huge eyes were rimmed with dark circles. "I mean, I feel fine—most of the time, anyway. I exercise a lot, sometimes two or three times a day, so I must be in great shape, right? It's just that, well, once in a while I . . . I notice my heart beats funny. Fast, you know? And sometimes it . . . feels like it stops or skips or something and . . . and I get dizzy too. Real dizzy, like I'm going to faint."

Harry nodded. "I see. So you've noticed that this is beginning to affect you physically."

Cindy nodded but would say no more. Yet the dizziness and the strange skipping of her heart were red flag warnings to Harry.

The second night in the hospital Cindy was restless. The mental health technician, who is trained to observe the patients and talk with them, noticed her walking up and down the hall every hour or so. By three o'clock in the morning Cindy walked past the nurses' station for the fourth time. A few seconds later the tech heard a dull thud. Cindy was lying on the floor, a few feet away from the station.

The tech yelled for assistance, and a nurse ran from a room down the hall. She felt for Cindy's pulse. None. "Code Blue!" the nurse yelled. She had trained in an intensive care unit so she quickly went through her past experiences to seek an answer. Cardiac arrest. She asked the tech to call for the doctor on duty in the hospital emergency room; then she yelled, "This patient has arrested. Get the crash cart."

In a few minutes another nurse wheeled the portable cardiac defibrillator, a computerlike mechanism with two paddles to stimulate the heart. The nurse applied one to the center of Cindy's chest and the other to the side. The electric surges finally shocked her heart into action.

This emergency procedure saved Cindy's life.

The physical effects of anorexia and bulimia can be life-threatening. You (or someone you love) may be damaging the body in many ways, so many that we can almost go straight through the alphabet with the physical side effects of these two eating disorders.

WHAT PHYSICAL EFFECTS CAN BE EXPECTED?

Eating disorders affect people in various ways, and the physical aspect is no exception. Many symptoms are similar in both anorexia and bulimia. In anorexia, however, others more often recognize the physical effects.

This section is not here to frighten you, but you must understand the importance of heeding your body's warning signals. Ignoring them could be fatal. Let's review some possible physical effects of eating disorders in alphabetical order.

A—Amenorrhea

Amenorrhea is the abnormal absence of menstrual discharge. Irregular menstrual periods can be brought on by experiencing the stress associated with bulimia and also by dropping the percentage of body fat to below 22 or 23 percent, as anorexics do. Bulimics tend to have irregular periods whereas anorexics often skip three or more consecutive menstrual periods.

Harry Beverly asked Cindy about her periods during that first interview.

Cindy's ashen face flushed slightly. Her jaws twitched. "Yes," she whispered. "In fact, I . . . I haven't had my period in almost a year."

Not only may menstrual periods stop, but breast tissue disappears as well. Of course, there are many ramifications to the whole area of sexuality, including the possibility of a poor sex drive.

When June sought treatment for bulimia, for example, she was already in the habit of purging several times each day and abusing laxatives. She was quite thin, leaning toward anorexic, in addition to having been bulimic for several years. One of her major concerns was her lack of menstrual periods. Also, she and her husband were having conflicts over her disinterest in sex. She received treatment in a behavioral medicine program, her weight began to increase as her stress decreased, and then her menstrual function returned to normal. With individual and marriage counseling, the marital and sexual problems were also resolved.

B—Blood Cell Functioning

Individuals with anorexia or bulimia often have either anemia or a decreased white blood cell count. Poor nutrition may be a factor in these altered blood counts, or the immune system may even be impaired. That's why we always do extensive blood tests on inpatients, like Cindy Briscoe, and why we ask our outpatients to see an internist or a general practitioner for a comprehensive medical exam. Cindy's routine blood counts revealed a low white cell count. That was followed closely by the doctors, and by the time she left, her blood had returned to normal.

C—Cardiovascular Complications

These are perhaps the most dangerous medical complications of all. Forced vomiting may alter the electrolytes, such as sodium, magnesium, calcium, and potassium. By altering the electrolytes, one may develop cardiac arrhythmia (irregular heartbeat), which is what happened to Cindy that second night in the hospital and can result in death.

Potassium is an element in the cells. When a person vomits, she loses some potassium, which alters the potassium level, affecting the functioning of the cell, putting it out of balance. That's why the heartbeat becomes irregular if the level is low. A low potassium level can be an ominous sign. Anorexia has a high mortality rate of 5 to 15 percent from cardiac arrest.[1]

The potassium level in Cindy Briscoe's blood looked okay when she entered the hospital—in a range of 3.8. However, sometimes the intracellular level can be low, even though the blood level is okay (unfortunately, we cannot measure this level, yet it is even more critical than the blood level). That low intracellular level caused Cindy to suffer cardiac arrest. She spent several days in the intensive care unit where she was monitored carefully and fed potassium intravenously. Then we were able to transfer her back to the Minirth-Meier unit.

As a young resident, Dr. Minirth worked with a teenager named Mary who had bulimia, although at that time the disease was not well known. Mary and her mother fought the medical and psychological suggestions made by Dr. Minirth. He did what he could, and Mary seemed to recover—at least she convinced the staff that she was okay—so they discharged her from the hospital. Dr. Minirth still recalls the day, less than a week after her discharge, when Mary was brought into the emergency room, dead. He believes that she probably vomited extensively that day, which triggered an irregular heartbeat and cardiac arrest. Dr. Minirth promised himself he would always look at the medical and psychological complications of eating disorders with serious concern.

Several years ago, another patient, Betty, arrived at the behavioral medicine unit of the Minirth-Meier Clinic for treatment of her eating disorder. She gave a typical history of binge eating and purging several times a day as well as abusing laxatives. She seemed extremely confident. Doctors were not as aware of the tremendous psychological and medical dangers of eating disorders as they are today. Betty had already visited several physicians who had dismissed her case. After she entered the hospital, tests revealed that she had low potassium. How fortunate that it was discovered as soon as it was, or a beautiful lady could have been found dead, and no one would have known why.

D—Digestion

Many digestive problems can arise from eating disorders. Perhaps the most common is a deficiency of digestive enzymes, which results in impaired digestion. Also, because the bowel becomes dependent on laxatives, the individuals become constipated without laxative use. In other words, these people literally become addicted to laxatives because the bowel loses its normal tone and motion. Medical doctors working with these individuals must be careful when eliminating all forms of laxatives; the problem has gone from being psychological to being partially medical.

At the time of her hospital admission, Tina Morgan was taking several laxatives every day. She was addicted to stimulant, irritant laxatives, such as Cascara® and Dulcolax®. Her bowels had become dependent on these stimulants to function normally because they had lost some of their peristaltic contractions. Dr. Minirth gradually replaced these laxatives with more natural types, such as Colace® (100 milligrams at bedtime), a water-drawing agent, and Psyllium C, a fiber agent, or Metamucil® (1 teaspoon in fluid two times a day). Tina was fortunate. Some patients develop syndromes such as inflammatory bowel disorders, similar to ulcerative colitis.

Because of the repeated vomiting, inflammation of the esophagus (known as esophagitis) can result. Tina Morgan came to the hospital because she noticed blood when she vomited, which was an indication of this inflammation of her esophagus. Since that was the first sign of bleeding, Tina had little damage to her esophagus, and the bleeding soon stopped. An especially dangerous condition of some persons is a torn, bleeding esophagus.

Hiatal hernias have been reported. And various other digestive problems can appear, such as accumulation of fluid around the stomach area. The individual looks potbellied, the complete opposite of what anorexics and bulimics desire. Perhaps the most common digestive disorder is a slower emptying of food from the stomach, which creates discomfort from bloating.

E—Erosion of Tooth Enamel

Persons with eating disorders are often very attractive, and it's a shame to see them come into the hospital with the beginning stages of erosion of their tooth enamel. The hydrochloric acid from the stomach causes this problem, and tooth pain may be one of the first symptoms. Also discoloration of the teeth occurs.

Tina Morgan had always been concerned about her appearance, and she had heard that throwing up discolored teeth. Part of her ritual was to wrap foil around her teeth before she threw up; therefore, she avoided the discoloration. Sally didn't know to do this. She was a beautiful young lady with few telltale signs of her bulimia, with the exception of her yellow-brown teeth. Fortunately for her, she sought help before significant damage was done.

Cavities are quite common because of the frequent vomiting and the limiting of the diet to citrus fruits and an abnormal carbohydrate intake.

F—Forgetfulness

Anorexia (or more specifically the malnutrition that results from it) can affect the primary organ of the body, the brain and the central nervous system. It can slow down your thinking. It can keep you from talking coherently. It can make you forgetful and delirious. A frequent assumption is that these manifestations are largely psychological, but anorexics and bulimics have deficiencies in nutrients such as vitamins, minerals, proteins, and fats that are essential to correct thinking. When Cindy Briscoe was admitted, for instance, she was quite dehydrated and was not thinking clearly. She had a short attention span and got confused about the current date.

Shelly admitted herself to the hospital because she felt humiliated after her boss had to show her for the third time how to work the new copy machine. Shelly felt stupid, even though she knew she had a high IQ.

Proper nutrition will correct this condition so it does not result in permanent brain damage.

G—Glandular Functioning

Many glandular dysfunctions, especially thyroid abnormalities, have been associated with eating disorders. It is possible that the thyroid could be altered as the body attempts to diminish metabolism and conserve energy. As a result, the individual feels lethargic. Also, for some not fully understood reason, the parotid gland is affected, producing a chipmunklike appearance.

For instance, Elaine came to the clinic suffering from the effects of bulimia. Her lab evaluation showed that she had a low thyroid level. The question arose: Was her abnormal thyroid a result of her eating disorder, or had her body always had a low thyroid level, which made it difficult for her to keep her weight down?

In Elaine's case it was a little of both. We put her on a low dose of Synthroid to help her stabilize her weight as we talked to her about the underlying problems that caused her to deal with her overweight in such an extreme manner.

Thyroid disorders also may lead to a lowering of body temperature, dry skin, brittle nails, decreased reflexes, and mild fluid retention.

H—Hypoglycemia

A person with an eating disorder may have a low blood sugar count (hypoglycemia) in response to a binge intake of high-calorie, simple sugar foods. The body overcompensates by releasing excessive insulin, which then drives the blood sugar too low. As a result, the body craves more sugar. Hypoglycemia may manifest itself by fatigue and feelings of anxiety. Complaints of dizziness and headaches are common; Debi Newman was not surprised when Tina Morgan mentioned these symptoms during their first interview.

"The dizziness and the shaking are getting to me," Tina explained. "It's been happening more often lately. At first it was hardly noticeable—nothing I couldn't ignore anyway. You know, like the stomach cramps and the headaches. No big deal. But lately . . ." She shook her head. "I can't ignore it anymore," she sighed, her radiant smile gone. "It's getting to where I'm reluctant to drive my car for fear I might pass out. I knew it was time to get help."

Tina Morgan put so much sugar in her body that her whole system was out of whack. The doctors at the health center had been prescribing a diabetic diet and could not understand why her symptoms persisted.

I—Impulse Control Disorder

Individuals with either bulimia or anorexia have long been said to have impulse control disorder (a loss of control of oneself, which results in impulsive actions and extreme emotions, such as anger and rage). It has been hypothesized that innate abnormalities in the food regulatory centers of the brain exist. It has also been thought that antidepressants work by regulating this abnormality. Some doctors do not accept this explanation, and the research is certainly far from conclusive. It is known, however, that impulse control problems exist in such areas as drug abuse, alcohol abuse, and sexual addictions.

We use behavioral treatment in our inpatient unit to address impulse control. We monitor our patients; we stay close to them so they cannot act out impulsively and run to the bathroom to vomit. The bathrooms are locked, and patients have to get permission to use them. There are no candy or soda machines. We do for them what they cannot, at that moment, do for themselves. We exercise control.

And when our patients succeed—when they eat everything on their breakfast, lunch, and dinner trays, for instance—we reward them, both verbally, "Hey, that's really good; we're glad you're doing so well," and monetarily by giving them a pass to go out with a friend or spouse.

J—Judgment

Obviously, the process of making good judgments is affected in persons with eating disorders. One argument centers on whether this problem is caused by the medical complications or whether it is purely psychological. Perhaps the neurotransmitters of the brain are altered, and perception is affected.

Cindy Briscoe, who was eighty-four pounds and five feet four inches tall, would stand in front of the mirror and complain of being overweight. Impossible, you might say. Not so. It was as though her perception was affected medically.

M—Musculoskeletal Problems

Various musculoskeletal problems can be seen in those with eating disorders. Because of the potassium deficiency, muscle spasms, pain, and muscle atrophy in general can result. Early on in the disease, these effects are not noticed because many persons exercise excessively. Yet if the disease continues, the damage can be permanent.

Francis was thirty years old, yet she had to walk with the support of a cane. Her bulimia was complicated by her diabetes, and the combination led to arthritic problems. Simple daily tasks such as showering and walking would take hours to complete. She was old beyond her years.

O—Other Physical Problems

Dry skin is common. Head hair may be thin (and also fall out when it is washed or combed), and downy fuzz may appear on other parts of the body. During Harry Beverly's first interview with Cindy Briscoe, he noticed the dryness of the skin on her arm and a downy fuzz of white hair. When he looked at her face, he saw the same white fuzz on her cheeks. Many anorexics' hair is limp and thin, and this downy fuzz will appear on their bodies to insulate them from cool weather because the natural fat layer has been depleted. The anorexics' hands, feet, and other parts of the body are always cold.

Cindy Briscoe hated winter. She literally froze for six months. She didn't use air conditioning in the summer—she called it her "thawing out time." Her body developed lanugo, the downylike white fuzz Harry noticed in that first interview, to help her stay warm.

Broken blood vessels in the face and bags under the eyes are two other physical symptoms of this disease. Fainting spells and rapid or irregular heartbeats are also common.

Marian Grier admitted to Pam Vredevelt: "I'm so scared about what my bulimia's been doing to me physically in the last sixteen years."

"Have you noticed any symptoms?"

"Yes," Marian admitted, lifting her head to look at Pam. She pushed a stray lock of short blonde hair from her forehead. "Headaches, stomach cramps, that sort of thing. Nothing I can't

PARTIAL LISTING OF PHYSICAL PROBLEMS BROUGHT ABOUT BY EATING DISORDERS*

	EXTERNAL PROBLEMS	INTERNAL PROBLEMS	CAUSE
SKIN	Dryness. Fine rash. Pimples.	Dehydration.	Reduced fluid intake. Excessive fluid elimination. Frequent vomiting. Laxative abuse.
SALIVARY GLANDS	Swelling. Pain. Tenderness.	Possible infection but usually not.	Frequent vomiting.
CONSTIPATION		Insufficient material. Insufficient fluid. Dulled intestinal nerves.	Failure to take in or retain sufficient food and fluid. Laxative abuse.
EDEMA (water retention)	Swelling and puffiness, frequently around the ankles and feet.	Electrolyte imbalance.	Malnutrition. Frequent vomiting. Excessive laxatives or diuretics.
BLOATING	Swelling over stomach or abdominal area.	Electrolyte imbalance? Time required for body systems to adjust? Insufficient protein intake.	Long periods of starvation and probable excessive vomiting, laxatives, or diuretics.
ABDOMINAL PAIN		Peptides? Hunger pangs? Changes in the bowel.	Failure to identify hunger? Emotional attitudes? Insufficient intake.
FEELING OF FULLNESS	Slight distention after eating is normal.	Normal feeling after eating for everybody.	Fear? Emotional attitudes.

*Provided by National Association of Anorexia Nervosa and Associated Disorders (ANAD), Box 7, Highland Park, IL 60035.

live with. But the last few years it's been getting worse, even though I try so hard to stay in shape." Her eyes brightened. "I run, you know. Six miles every morning, and six to ten every evening, five days a week."

"It sounds like running is extremely important to you," said Pam.

"Definitely," Marian agreed. "I even compete in one or two marathon runs every year. I've been doing that for six years now, so I should be in great shape, but . . ." Her voice trailed off, and her face seemed to sag. "But I'm not," she finished. "I'm not in great shape at all."

The chart on page 43 lists minor physical problems brought about by eating disorders and the causes of these problems.

R—Renal

Sometimes individuals with eating disorders develop complications with their kidneys. Dr. Minirth worries about anorexics' starving themselves to death. If the body weight gets low enough—fifty pounds or so, and Dr. Minirth has seen patients at this weight—the kidneys will shut down. The person then goes into kidney failure and dies.

Anorexia is similar to starvation, and people who starve to death go through these same body organ failures as they are deprived of the nutrients and proteins the organs need to survive.

S—Seizures

For some not-fully-understood reason, seizures occur in persons with eating disorders at a higher rate than in the general population. Further research is needed. If a patient is subject to seizures, she must receive treatment for them while at the same time receiving treatment for the eating disorder.

V—Vision Impairment

Rarely, but occasionally, night vision will be impaired, perhaps because of poor nutrition and decreased amounts of vitamin A in the body. One of our patients, Karissa, had her husband drive her to evening outpatient sessions because her night vision was so poor. It kept her from doing many things she enjoyed, but the payoff—in her thinking—was increased dependency on her husband.

W—Weight

For anorexics, loss of weight is the most ominous sign of all. For bulimics, extreme weight fluctuations can occur within short time periods. Michelle called herself a bulimic failure. Although she consistently purged her food, she remained twenty pounds overweight; her metabolism was so far off that she was unable to maintain a healthy weight. Yet when she developed healthy eating habits, she was able to control her weight better.

X—X-ray Abnormalities

Young women may have degrees of osteoporosis because of the loss in calcium due to poor nutrition. Sometimes there are fractures of the vertebrae, which shorten the person's stature. Clarisse, for instance, was referred to us by her general practitioner. Her foot was hurting, so she went to the doctor, who discovered she had a fracture. Yet Clarisse couldn't remember when or how she injured her foot. That was a sign of bone deterioration.

HOW CAN THE MEDICAL FIELD HELP TREAT EATING DISORDERS?

Currently the medical field can treat eating disorders in three ways. The first is to treat the physical complications that arise from these disorders, as outlined in the first part of this chapter. Dr. Minirth orders a comprehensive medical exam for all anorexic and bulimic patients (a complete physical, a neurological exam, a gynecological exam, and a comprehensive laboratory evaluation). With the results of this workup, he can eliminate any other possible diseases that might be causing weight loss and the other symptoms (for instance, blood tests will determine if the patient has any blood infection or disorder, such as leukemia, rather than an eating disorder), and he can identify the extent of the patient's physical side effects and the proper treatment (such as a potassium supplement if that level is found to be low).

The second way is to provide a controlled environment in a hospital setting. The behavior of individuals with severe eating disorders can cause medical complications. That behavior must be controlled. The diet needs to be controlled, and these patients must be monitored while they eat. Dr. Minirth put Cindy on a refeeding plan of 1,200 calories a day right after her admittance. She had to eat 100 percent of her meals. If she didn't, she had to take a supplement (for example, Ensure®) to replace the calories she missed that day.

Getting only 1,200 calories might seem like a diet to lose weight—and it can be. However, in Cindy's case a gradual readjustment of nutrients to the system was needed. Metabolism slows down during starvation. And it's not healthy to overwhelm the body with food all at once because of the stress placed on the organs. The body must readjust slowly. (If patients resist a refeeding plan, we may recommend intravenous or tube feeding to save their lives.)

The patient's weight and exercise must be closely monitored. She must be watched for ways in which she will attempt to deceive (e.g., placing weights in her pockets before being weighed). In short, an extensive behavioral medicine approach must be instituted.

In severe cases, an inpatient program is highly recommended. In less chronic cases, many individuals have made great progress recovering from an eating disorder while counseling on an outpatient basis.

The third way the medical field can aid in treating eating disorders is to use antidepressants. Those with eating disorders are usually depressed because of the psychological problems that cause them to abuse food, as well as the physical effects of their disease (anemia, dehydration, and poor physical condition). This stress alters their brain chemistry, and antidepressant medications often help. Prozac® (fluoxetine) has been used most often with good results, along with tricyclics such as Desipramine® or Nortriptyline®. Monoamine oxidase inhibitors (MAOIs) and lithium carbonate are sometimes used. These have had good results because they treat the physiological symptoms of depression. These medicines have also been postulated to work because of some other effect on the body, such as on the appetite center of the brain.

At the Minirth-Meier Clinic we use antidepressants with caution. After several weeks of treatment, when the body's physiology has returned to normal, their use is discontinued. (If you stop the medicine suddenly, so that the body hasn't had time to adjust, the patient will be medically depressed, and you're right back where you started.)

Cindy Briscoe was scared by her sudden death episode. For the first week or so, she had chest burns where the defibrillator shocked her out of the heart stoppage, which were a continual reminder of the severity of her disease. She slowly began to eat her meals and to look at the issues that caused her to abuse food. We will begin to consider these issues in the next chapter.

Before that, let us stress again that this section on medical complications was not intended to scare you; however, you must realized how serious an untreated eating disorder can be. If you recognized any of your own physical symptoms (or those of someone you love) as you read through this list, do not hesitate to contact a physician immediately. Help is available, but you must seek it—before it's too late.

4

WHAT KEEPS
THE CYCLE
GOING?

Ever since she was a baby, Linda had been fat. Her parents used to call her their little teddy bear because she was so cuddly and pudgy. One of their favorite scrapbook pictures of Linda showed her grinning from ear to ear, her arms puffed out of a sleeveless shirt that was partially buttoned over a pregnant-looking tummy. Linda hated that picture and all the memories attached to being known as a "fat kid." She swore that someday she was going to take that picture out of the scrapbook and burn it.

Months before Linda first sought treatment, she tried out for cheerleader. Her close friends told her she was the most skilled of all those competing. When the big day of tryouts came, she performed perfectly. Everyone, including Linda, thought she would be selected.

The next morning she left for school, excited as she anticipated seeing her name on the list of the new rally squad members. Then came the shocking truth. Her name wasn't on the list. She couldn't believe it. What had gone wrong? She knew she had done better than the other girls at tryouts. Why wasn't her name posted?

Linda ran down the hall to find the cheerleading adviser—

maybe she could give her some answers. Mrs. Anderson stood up as Linda walked into her office in tears.

"Why didn't I make the squad when everyone, including you, said I was so good?" Linda cried.

Mrs. Anderson's frank reply made a scarring impression on Linda. "You're good," she said, "but you're also overweight. We can't put fat cheerleaders out in front of everyone. Besides that, we don't have a uniform big enough to fit you."

Stunned, Linda turned and walked out of Mrs. Anderson's office. She hated herself. She hated her fat. She determined at that moment never to put another fattening food into her mouth. During the following weeks, she lived on water, lettuce, and celery.

Two months later, Linda had lost 40 pounds and had gone from a size thirteen to a size four. At five feet seven inches tall, she weighed 102 pounds. She had become anorexic at fifteen years of age.

When Linda first came to see Pam Vredevelt for treatment, Pam sensed her tremendous fear of "getting fat." Looking in the mirror at her thin body, Linda saw only the image from the scrapbook photograph. Though others expressed concern about her frail appearance, she was convinced they were trying to control her and wanted her to be fat. She felt as if everyone were on one side of a line, ganged up against her, while she stood on the other side—alone.

Linda sincerely believed that her acceptance by others hinged on keeping her weight at or below 102 pounds. Even a one-pound gain could mean rejection. Since her weight loss, boys were suddenly beginning to notice her. She loved the attention and the dates but was paranoid that all interest would be lost if she ate normally.

Like Linda's, Karen's story is somewhat typical of those with eating disorders. Karen grew up in a dysfunctional family. Her father was extremely abusive, both physically and verbally. An alcoholic, he often came home drunk and angry, taking out his anger on anyone who got in his way. If Karen accidentally left a toy out, her father would fly into a drunken rage and berate her for being "bad." In her little girl mind, her father was right. If only she'd been good and remembered to do everything perfectly, he would not have gotten mad. And so, in an effort to control her father's outrageous behavior, Karen became a pleaser.

By the time she was a teenager, Karen thought that being perfect included her physical image. Living in a society that promotes and applauds thinness, equating it with beauty and success, she felt that she was failing if she put on a few extra pounds. When her friend's big sister let it slip that she had discovered the secret to staying thin—eating all you want and then vomiting it up and/or using laxatives—Karen knew she had found her answer. It wasn't long before she was bingeing and purging on a regular basis.

HOW DOES IT START?

Linda and Karen don't know it, but they are caught in the vicious cycle of addiction. We often compare this cycle to a Ferris wheel ride. Linda and Karen are stuck at the top of the wheel, high in the sky, wanting to come down to the ground but unable to because the wheel seems to be controlled by someone else, that man on the ground who is loading on new passengers. They've lost control.

The addiction cycle has four major components: pain, faulty thinking, anesthesia (which seems to numb the original pain), and guilt and shame. (See the chart on page 51.) We walk patients through these stops on the cycle so they can understand their uncontrollable Ferris wheel ride and how they can get out of this crazy cycle.

Pain

Although Linda's and Karen's stories are different, they both start at the same point—pain. Linda suffered from the pain and humiliation of rejection. Karen's pain was a result of her father's abusive behavior. She turned the rage inside and sought to keep

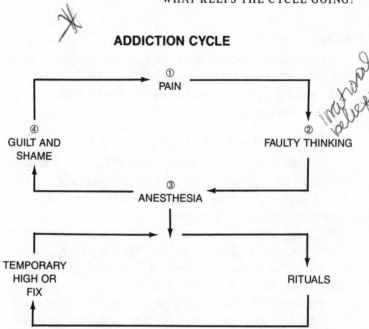

ADDICTION CYCLE

peace by being perfect. The quest for perfection created more pain and drove her straight to bulimic behavior. In Linda's and Karen's case, food was not the real problem.

Food is not the issue with anorexics or bulimics. That is why behavioral treatment is rarely effective. To concentrate solely on teaching an anorexic or a bulimic proper eating habits is to ignore the real issue—the pain. Although a person might learn to eat properly in a controlled hospital or outpatient setting, as soon as she leaves that environment, the old eating patterns will resurface because the pain is still there.

As you can see from the illustration on page 51, the cycle always begins with pain. That pain can have its origin in some major life trauma, family issues, or low self-esteem. Regardless of how the pain starts, it inevitably leads to faulty thinking. People with eating disorders hold to numerous irrational beliefs, which fuel their obsessions with food.

Faulty Thinking

We hear twelve typical lies as we talk to anorexics or bulimics. Ask yourself if you (or someone you love) could be trapped into faulty thinking as you read through the lies people with eating disorders tend to believe.

1. "The best way to stay thin is the way I'm doing it now."

Cindy Briscoe believed this lie. When she was forced to eat everything on her hospital tray, she complained to Harry Beverly, "I'm going to get really fat now. All this food. I don't have a chance to keep my weight down."

She went on to tell Harry, "Before I began controlling my weight, everyone told me I was fat. Mom would say, 'You need to lose some weight on your hips.' Or 'You need to get rid of that tummy.' Or 'You look horrible in a bathing suit.'

"But no one says that to me now. In fact, at first Mom complimented me on how good I looked. And so did my friends."

Cindy's fear was typical of our patients. It helps them to realize that a lot of thin people in the world know absolutely nothing about starving, bingeing, or purging. Harry confronted this lie by simply saying, "Sounds like faulty thinking to me. Your eating disorder is not the only means you can use to stay thin. Think of the girls in your school who are thin. Do all of them have an eating disorder?

"Your way of staying thin is one way. It is also a life-threatening way. Many alternatives in weight control are successful and healthy. Don't be duped by the lie that says, 'My way is the only way.'"

When they begin to eat normally again, many anorexics and bulimics are amazed at the amount of food they can eat without gaining huge amounts of weight. In fact, some bulimics who were slightly overweight at the beginning of treatment may lose weight rather than gain it as they learn to eat normally.

2. "The worst thing that could happen to me would be to gain weight or become fat."

We tell our patients to think about that statement for a moment. Is that truly the worst thing that could happen to you? Wouldn't it be much worse to be in a severe car accident, to lose a limb, or to become paralyzed? Let's take it a step further. What about losing your job or a loved one? By continuing in a destructive eating disorder, you increase your chances of experiencing just such a loss.

3. "This eating behavior is my life. If I give it up, I will have nothing to do."

Anorexics become more and more obsessed with food. Cindy Briscoe spent so much of her day counting calories and restricting her diet, she had little time for her friends at school. Anorexics unconsciously wonder, "If I give up this eating disorder, what will fill my days?"

In counseling we try to help these patients see that although eating is a way to reduce boredom, it certainly is not the most fulfilling way, especially when done to an extreme. We try to show them what a normal day is like. Harry Beverly asked Cindy Briscoe to think back to her junior high school years. "What was your day like then?"

"Oh, well. I spent a lot of time involved in school activities, like chorus and intramural sports. And sometimes I would just watch television."

"Did you feel as if your day was fulfilling?"

"Sure. I loved the girls I hung around with. We did lots of things together."

"Why not go back to that, then? And remember, you don't always have to be busy," Harry said. "Sometimes it's good to be quiet or alone. Like taking a walk by yourself. Or reading or sewing—or watching TV."

Harry also told Cindy to ask a few of the recovering patients on the unit about this fear of boredom. "Any recovered anorexic or bulimic whose eating disorder began out of boredom will tell you that food is a false substitute for fulfillment. The despair and guilt for the behavior far outweighed any satisfaction she felt," he assured her.

4. *"My favorite escape from my problems is food. If I give up this area of my life, I'll have to deal with all those other sore spots, and I don't want to."*

In one of the early group sessions Tina Morgan attended, she listened as a twenty-five-year-old woman who was bulimic told about how her father had abused her sexually as a child. Her pain was all too evident. She could hardly tell her story because she was crying so much.

Afterward Tina remarked, "Is that better than what I'm doing to my body? Is getting in touch with all these feelings really good?"

Debi Newman encouraged Tina to ask the young woman those questions at the next group session. The twenty-five-year-old answered immediately, "I feel so much better now that I've gotten this out in the open. Yes, I cried a lot yesterday morning—and afternoon and evening. But as you can see, I'm better now. I may cry a lot more in the coming days, but it's still worth it, believe me, Tina."

As the overpowering problem of bulimia or anorexia diminishes, an individual may become more aware of other parts of life that need attention and repair. But that is nothing to dread.

Be encouraged. In the process of overcoming an eating disorder, you will collect tools to use in other problem areas of your life. These tools will help you cope with a variety of stresses. You will build a track record of victories. You will gradually become more skillful at handling new challenges.

Many people think that once the eating disorder is cured, the rest of life will be total bliss. That is a misconception. You might have said to yourself, "If I could just get out of this bondage to food, my life would be free from problems." Don't delude yourself. No one lives problem free. Problems are a natural part of human experience. But with God, all problems can be faced. In fact, many times those problems provide platforms from which we can watch God do the miraculous.

5. "I'm happy with my life the way it is."

Have you ever made that statement? If you have, do you believe you were really being honest? Picture yourself in your favorite bathroom purging the food from your last binge. Are you happy? Picture yourself taking all those laxatives and feeling the cramping and pain that follow. Are you happy with yourself?

Denial can be deadly. Although you may thoroughly enjoy parts of your life, happiness will become progressively less apparent the longer you deny an eating disorder.

6. "I have to continue this pattern because my friends won't care about me if I'm well and don't have this problem anymore."

Some families are not able to deal with negative feelings, but they can deal with illness so they will reach out to someone with an eating disorder. "We want to help you. We want to take care of you," they say. And that becomes part of the reason the bulimic does not want to give up the behavior. She thinks she will lose the positive attention.

Sometimes being sick does have payoffs. You get a lot of attention and tender loving care from friends. Chances are, you have had extra attention since you developed your eating disorder. That's fine right now. But the fact is, people eventually get bored, tired, and exasperated with someone who doesn't take responsibility for problems that can be remedied.

Everyone has problems. Some are more difficult to cope with than others. Your friends have their own struggles to resolve. If every time they are with you, they are emotionally drained and frustrated because of your irresponsible behavior, they might not stick around very long.

You might like to practice combating this personal lie with statements like these: "My friends will enjoy me more when they know I'm taking charge of this area of my life. They'll respect me for taking responsibility to get help. I'll enjoy my friends more too. I don't want them to feel sorry for me anymore or to give me attention for being sick. I want to take steps to recover so that they can spend time with me because they like me, not because they are worried about me."

7. *"I don't want sensual advances from the opposite sex. If I give up my eating disorder, I may become more appealing, and I'm not sure I could handle a come-on. This way I can avoid my sexuality."*

Sometimes anorexics have experienced sexual abuse in their pasts. They unconsciously think, *If I lose my female features—my breasts, my hips—I'll become less attractive, and men will leave me alone.* Cindy Briscoe thought she didn't have to deal with guys at school making advances because she wasn't as sexy as the other girls. She would fix herself up and try to look pretty, but she didn't want to emphasize her figure. That was her way to control men.

Her rationalization was built on fear. And she couldn't be sure that some boy wouldn't try to come on to her. Harry suggested that she have a battle plan, instead. "Keep a few statements on the 'back burner,'" he advised, "just in case you run into this situation. If you are not interested in someone who is making advances toward you, remember that honesty is the best policy. Politely tell that guy, 'I'm not interested.' It's amazing to see the profound impact those three little words can have."

(Or if you're married and a man asks you for a date, you might reply, "Only if I can bring my husband along," or "I'm happily married and really not interested.")

*8. "My family is so preoccupied with the way I eat that if I
start eating again, everyone will be on my back about
everything I put in my mouth."*

Anorexics sometimes think this way since their eating disorder
is more obvious than the bulimics who often eat fairly normally in
front of people and hide their binges. Often family members can
be so concerned about the person with an eating disorder that they
act like detectives and watch every move made toward the kitchen
or every bite eaten during meals. Cindy Briscoe felt that her family was watching her this way. Often individuals can be so obsessed with their eating disorders that they project this obsession
onto their families. Yet in Cindy's case, and that of others, her
fear was accurate. Her mother was watching her. She was
alarmed, and she had reason to be.

Harry reminded Cindy, "If your family didn't care about you,
they wouldn't give your behavior a second thought. If you are feeling watched over, it's because those who love you want to help
you. They just don't know how to offer assistance. They may
think the only help they can give is to make you eat if you have
been starving."

"It doesn't work, though," Cindy said.

"Still you can realize that your mom's intentions are good. The
bottom line is that only you can take responsibility for your problem. No one can do it for you."

Tremendous healing has occurred in families when they received insight concerning what does and does not help a recovering anorexic or bulimic. After you have had a chance to talk
confidentially with a counselor, your recovery speed can be
boosted if you take the risk of involving your loved ones in therapy. You might get a chance to watch the Sherlock Holmes in your
family enter retirement.

We often tell moms or other family members or spouses to talk
to their loved ones about something besides food, such as their
feelings about what's happening in the family or what's going on

at school. This approach may lead the patient to talk about her eating disorder. We also suggest that loved ones become involved in activities or hobbies with the patient. Often parents need to show interest in their child rather than the eating disorder, and husbands need to express their love for their wives more obviously. The individual is really starving for attention. (Chapter 16 will give loved ones more helpful hints about ways to support an anorexic or a bulimic as she works toward wholeness.)

9. *"I can use my eating disorder as a scapegoat now. If people reject me, I can say it's because I'm anorexic or bulimic. If I give up this eating disorder, I'll have nothing safe on which to blame rejection."*

Tina Morgan unconsciously thought this way. Just before she came to the clinic she had been dating a guy who really liked her and wanted to share more with her than fun social events, the deeper thoughts that included their hurts and problems. Tina discouraged such intimacy. "I don't have any problems," she told him. Their relationship soon failed, even though deep inside Tina wanted to respond to his desire to know more about her. She blamed their breakup on her bulimia. "He couldn't understand why I wanted to be alone during the week rather than spend time with him," she told Debi. "I know he knew I had a problem. He just wouldn't admit it."

We all look for scapegoats. It seems so much easier to shift responsibility than to come to grips with problems. However, as we gloss over rejections by saying, "It's because I'm fat or bulimic or anorexic," we also pass up opportunities to learn about ourselves and our relationships with others. Chances are, your eating disorder may have nothing to do with the reasons others keep their distance from you. Maybe people feel that you don't like them or that you aren't interested in their lives. Maybe they don't realize your desire to make friends.

In the process of making new friends, we all experience the

sting of rejection at one time or another. Sometimes there are no good reasons for the rejection. And that hurts. But with God's strength you can handle it. There is no need to let one person's rejection destroy the rest of your life.

10. "I would be better off killing myself than trying to fight this eating disorder."

Bulimics can feel so out of control and powerless that they consider suicide.

Tina Morgan admitted to Debi Newman: "Many times after I binged and purged I would go into the living room of our apartment and forget about what I'd done because there was always something going on. But on the weekends, no one would be around. And if I didn't have a date, I'd just sit in my room and think about what I'd done. I'd feel so guilty. So awful. And so sick! I often thought I'd be better off dead.

"I even had a plan," she continued. "I'd mix alcohol with an overdose of tranquilizers. But I never got up the nerve to ask the doctors at the health center to prescribe the pills for me—or to get them from someone on campus."

Debi tried to show Tina that this was desperation thinking. "Look at the people in your group who are overcoming their eating disorders," she said. "Healing is possible. You've begun the road to recovery by coming to the clinic. Now just stick with it for a while."

Bulimics sometimes plan a suicide attempt. Anorexics are more passive, but starving oneself is a form of slow suicide. They unconsciously think, *I don't care if I die. If my heart stops, as some people say it could, that's okay.*

Family members need to be careful if either an anorexic or a bulimic makes statements like, "I want to disappear," or "You'd all be better off if I'd just go away." These statements are red flags that indicate suicidal thoughts; hospitalization is often necessary.

11. "My eating disorder doesn't affect other people."

Anorexics and bulimics often believe that what they eat or don't eat is no one else's business and affects no one but themselves. However, families and friends of people with eating disorders are affected in many ways. Tina Morgan's secrecy meant that nobody knew about her eating disorder, so she thought it didn't affect anyone else. Yet when she entered the hospital, her roommates felt very sad. They felt as if they'd failed her. We know husbands and parents and children who feel the same way.

12. "I don't want to try to quit this behavior because I know it will just happen again."

Anorexics and bulimics feel a sense of powerlessness. Will it happen again? You are assuming the worst. You can set yourself up for failure by believing you will fail. Try something new. Instead of focusing on failure, focus on this idea: "If I get help, there's a good chance I will recover and my eating disorder won't paralyze me for the rest of my life." See yourself getting help and being successful; your behavior will follow suit. Say, "I do want to quit. There are no guarantees that my eating disorder will suddenly come back once I'm well. I have good cause to think that if others can do it, there's hope for me. Nothing is impossible with God's help."

Tina Morgan discovered this truth once she'd walked through the recovery process. She got a pass from the hospital for Easter weekend. She went home, but no one was in the apartment since most of her roommates were away for the holiday. She felt very lonely as she walked into the kitchen and saw a great big basket of Easter candy sitting in the center of the table. She looked at the big pink ribbon on the handle and then at the chocolate eggs and jelly beans and pink marshmallow bunnies inside the basket. Quickly, she picked out a chocolate egg and ate it. The chocolate tasted so good. It had been several weeks since she'd had any.

In the past she would have eaten most of the chocolate eggs in the basket as well as many jelly beans and marshmallow bunnies. She'd have thought, *I've blown it already, so why not?*

This time she stopped and turned that thought around: *I ate one little piece of candy. It's not going to kill me. It tasted good, but I don't have to eat five more. I can stop right now.* And she did.

Remembering to view success and failure from a long-term perspective is important. Try saying, "I'll eat normally today. And if I fail tomorrow, well, I'm sure it will be a disappointment, but at least I'm a few steps ahead of myself by tackling today successfully."

These twelve irrational beliefs make life more unbearable, and in desperation, the person again turns to some sort of anesthetic to ease this new pain. For anorexics or bulimics, that anesthetic is food.

Anesthesia

The bulimic consumes huge amounts of food and then purges to keep from gaining weight. The anorexic, on the other hand, avoids food at all costs, even though her mind is constantly obsessed with thoughts of food. Both try to mask the pain by controlling food in different ways. They develop rituals to show this control.

Rituals

Anorexics and bulimics devote a lot of time and energy to developing rituals associated with their eating disorders. Although the rituals may seem bizarre to others, those with eating disorders are comfortable with their rituals because they are familiar and safe and because they give the individuals an illusion of control. However, if rituals are not addressed for what they are—a self-imposed means of continuing a destructive lifestyle—they cannot be overcome.

Rituals can range from the time and/or place food is eaten to the type(s) of food eaten to the way it is consumed. Calories or portions may or may not have anything to do with rituals.

For instance, as Harry Beverly got to know his new anorexic patient, Cindy Briscoe, he discovered that she smelled each bite of food before eating it and never allowed the food to touch the sides of her mouth. When asked about it, she was unable to express her reasons for the particular ritual, other than it was the only way she could eat even the smallest amounts of food without feeling overwhelmingly guilty.

Marian Grier revealed to Pam Vredevelt that she never allowed herself to eat anything before 2:00 P.M. She had rationalized that, by depriving herself during the early part of the day, she deserved to binge and purge throughout the afternoon and evening. To her, any food eaten before 2:00 P.M. was proof of a terrible weakness on her part, convincing her that she was, indeed, a total failure. She deviated from her rigid schedule only during her pregnancies. The desire to protect her unborn children was strong enough to enable her to stop bingeing and purging temporarily. To maintain her illusion of control, however, Marian put herself on such a strict diet that she ate the exact same thing every day from the day she learned she was pregnant until each of the babies was born. Then, almost immediately after each childbirth, she resumed her previous cycle of bingeing and purging.

Debi Newman's patient, Tina Morgan, also had developed rituals in keeping with her lifestyle. A few months before she entered counseling, Tina began to limit her bingeing and purging to the late evening hours. She would cruise from one fast-food restaurant to another, bingeing in her car until she could eat no more. Then she would head back to the apartment she shared with her friends, where she would purge. If she wanted to eat again, she would get back in her car and go to different fast-food restaurants, alternating her route so the cashiers at the drive-up windows would not suspect her.

One common ritual among anorexics is that of limiting food

intake to two or three specific items, such as carrots, bran muffins, and/or strawberries. Anorexics have also been known to deprive themselves of healthy foods while sucking on an M & M® or a Life Saver® to appease their hunger pangs. Although candy would not normally be thought of as a dietary aid, the anorexic may consider it safe because it is small. And if it is not chewed, it lasts quite awhile.

This abuse of food gives the person a temporary high or fix. The frustration or anxiety is gone for the bulimic, and the anorexic feels in control because she has been able to starve all day, to command this one area of her life.

The Fix or Temporary High

We often compare this temporary high to that moment on the Ferris wheel ride when you first reach the top. High up in the air, with a view that seems godlike because it stretches for miles around, you feel exhilarated. You control the world. Or so you think—until the seat begins to sway back and forth and you think you might topple down from your lofty throne. Another dip and you panic. You have to get down, or you will scream.

That's the way the anorexic or bulimic feels when the fix wears off and reality sets in again. It's just like alcohol or drugs. The fantasy world of the high disappears, and the real world—with its problems—becomes all too apparent. So does the sickness. Now the cycle veers to guilt and shame.

Guilt and Shame

Anorexics and bulimics have two options when they reach this point in the cycle. The first is to deny the feeling of guilt. They say, "Oh, this is just my little vice. I don't drink too much or do drugs. And I can stop this anytime I want."

At the same time, however, the eating disorder is a little vice they don't reveal to anyone. And that's where shame sets in. Tina Morgan acknowledged to Debi she would rather tell her friends she had a drinking or drug problem than admit to her bingeing and purging. "I feel like such a pig for eating all this food. And vomiting is a disgusting habit. I hate the way it makes me feel."

Tina felt shame about what she was doing. She had heard guys on the campus talk about how gross bingeing and purging seemed to be. "I don't know how any girl could do those things," they'd said.

People delude themselves into thinking, *If I stuff my guilt and shame deep down inside me, they will go away.* Of course, they don't. Instead guilt and shame produce more pain—and start the cycle spinning all over again.

The person with an eating disorder is not aware of this cycle. Anorexics and bulimics live in a deep state of denial: denial of body image, denial of body damage, denial of family issues, and denial of rage and other negative emotions. As painful emotions are stuffed inside and avoided, the drive to eat or starve escalates, and the cycle repeats itself. Anyone with an obsessive-compulsive behavior like an eating disorder is doomed to sway back and forth at the top of that Ferris wheel. The view below, which once seemed so exhilarating, now becomes an enemy, which will destroy her if the seat swings too far and sends her hurtling to the ground.

Fortunately, some anorexics and bulimics scream out for help, which is a second response to guilt. This feeling can be a gift from God. Guilt often causes our patients to seek counseling. Then we can work them through the recovery steps described in Part Two of this book. Linda, the teen who didn't make the cheerleading squad, is now sixteen and making good progress in fighting against self-starvation. But the road to healing has been one of dedication and commitment on her part. She has worked hard to understand herself and those things that contribute to her anorexic behavior.

In this chapter we have discussed the cycle of addiction and some irrational beliefs and reasons used by anorexics and bulimics. After reviewing these last pages, you may be ready to take the next four steps: (1) admit to yourself that you struggle in these areas; (2) read on to learn what you can do about it; (3) share your problem with someone else; and (4) consider seeking professional help.

Above all, don't be discouraged. When you are honest with yourself and with God, He will honor your efforts and back you up 100 percent. Even when everything seems to be crumbling down around you and you feel like a hopeless case, remember that you and God as a team are a majority! Together you can walk the pathway to recovery, which we will explore in Part Two.

We will begin by helping you break the cycle of secrecy (Chapter 5). Then we will consider your family background (Chapter 6) and the mask that you have assumed because of your past experiences (Chapter 7). One dominant mask that a person with an eating disorder tends to wear is the mask of perfectionism. We will examine how you can be free from the pain of perfectionism (Chapter 8) and from painful emotions like anger (Chapter 9) and the shame you have attached to your sexuality (Chapter 10).

Once you have said good-bye to all the losses that have resulted from your eating disorder and grieved them (Chapter 11), we will walk you into recovery and maintenance by discussing how to establish healthy eating patterns (Chapter 12), how to be comfortable with your body image (Chapter 13), how to set up a support system (Chapter 14), and how to eat healthy for life (Chapter 15). Finally, we have a special word for those closest to you, your family members, who can support you in this journey (Chapter 16).

Come with us now as we throw off the thin disguise.

PART TWO

THE PATHWAY TO RECOVERY

5

BREAKING THE CYCLE OF SECRECY

It's 2:00 A.M. Your family has been asleep for hours, but you're awake, lying in bed thinking through every item in the refrigerator. You give up trying to sleep, crawl out of bed, and sneak down the stairs to the kitchen. The next hour is a blur as you consume all the leftovers and sweets you can find.

Gathering together all the cartons and wrappers, you stash the evidence in a trash can so no one will notice. Next, you force yourself to vomit so that the food won't turn into pounds. Feeling numb and dizzy, you tiptoe back up the stairs and climb under the covers once again. Suddenly, your husband startles you by asking, "Is everything all right?"

"Oh, sure," you reply quickly. "Everything's fine. I just had to go to the bathroom."

You feel guilty because you know he would be concerned if he was aware of your consistent bingeing and purging. Openness and honesty were values that you both agreed were vital to your relationship—and yet here you are, lying again. As you try to go to sleep, you find yourself praying the same old prayer you did the night before: "God, there's got to be more to life than this senseless routine. Forgive me for lying. I'll never do it again."

LYING AND STEALING

Anyone who seeks counseling for an eating disorder will, sooner or later, have to face the issue of secrecy and dishonesty. It is as much a part of the disorder as food. Many bulimics take exhaustive steps to cover up their bingeing. Lying, stealing, and secret rituals are woven into their daily routine. Lindsey is a classic example.

"During the five years of my first marriage," she told Pam, "my husband never uncovered my closely guarded secrets. No one knew. Covering my tracks was a part of my daily routine. Lying about food was second nature to me. For example, for several months I went to the same grocery daily to buy large quantities of binge foods. I told the checker I was a nursery school teacher buying snacks for the children."

Judy was involved with a different form of secrecy, which paralyzed her family relationships: "For thirteen years I was anorexic. My children never saw me eat a meal until two months ago. Stan always asked me to eat with the family, but I refused. Family food wasn't a part of my 'safe foods' or a part of my ritualized routine. To keep peace, I told them I had eaten so much fixing the meals, I couldn't eat with them during mealtime. I lied through my teeth. My regular routine was to starve myself all day, and then at 11:30 at night have a salad, yogurt, and an orange after everyone else was in bed. I hated the lies, but I was so comfortable with my rituals that I did anything to hang on to them."

Lying is not the only form of secrecy that accompanies eating disorders. Research indicates that 24 percent of those with eating disorders steal compulsively.[1]

Anna and Melanie were part of that 24 percent. For years they shoplifted consistently. "We had been best friends all through high school," Anna explained to Pam. "We wanted to go to a Christian college together, so we did. Our first year we were roommates, and that's when we began to eat pizza at midnight. Both of us started gaining weight. We were really depressed one night after consuming a giant combo pizza and decided to figure out a plan to get skinny again. We had tried the vomiting route but hated it because it was too hard and never worked real well.

"Our new plan was to try laxatives and diet pills. We wanted more pep for studying, and we knew that certain diet pills were loaded with caffeine. So we hopped into the car and drove to the nearest drugstore. We searched the aisles and found the laxatives and diet pills but were too embarrassed to take them to the cashier. We thought she might tell someone from school what we were doing. Stuffing the pills into our coat pockets, we bought nail polish to make it look like we had found what we wanted. All the way back to school we rationalized our dishonesty by telling ourselves they would never miss one package of laxatives and one of diet pills. After all, they had so many things in that store, what's the difference? And we were only going to try our plan for a week. We would just pay them back by buying more of the things we needed at their store instead of somewhere else."

But the stealing didn't stop that Friday night. A week later when their supplies ran out, they were back in the store doing the same thing again. Gradually, the laxatives and diet pills lost their effectiveness, so they had to double the amounts. One package of each item eventually turned into seven. Binges are also expensive, so to cut costs they began to steal their favorite binge foods. They knew when store managers were off duty and developed elaborate schemes to steal high-cost foods when only a few employees were in the store. This pattern continued throughout their college years.

After four years of compulsive laxative abuse, diet pill consumption, and stealing, Anna and Melanie had established some strong behavioral patterns. Could life ever be different for them? Could they be free from the stealing and pill popping? The answer is a resounding "Yes!"

OVERCOMING THE HINDRANCES OF RECOVERY

The first step you must take to begin walking the pathway of recovery is to learn to be honest with yourself and with others. Our patients must begin by admitting that there is a problem. This step may sound simplistic, but in reality, it can be the most difficult one of the entire recovery process.

Being Honest with Yourself

Without a doubt, the first hindrance you will come up against in recovery is denial. Breaking through denial requires complete honesty, first with yourself and then with others. Often our patients won't even use the word *anorexic* or *bulimic* when they first come for counseling. One reason that individual and/or group therapy is so important in the recovery process is that it often becomes the only place where the anorexic or bulimic can finally express herself honestly. Sometimes this happens through confrontation. A patient who is anorexic will boldly tell a new patient: "You're anorexic." Since we all realize "it takes one to know one," the new patient cannot convincingly deny this accusation. Individuals with eating disorders have been lying to themselves and others so long that they cling to the pattern, but they must let go of it if healing is to begin.

Take the time to carefully and honestly consider the following questions about your eating disorder (or that of someone you love). It will lead you to specific insights about yourself (or your loved one). Sometimes looking inside yourself is not a comfortable adventure. It's never fun rummaging through dirty laundry, but before clothes can be cleaned, the items need to be organized into piles. This exercise will help you sort through some of your thoughts and feelings. It may be painful, but it is in no way harmful. In fact, it will be healthful.

1. I first got involved in anorexia nervosa or bulimia when I

was (age) _____. I have been involved with this disorder for _____ years.

We ask patients to look back at the years they have been addicted to an eating disorder so they can realize the extent of their illness. It's hard to deny a problem that has been occurring for quite a few years.

2. I became involved in my eating disorder because (Tina Morgan would answer, "I saw my sorority sisters using this seemingly easy method of controlling their weight. It seemed to be a good thing to do."):

_____

_____

_____

We also ask our patients to remember if there was a reason for their eating disorder; often the beginning of this problem is associated with a major trauma in their lives, such as the onset of puberty (the girl is unconsciously thinking, *I don't want to become a woman*) or physical or sexual abuse. (Lisa realized that her anorexia began right after she was date raped. In counseling we showed her that this eating disorder was directly tied to that experience. She thought, *If I'm thin and unfeminine looking, no one will harm me in this way.*)

3. Over the years this eating disorder has caused me to lose the following things:

_____ Some of my friends. I don't have time for them any longer because I am so obsessed by my eating disorder.

_____ A close relationship with my family (my spouse or my children or my parents). I spend so much time thinking about how I can control my weight that I do not think about these important people in my life and share their joys and problems with them.

_____ My self-esteem. I'm ashamed that I binge and purge or starve myself or use laxatives to control my weight. I know these are extreme measures.

_____ My physical health:

        _____ My hair is becoming thin and tends to fall out when I comb it.

        _____ My skin has become very dry, and I have a downy fuzz on my face and arms.

        _____ I feel dizzy at times and have headaches.

        _____ My period is irregular or has stopped for three months or longer.

        _____ I have frequent cavities and/or my teeth are becoming discolored. My appearance is suffering from my disorder.

        _____ I might have suffered some impairment of my heart, my digestive tract, or my other organs because my body is not receiving the proper nutrients.

_____ My emotional health. I feel depressed and irritable a good bit of the time.

_____ My honesty. I have hidden my disorder from my family and my friends and sometimes have to lie to keep them from knowing how little I eat or how much I binge and purge.

_____ My grades at school are suffering, or my performance at work is becoming substandard.

_____ Other: _____

_____ .

    We ask our patients to list their losses so they will honestly face the toll these diseases have had on them. Cindy Briscoe's physical losses were all too evident. When she did this exercise, the redness from the defibrillator burns was still present on her chest, an ominous warning of the damage she was doing to her heart. She checked many of the other physical losses—dry skin, downy white fuzz, thin, limp hair, lack of a menstrual period—and the emotional losses of depression and irritability. The only losses she didn't check were the ones that are typically bulimic, not anorexic, such as discolored teeth.

Tina Morgan also checked many of the items above—and then added two of her own: the fun of her sorority activities and the close relationship with her boyfriend. Thinking back on the months they dated, she realized he would have been willing to accept her eating disorder and help her walk into recovery. She hoped that someday she would meet another young man like him.

Like the two married women at the beginning of this chapter, Marian Grier was losing an honest, intimate relationship with her husband and years of sharing her children's joys and sorrows. She had already admitted the physical losses, and now she added the emotional ones. Each of these patients concluded that the price of continuing her eating disorder was too high. She determined to get off the Ferris wheel of addiction for good, and she made a pact with herself that she would stay in counseling until we said she was healed.

Obviously, being honest with yourself means rejecting faulty thinking. Being honest with yourself also means you must realize that food is not the issue. As you learned in Chapter 4, food is merely the chosen anesthetic to deal with the underlying pain. Until that pain is dealt with, healing is impossible. A strong advantage of group therapy is that those involved will hold each other accountable to this fact. When a member gets off on her favorite "safe" subject—food—the others quickly remind her that "food is not the issue." Realizing this truth is a major releasing point in the recovery process.

Being Honest with Others

How did Melanie and Anna break free from the destructive chains of their dishonesty and secrecy? By taking responsibility for their actions. When they were willing to admit that they were stealing, Melanie and Anna took a major step toward freedom. While talking with someone they trusted, they confessed the deception that had been a regular part of their daily interaction with others. The admission opened the door for their friends to support them and to hold them accountable.

Next, they chose to change. In biblical terms, they "repented." Repentance occurred when they made a 180-degree turn and chose to walk in the opposite direction away from their former behavior. Melanie and Anna determined to stop stealing. They stopped rationalizing and recognized that their actions were destroying them.

Melanie and Anna made a commitment to themselves and to each other to consciously work on speaking the truth. They made a pact not to tell even "little lies." But they didn't stop there. They went a step further and prayed to God for added strength to be transparent and to quit hiding behind secret rituals. They also committed themselves to pray daily for each other to be open and truthful.

When they risked vulnerability, they began to get well. Being honest with others became more important than being liked by others. An exciting by-product of their commitment to transparency appeared. Their friends began to invite them out more often and told them how much more they appreciated the real Anna and Melanie. As a result, they were able to build deeper and more meaningful relationships.

Both of them are now free. It took some decisive action and hard work, but they'll be the first to tell you, "It's worth every bit of effort to live in freedom rather than in bondage."

God's Word has a lot to say about truth and honesty. While Jesus was teaching in the temple one afternoon, He said, "If you hold to my teaching, you are really my disciples. Then you will know the truth, and the truth will set you free."[2] The principle here is that truth brings freedom. Christ came to set us free and to help us walk in the light . . . and in the truth.

Can you see now why it is vital to break the cycle of secrecy that has held you in its power? And the only way to break that power is to face it head-on with honesty. As an anorexic or a bulimic, you have probably viewed yourself as a dishonest person for so long, you don't know how to start being honest again. But be encouraged. Although a large part of you wants to maintain the secrecy, there is also a part of you that wants to break free. If that weren't true, you would not be reading this book.

The truth is, you are not a hopelessly dishonest person. It is time now to affirm and strengthen the part of you that so desires to be honest with yourself and with others. Take that first step. Admit to yourself that you have an eating disorder, and then find someone else to share this truth with. That first small step will begin to break your eating disorder's hold over you, and you will be on your way to freedom at last!

Total freedom comes from "safe" exposure, which is another advantage of professional counseling for persons with eating disorders. In either individual or group therapy, the anorexic or bulimic is able to bring her problem into the light without fear of rejection or judgment. In her recovery she needs someone who will listen, understand, accept—and at the same time encourage change and healing.

And many of our patients have found that they need God to walk with them on the pathway to recovery. They need to see God as their friend.

GOD AS A COMPANION ON THE JOURNEY

Our patients frequently have trouble picturing God as a companion and friend. They see Him as a black-robed judge (or as a critical parent) who blames them for their problems. An anorexic or a bulimic has difficulty understanding that God loves her even when she is starving herself or when she is in the midst of a bingeing and purging session. Unconditional love is a foreign concept to almost anyone raised in a dysfunctional family, but when that concept is understood and appropriated, it is a tremendous point of release, enabling the person with the eating disorder to move out of denial and into honesty without fear of rejection and failure.

God's Rebuilding Process

In his book *Rebuilding the Real You,* Dr. Jack Hayford answers questions like, "If Jesus came to redeem and restore me, why do I still feel so broken?"; "Why does it take so long to get better?"; and "How can I get moving and rise above the things that cripple me?" Although his book was not written strictly to those with eating disorders, the principles certainly apply. Let's look at two of his main ideas.

Rebuilding the Real You is based on the Old Testament Book of Nehemiah, which tells of the rebuilding and restoration of the walls of Jerusalem. The story of Nehemiah opens with the prophet weeping over the news that the walls have been broken down. Nehemiah is a picture of God's Holy Spirit, Who grieves over His children whose lives have been crushed and broken. His desire is to see their lives rebuilt and restored to His original purpose and design. What's the point? God longs to see you healed and restored even more than you do. He desires it so much that He is committed to seeing you through the recovery process from start to finish, even in those times when you want to throw your hands up in the air and quit. As Philippians 1:6 promises, "He who has begun a good work in you will complete it." Once you have made that decision to walk the pathway of healing, God will walk it with you—and He will see that you make it to the end.

All the necessary requirements for rebuilding the real you are available if you truly want to access them. This principle is evident in Nehemiah 2:4–9, which tells of Nehemiah's going to the king requesting provisions to rebuild the walls. Nehemiah seeks four specific things:

1. Time—an extended period of leave from his duties at the palace.
2. Authority to enter the region of activity.

3. Resources for the actual building project.
4. Troops to secure his mission and support him in the event of opposition.[3]

Can you see the parallels here? The very first thing that Nehemiah asked for was *time*—several years, actually. He recognized that the rebuilding process was going to require a major investment of his time. The same is true for anyone desiring healing from an eating disorder.

Nehemiah then asked for *letters from the king,* authorizing him to enter the area of destruction. This may be one of the more painful steps in the healing process because the anorexic or bulimic herself must give permission for those broken-down areas of her life to be restored, knowing that this will require painful probing of some previously "off limit" arenas of her life. Keeping the desired results in mind, however, can ease the pain during restoration.

Nehemiah's primary *building materials* were the rocks from the former walls—debris, trash, rubbish. And yet, through the restorative process, the rubble was transformed into something strong and beautiful. The good news is that God can take the very areas of our lives that have been rendered seemingly useless through years of brokenness and destruction, and restore them to the point where we are able to bless and encourage others as well as be blessed and encouraged ourselves.

Nehemiah's last request was for *troops to secure his mission and support him in the event of opposition.* Nehemiah was a wise man, who knew with a certainty that his rebuilding project was going to face opposition. The person trying to overcome an eating disorder can expect no less. Opposition will come in the forms of frustration, temptation, pain, anger, despair, and confusion, just to mention a few. That's why "support troops" are vital. Those troops may be your family and/or friends, a trusted therapist or pastor, and members of group counseling sessions. Whoever they are, they are a necessary part of the healing and restorative process. It's just too difficult a task to try to "go it alone," as anyone who has tried to overcome anorexia or bulimia by herself can attest.

We also ask our patients to picture God walking beside them, holding their hand, as they go through the recovery process, just as David pictures God walking beside him in many of the Psalms. The king of Israel was continually surrounded by political enemies who wanted to kill and destroy him. In fact, many of the Psalms are David's cry for help. And many of them show his belief in a God who walked beside him. "You hold me by my right hand," he says. "You will guide me with Your counsel, / And afterward receive me to glory."[4] God promises you the same guidance and love and help and caring. Let Him walk down the pathway to recovery with you.

6

A FAMILY AFFAIR

As Cindy Briscoe's treatment time in the hospital progressed, Harry Beverly was becoming accustomed to her withdrawn, detached mannerisms. Almost everything he had learned from her to date had come through gentle, patient probing because she seldom offered any information on her own. Today seemed no different.

"How are you this morning, Cindy?" asked Harry, settling into a corner chair near the foot of her bed.

She sat huddled under a blanket, silently twisting a strand of hair around one finger. She shrugged, not looking up. "Okay," she answered.

Harry tried again, "Did you enjoy your breakfast?"

That got her attention. "No," she said, lifting her head as she looked into his eyes briefly. "It was huge, and they made me eat all of it. I feel so fat, I can't stand it."

"What do you mean, you feel fat?" Harry asked. "I'm not sure I understand how that feels."

Cindy seemed a bit impatient. "You know," she said. "Fat. Full. Like I'm going to explode." She dropped her eyes. "It was awful. Just like when my mom hassles me about eating. I really hate it when she does that."

"Do you feel that people hassle you quite a bit about eating?" asked Harry.

She raised her head again, but this time her gaze wandered around the room, as if she were afraid to look at Harry while she spoke. "All the time," she said. "Always. And I just don't understand why. I mean, it's nobody's business what I eat, so why don't they just leave me alone?"

"Is that what you want?" Harry asked. "For people to leave you alone?"

Confusion registered on Cindy's gaunt face, and she hesitated before answering. "I . . . I don't know. Sometimes I do. Especially my mom, but . . ."

Cindy's voice trailed off, and Harry waited a moment before asking his next question. "What about your mom, Cindy? Why do you want her to leave you alone?"

"Because . . ." She stopped, darting her eyes toward Harry, then back toward the wall. "Because she bugs me," she said. "All the time. About everything. She's always telling me what to do, what to say, how to act. My brothers get to do anything they want, but she treats me like a baby. She doesn't trust me. She watches every move I make. And when . . . I mess up, I think she's glad because then she doesn't talk to me for weeks. She just looks at me with that I-told-you-so face."

Harry was encouraged. This was the most feedback he'd gotten from her at one time. "And what about your dad?" he went on. "Does he do the same thing?"

Cindy shook her head quickly. "Oh no," she said. "My dad's not like her at all. But . . . when it comes to Mom, he's no help. No one is."

Cindy had been raised in a dysfunctional family. The relationships among the Briscoe family members were not healthy. In a dysfunctional family, parents use perfectionism or manipulation or shame and guilt or neglect or rage to teach their children what to do and how to behave, which results in the children's learning unhealthy patterns of relating to family members and other people. These unhealthy patterns often include an intense need for control and an enmeshment with the family; children lose their identity, fear acknowledging or expressing feelings, and have a heightened sense of worthlessness. Children in this type of family develop a love hunger because their parents are not showing them the love and affection they need to mature to healthy, happy adults.

Obviously, families are dysfunctional in differing degrees. One day, when we were discussing dysfunctional families on the "Minirth-Meier Clinic" radio program, a listener called in and said, "I'm really confused. I thought I was raised in a healthy family. But as I hear you talk about dysfunctional families, I see characteristics of my childhood."

Frank Minirth answered this listener by saying, "All families are dysfunctional to some degree. None of us was raised in a perfect family. And none of us will create a perfect family situation for our children. I haven't. That's because none of us is perfect. Neither do we live in a perfect world. When Adam and Eve sinned in the Garden of Eden, they destroyed the paradise God had created for them. None of us can expect perfection here on earth."

The three unwritten laws of any dysfunctional family are: don't talk, don't trust, don't feel. Persons with eating disorders have long since adopted these beliefs and are very uncomfortable discussing the family of origin. They believe they are betraying their families by saying anything negative about them. It is one of the most frightening aspects of their lives to focus on. And yet, it is vital for their recovery.

Types of Dysfunctional Families

We'd like you to look at five general types of dysfunctional families: (1) the upside-down family, (2) the perfectionistic family,

(3) the controlling family, (4) the rageaholic family, and (5) the rigid family. As we describe these families to you, place a mental check mark next to the one that applies to your family of origin. Your family may be a combination of two types. Cindy Briscoe's was.

_____ 1) The Upside-Down Family

Cindy's family was an upside-down family. In this family, the child meets the emotional needs of the parents—primarily the mother—rather than the other way around. At the same time, the father's love must often be earned by the child's behavior. This situation teaches a child that her own needs are not nearly as important as those of her parents since her parents are vital for the survival of the family. As the child learns to suppress and deny her needs, she eventually becomes so out of touch with those needs that, by the time she reaches adolescence, she is no longer aware of what her needs are. At this point, her unmet needs are so tremendous she begins to fall apart and demand that someone give her attention. The onset of an eating disorder often takes place at this time.

The father may very well be a workaholic. Upside-down families are usually middle class to upper middle class, and the children's physical and financial needs are adequately met. However, both parents often severely neglect their emotional needs.

The problems escalate when a girl reaches puberty. As her body changes, the father is unsure of the appropriate boundaries for his relationship with his rapidly changing daughter. He will often withdraw from her entirely to maintain a "safe" relationship. The child feels abandoned, and yet, because she has learned to deny her feelings, she tries to ignore the hurt. As we learned in Chapter 4, unacknowledged hurt and pain do *not* go away.

The unwritten rules in an upside-down family are:
- The child should meet the emotional needs of the parent (or parents).

- Self-sacrifice is the prized quality.
- Therefore, the child learns to deny her needs and feelings.

———— 2) The Perfectionistic Family

In healthy families, children are taught to excel, to capitalize on their strengths, to recognize their weaknesses, and to recover and learn from their mistakes. In the dysfunctional family, each member must be an overachiever, never falling short in anything—standards that are, of course, impossible to achieve.

This family has a need to be regarded as all-good and picture perfect, even though an individual in the family (usually the daughter) may be seen as bad. One patient of ours, Linda Jeffers, came from a family in which her mother had a master's degree in education, but she stayed home to raise her children instead of pursuing a career in the marketplace; her father was a trial lawyer who made a lot of money and was on the board of several Christian institutions. Linda was the middle child of three daughters.

Each girl had to wear the latest designer clothes, make the best grades, be active in school plays and clubs, excel at every opportunity because the family was able to provide all the amenities—singing and piano and horseback riding lessons—that would make this possible.

The greatest emphasis in her family was on appearance. Her father commented to her, "Men don't like fat girls," and warned her, "Don't ever start gaining weight, or you won't be popular."

Linda knew that everything she did individually had to be evaluated by whether or not it was in the best interests of keeping up this facade of "the perfect family." If she felt angry or resentful, for instance, she had to go to her room until she could get over these feelings and come out with a smile on her face.

Linda eventually shared with Pam Vredevelt what it was like when her family went to church on Sundays. All the way to church, her parents would yell and scream at each other, but as soon as they walked into the sanctuary, everything changed. They all put on smiles. Mom made her way to the piano, and Dad portrayed his part as the respectable church deacon. To everyone else, the Jefferses were the ideal family. In Linda's eyes, they were not. Therefore, she reasoned that she must, indeed, be the bad one.

In other perfectionistic families Dad might constantly tease Mom: "You'd better watch it, dear. Your clothes are really starting to get tight. You'll be a size sixteen before you know it." Or Dad might say, "You'd look so much better if you'd just lose twenty pounds." And Dad might even take food away from Mom: "You don't really need that piece of pie." Or he might suggest that she order a light meal at a restaurant. Linda heard enough of this kind of talk that she unconsciously vowed, "I'll never be overweight like my mom." Yet Linda resembled Mom's side of the family. She told us, "I have 'fat genes.'" And she was partly right; her metabolism was low.

In perfectionistic families, children are told, "Well, just do the best that you can." But when they do the best that they can—get a *C*, for instance, on a math test—that's not quite good enough.

The unwritten rules in a perfectionistic family are:

- Every family member must "measure up."
- Every family member must make the family look great.
- Every family member can have only positive feelings.
- Every family member must look good on the outside at all times.
- Therefore, the child learns, "I'm unacceptable if I'm not perfect."

_____ 3) The Controlling Family

A healthy level of protection is necessary for the nurturing and survival of any family. A dysfunctional family carries that to extremes. In an anorexic's family, children are sometimes overprotected. They have different rules from those of their friends; they may have to come home an hour or two earlier than everyone else, for instance. Children are smothered in an effort to control every possible danger or problem.

Often parents in a controlling family are trying to live their lives through their children. They have "unfinished business"—a major goal, need, or expectation that was not fulfilled—from their own pasts, which they are passing on to the next generation.

Karen was obviously entrapped by her mother's unfinished business. Her mother had always wanted to be a concert pianist, but because she came from a poor family, the money for year after year of piano lessons with the finest teachers was not available.

Karen's piano lessons began at age three. Once Karen started to perform in concerts at school and in the community, her father began to receive compliments about her obvious talent so he, too, pushed her to excel. He sent her to expensive summer camps where she could concentrate on perfecting her performance and enrolled her in the local music conservatory for further studies.

Parents in controlling families often exert influence on the children through guilt and shame. Karen's dad reminded her: "You are so fortunate that your mother and I are willing to spend so much money—and time—encouraging your talent. Lots of kids aren't able to do all these things. Your mother is just one example."

And then Karen's mother would chime in: "I would have given anything if I could have been a concert pianist. Your achievement doesn't just come from your natural talent. It's because of what we've done to help you, all the money we've spent on your lessons." And on and on and on.

Karen didn't have many friends at school because she had to practice three to four hours a day. Yet if she wanted to go to a slumber party with the few friends she had or spend time with them, her parents would shame her by saying, "You can't do that. You'll miss practicing that day. You just don't appreciate us or what we've done for you." Guilt and shame—two strong persuaders that held Karen captive.

In Karen's case, both parents were controlling. In other families it may be just one parent. Sometimes the parents are divorced or separated but not always. We can usually predict that the marriage is weak, however, and in most cases there is little love or intimacy between the parents.

Hostile controlling comes most often from the mother and may be in the form of overt or covert (hidden) controlling. It can include yelling, screaming, or hysteria over something as minor as leaving a wet towel on the floor. Yet there is little consistency in that the same infraction may cause no reaction whatsoever the following day.

The unwritten rules in a controlling family are:

• The parents' unfinished business becomes the child's business.

• Parents assume that it's okay to control the family through guilt and shame.

• Therefore, the child learns, "My feelings and thoughts or opinions don't count. It is wrong to have them."

———— 4) The Rageaholic Family

In the rageaholic family only the parent or one parent is allowed to express feelings. And the predominant feeling is obviously rage or anger. Unfortunately, the children are taught to believe that they are responsible for that anger. "If you hadn't left that toy out, Dad wouldn't have hit you (or gotten mad). It's all your fault." Often these words are said over and over again. Just as often the thought is unexpressed but evident by the way one parent does anything he or she can to keep the rageaholic calm. "Be quiet," Mom may say. "Dad's had a bad day." Or Dad may say, "Keep your room clean. You know how mad Mom gets when you don't make your bed and clean up."

Mothers in rageaholic families may have anger and rage from the family of origin, and in some cases the daughter becomes an "emotional receptacle" for that rage. Although the mother is, in actuality, angry with herself and her parents, she pushes that anger onto her daughter. Mom may consider herself selfish, and whenever she sees her daughter doing something, she'll tell her daughter that she's selfish or evil or bad. She'll say, "What's wrong with you? Why do you act this way? No daughter of mine would act this way." Every negative thing that the mother throws out, the daughter receives and believes. If the mother tells her daughter that she is evil and selfish, the daughter assumes it must be so since a child does not have the cognitive abilities to decipher whether or not Mom is right or wrong. Mom is always seen as right when she criticizes the daughter.

As Harry Beverly got to know Cindy better, he recognized this pattern in the Briscoe family. Cindy's mother, Christine, had been raised in a dysfunctional family. Her father was an alcoholic who regularly disappeared from home for several days at a time; her mother was a controlling enabler. Although Christine resolved early in her marriage to be a good mother and to raise her children differently from the way her parents raised her, she eventually saw her daughter as an extension of herself—a self she wasn't too happy with.

Cindy's father, on the other hand, was raised by his grandmother until, at the age of sixteen, he struck out on his own. Cindy had always looked to her father for affection, but although he loved his daughter, demonstrating that love was difficult for him.

Cindy firmly believed that her parents cared more for her two brothers—one older and one younger than she—because they were allowed many more privileges and were seldom the objects of their mother's negative emotions. She reasoned that if she had been born a boy, her mother would have loved her the way she did Cindy's brothers.

Sometimes alcohol or drugs cause the parent to be rageaholic. Sometimes the physical abuse also extends to sexual abuse. Whatever the abuse, there is an unspoken understanding that it's okay for a parent who is angry to abuse you because Dad (or Mom) never admits being sorry or being at fault. The child learns to hate this rageful parent (or parents), and whenever she feels angry, she represses it completely for fear she will lose her temper as her parent does.

The unwritten rules in a rageaholic family are:
- Parents are the only ones who are permitted to have feelings.
- The child is responsible for the parent's rage.
- The unspoken standard is that it's okay to abuse a child when a parent is angry.
- Therefore, the child learns to completely repress her anger.

_____ 5) The Rigid Family

Healthy families are warm and affectionate. The members give and receive hugs, kisses, and other appropriate touches and physical closeness. Rules, as well as people, are flexible. That is not so in dysfunctional families where flexibility is a nonexistent concept and affection is seldom expressed.

Fathers who are very logical and intelligent tend to be as obsessive about the standards in their families as they are about bottom-line profitability or the exact specifications of a product. Tina Morgan's dad was a lineman for the power company. There was a certain way to do things and a certain way not to do things.

Tina's dad did not abuse her physically, but there was no warmth in her family; no emotions were expressed. Nor was there any kissing or hugging or expressing the words, "I love you." The unspoken message was: each family member should be able to take care of himself or herself. We call this emotional neglect.

Tina naturally wanted to be loved and touched and nurtured, and when those needs weren't met, she filled her hunger for affection with food. She also thought that it must be wrong to want to be loved and touched and cared for, so she grew up feeling that emotions and longings are wrong.

The unwritten rules in a rigid family are:
- As long as a child's physical needs are being met, the child is okay. The child's emotional needs are not considered.
- Nurturing—hugging, kissing, or saying, "I love you"—is wrong.
- Family members are supposed to take care of themselves.

- Therefore, the child believes that emotions and longings are wrong.

Because of the unwritten rules in these dysfunctional families, children learn to respond to situations in unhealthy ways, which become a way of life for them.

THE ADVERSE EFFECTS OF DYSFUNCTIONAL FAMILIES

Let's look at five negative influences a dysfunctional family can have on a child.

1. Abnormal Desire to Please People

In a dysfunctional family, there are two primary ways of dealing with conflict: deny it entirely or become completely engulfed in it, resulting in ongoing chaos. Whereas in a healthy family, children learn that conflict is inevitable and there are constructive ways of resolving it, the child from the dysfunctional home has no resources for handling conflict. She therefore avoids it at all costs.

Cindy Briscoe came from a religious home where conflict was not acceptable. She never really learned that conflict and disagreement between people were okay. Everyone in her family always had to agree. As Cindy got older, she was reluctant to disagree with her peers. She became a people pleaser who felt it better to sacrifice her thoughts than to confront other people.

2. An Inability to Cope with Painful Feelings

Some children from dysfunctional families learn to control their emotions by starving or bingeing and purging, which bring a temporary calm. Their eating disorders become their only method of reducing their anxieties since they have not learned how to approach their negative feelings or soothe themselves in the ways most of us do, through support from loved ones—talks with Mom or Dad and hugs from family members.

3. A Lack of the Ability to "Be Oneself"

A healthy family establishes reasonable levels of togetherness, but it also encourages individuals to discover their own identities. Although the family unit is important, so is each family member, and each is affirmed for differences. A dysfunctional family has no concept of individuality. Family members work together for the good of the whole, even if one (or more) gets lost in the process.

Parents are overinvolved in the child's life. The child, then, does not feel confident to make her own decisions. Family members will try to tell the child how to act or how to be. Then when the child is an adult, she feels as if she can't cope with life by herself.

When these girls try to separate themselves from their parents and make their own decisions, which is a normal part of the maturing process, they are criticized, ignored, or pulled back to meet the needs of the family. The message is that it is not okay for them to have their own feelings or thoughts or needs. They feel a sense of shame because what they consider acceptable obviously isn't to the family as a unit. A dual fear enters here; these girls fear abandonment by their families if they go their own way, but they also fear becoming so enmeshed in the family that they lose their own identities.

4. An Unhealthy Defense Mechanism—Splitting

A basic concept for any anorexic or bulimic to understand is "splitting." Throughout childhood, the person has "split" herself into two parts—the good part, and the bad part. The good part does everything she is told, maintains the family image, is always sweet and kind, and never, never gets angry. The bad part hides those angry feelings that are not allowed to show, the frustrations and hurts and needs that have no place in a dysfunctional family. As the child gets older, she lives in constant fear that the bad part will gain control and take over the good part entirely.

Splitting is the child's unconscious attempt to defend herself and separate the good in her mom from the bad. The child wants to look only at the good in Mom and to deny the bad. If she acknowledges that part of Mom is bad, then Mom might do something bad, like leave her. For her own emotional survival, she chooses to see her parents as perfect. Of course, if they are perfect and they reject her, then she must obviously be the imperfect one.

All young children are basically egocentric and selfish, believing that the world revolves around them. As a result, they tend to compartmentalize their parents to some degree, but as they mature, they realize that good and bad are in everyone. They are therefore able to perceive their parents more realistically. Children with eating disorders do not mature normally, and they become stuck at the compartmentalization stage, believing that everything is either good or bad. They develop a pattern of unrealistic black-and-white thinking in every area of their lives.

Cindy, for instance, had intense resentment and hatred for her mother, and buried those feelings deep within her "bad" self. At an early age she was convinced that if she acknowledged those feelings, she would be rejected by her entire family. It wasn't until Harry asked her to write a letter to her parents—one that she would never mail—expressing those long-buried feelings that Cindy was able to begin integrating her two selves. By identifying the offenses and feeling the hurts, she could finally begin to work through the healing process.

5. Low Impulse Control or "I Want It Now!"

Children from dysfunctional families have problems delaying gratification of their needs simply because they are so very needy inside. Anyone who shows them attention is immediately overwhelmed and smothered by these needy young ladies, who come from families that have rarely made them feel special in any way.

A LIVING FAMILY SCULPTURE

Persons struggling with eating disorders, and especially anorexics, often feel powerless to change their circumstances. Creating a living family sculpture gives them a chance to express what they would like to have changed in the family if they had been given the opportunity.

This sculpting is done in group therapy. The patient "directs" the exercise, with members of the group playing different roles in her family. In the first part of the exercise, the patient arranges the actors to represent the way she saw her family (the way she felt they related to each other). For example, Cindy placed her father on a chair because she saw him as the head of the family. She then placed her mother directly beside her father, with his arm leaning on her shoulder, because in reality she regarded her mother as the strong one. Next she placed her older brother and sister slightly removed from her parents because she felt they did not really care about their parents' anger. Nearer to her parents, she placed herself and her little brother. Finally, she had them all kneel down before her parents because she saw her parents as being in total control of every aspect of their lives.

Cindy's family sculpture told a lot about the Briscoe family. Dad brought home the paycheck; he was the head of the household who made decisions about whether or not the family could afford to send the kids to camp or whether or not the family could buy a new car. But Dad's arm was leaning on Mom's shoulder because Mom was the one who helped the kids with their everyday problems and disciplined them when they did something wrong.

The next part of the family sculpture exercise is to rearrange the family members as the patient would have liked the family to be. When Harry asked Cindy to rearrange her family into a new sculpture, things changed dramatically.

"I want my mother over there in the corner," Cindy announced. "And I want to be on the other side of the room—invisible—so she can't get to me." Invisible. Even as she said the word, Cindy began to make the first connection between her feelings of powerlessness at home and her anorexic behavior. We helped her recognize that she wanted to be invisible. She wanted to be away from her family. A light bulb went on for her when she realized she was starving herself so she could make herself disappear.

Draw your own family sculpture in the space below. Think about the relationships in your childhood family. Where would you put your father? Your mother? Would they be close beside each other or far away, with your father's or mother's back turned away from the other spouse? Where would your sisters or brothers be in relationship to your parents? Would one of them be very close—almost too close—to your mother, for instance? And where would you put yourself? Close to a parent? A sibling? Or far away from anyone else, off by yourself?

Think about how you felt in that family situation. Safe and secure? Or lonely and unhappy? Which feelings are still with you today? Could some of them be feeding your eating disorder as Cindy's feelings made her want to disappear? (We will examine negative emotions and how to overcome them in Chapter 9.)

Now do the second part of the sculpting exercise. Redraw your family—this time as you would like to have seen it.

Although the anorexic or bulimic must gain a new understanding of the dynamics of her family of origin, the purpose is not to place the blame for an eating disorder on anyone. One of the keys to healing is to realize that individual members of the same family can perceive things in very different ways. It doesn't make one way right and the other wrong. The different perceptions simply affected the way each family member reacted to (and coped with) given situations. Many other factors of a person's life, social and educational experiences, for instance, can contribute to the tendency to have an eating disorder. In this chapter we have just identified the common themes in families.

As Harry Beverly was meeting with Cindy Briscoe, he was also meeting with her parents. His experience in working with people with eating disorders led him to know that family involvement is a crucial part of the recovery process. His aim was not to blame the parents but to help the family know how they could be a part of the solution. Harry asked Cindy's parents to consider the following family contract, which would guide their relationships with Cindy in the future. With the whole family working together, her recovery process could begin.

FAMILY CONTRACT

The contract on page 97, which is similar to the one Cindy's parents signed, will assist you in knowing how to work with your child or spouse. It is best for you to sit down with your child or spouse and go through this contract step by step so you can talk through the statements. Then post it where it can be easily referred to. We hope this will be a valuable tool in understanding your loved one.

PARENT'S (OR SPOUSE'S) VOW

1. I'm going to give you the permission to "run your own life," the right to make decisions, even if I or others disagree with you.

2. I'm going to give you the permission to stop being a pleaser. You do not have to do or say what I want you to.

3. I'm going to give you permission to have your privacy. I will trust you without your needing to prove your actions to me.

4. I acknowledge that you are not the only person with problems. I will agree to seek counseling for myself and address my own issues, not yours.

5. I know that I cannot always protect you. If you are old enough (age ?), you need to be on your own, making decisions for yourself.

6. However, as a parent (or spouse) I have the right to intervene to save your life. I will get you professional help if you will not do it yourself.

7. As a parent (or spouse) I must trust you to work on your recovery without having to feel as if I have to do it for you.

8. I retain the right to express my anger and not feel guilty for it later. This anger does not negate my love for you.

9. I also retain the right to express my disappointment with you and not feel guilty for it later. Again this does not negate my love for you.

Signed: _____

_____

ANOREXIC'S (OR BULIMIC'S) VOW

1. I have the permission to eat three meals a day without feeling guilty.

2. I have the permission to ask for what I want, knowing that I cannot demand that you give it to me.

3. I refuse to "mind read" your thoughts and opinions. I want each of us to communicate without having to guess what the other is thinking and feeling. If you cannot tell me what you think or feel, then I'm going to "act as if" you are not bothered by me.

4. I retain the right to express my anger and not feel guilty for it later. This anger does not negate my love for you.

5. I also retain the right to express my disappointment with you and not feel guilty for it later. Again this does not negate my love for you.

6. I ask that we decide as a family when we will talk about my relationship with food.

We will talk about food only _____ a week.

Signed: _____

Cindy Briscoe and her parents signed this contract when she was in the hospital. In the next weeks we would help her work through the anger she felt toward her mother. But first let's look at the masks she and Marian Grier and other persons with eating disorders wear in their relationships.

7

UNVEILING
THE MASKS

When I was a little girl, I desperately wanted to be accepted by my parents." Marian Grier sat opposite Pam Vredevelt. "My father is a perfectionist; my mother, strong-willed and assertive. My older sister is an extrovert and was always voicing her opinions and criticisms. The stage was set for me. As an insecure younger child, I was always trying to find a way to belong. I deeply desired to please all three of them, and I quickly learned that when I agreed with everything they said, they accepted me. To disagree meant rejection, which I avoided in every possible way. My mission in life was to keep peace at all costs."

Pam nodded as Marian continued.

"I saw constant confrontation between my older sister and my parents. Her honesty sparked friction in our home. It was obvious to me that openness only meant trouble. I decided that I'd be smarter than my sister. My battle plan was emotional hibernation. I withdrew into a shell when any differences began to surface."

"And did you find this worked for you?" Pam asked.

"Yes. It worked so well that I formed my friendships with others the same way. I tried to read their minds, to make sure that what I said was what they wanted to hear. I watched them intently for cues to see what they liked in others and then tried to conform. I could easily have run away with a National People Pleaser Award had one been offered."

"Did you continue relating to others this way during college?" asked Pam.

"Yes, I actually quit dating a guy when I found out my roommate had her eye on him too! It was the safe thing to do. I was afraid Karen would reject me if I didn't end the relationship. I was also fearful that Jim would drop me if he knew Karen was interested in him. To eliminate both possibilities, I told Jim I didn't want to date him anymore. But the cost of my emotional hibernation outweighed the benefits, and something in me snapped. I remember crying angrily all night. I hated Karen for liking Jim. I hated everything."

"It seems like people pleasing had taken its toll," Pam said compassionately.

Marian nodded.

"I resented the control that other people had over me. I was exhausted from trying to be perfect. I didn't care if everyone was happy anymore. I desperately wanted to be myself but was afraid of being different. I had played the game of being what other people wanted for so long, I wasn't aware of a unique identity of my own. I felt trapped . . . confused . . . frustrated. That's when I began to find relief through bingeing."

As you can see, Marian Grier had compromised who she was in her efforts to please people. She had allowed others to control her, starting with her parents and continuing with her husband, Bob.

One of the things Pam Vredevelt worked with Marian on during the course of her therapy was learning to replace the doormat approach to life with healthy relationship-building skills. While growing up, Marian had learned to equate closeness and acceptance with agreement, and rejection and alienation with disagreement. That outlook was crippling her. But in time, Marian learned that she didn't always have to be what other people wanted or expected.

The rest of this chapter discusses some of the things Marian—and countless others—learned about the high cost of wearing masks to please others and the benefits of being herself.

THE MASKS

People Pleaser

One of the most common masks anorexics or bulimics wear is that of the people pleaser. As we discussed previously, the people pleaser is the "good girl" who disregards herself and her feelings, focusing solely on pleasing others, meeting their needs, doing what they want her to do, denying the validity of her own needs. Brenda, for example, is a bulimic who had experienced extreme physical and mental abuse from her father. However, years later when her father was stricken with cancer, she took him into her home, nursing him day and night in addition to caring for her own family. This situation put a great strain on Brenda physically and emotionally, yet she felt she had no right to do otherwise.

OPD (Obnoxious Personality Disorder)

This mask is much less common than that of the pleaser. She wants to appear "together" at all times, so she keeps people at a distance through her aggressive behavior, attempting to hide her vulnerability.

Most of the other girls on the floor walked on eggshells around Faye. They were afraid of conflict (people pleasers, actresses) and no one wanted to be the one to set Faye off. One night while watching the show "Designing Women," one of the characters was described as having OPD (obnoxious personality disorder).

"That's you, Faye," Denise blurted out unexpectedly. The killer look Faye gave after her comment made Denise regret she had been so hasty in her words. Denise stopped regretting them the next day when Faye finally opened up in group. Faye covered up her vulnerability and insecurity with her rough exterior. Inside, she shared many of the same feelings as the rest of the girls. Faye recognized the mask she wore and took it off in group that day. Her fear was that if she really let others see how needy and vulnerable she was they would respond by hurting her. Instead, the group responded by accepting her on a deeper level than she had been accepted in her life.

Actress

No one ever suspects that this happy-go-lucky girl has a problem of any kind. Underneath her bubbly exterior, however, is a pain-filled young lady who hates herself and feels completely worthless. Although on the surface her relationships are pleasing to others, they are not close or fulfilling. April fits this description perfectly. A cheerleader in high school, she is on the student council and will probably appear in her senior yearbook as "Most Likely to Succeed." Inside, April wonders if life is worth living long enough to graduate.

Until Brenda and Jane and April can get in touch with their feelings and take off their masks, they will never learn to relate to others in an honest, healthy way. And they will never move into the healing necessary to overcome their eating disorders.

MASK INVENTORY

Now let's learn how to take a "mask inventory." This exercise is often used in therapy to enable individuals to peel off that outer mask and find the real self underneath.

The exercise is quite simple. It requires only a small paper bag and some crayons. First, the patient is instructed to draw a picture of herself on the outside of the bag—the face that she normally shows the world. Almost always the picture is of a smiling, happy, people-pleasing face, although anorexics occasionally draw an ugly picture because they do not want to appear attractive to others. After the patient has drawn the picture, she writes about that face.

Immediately afterward, the patient is told to draw a picture of herself on the inside of the bag. Because of the size of the bag, the patient has to struggle with this part of the exercise. The harder she works, the angrier and more frustrated she becomes. Before long, she is complaining to her therapist about the difficulty of drawing a picture within the small bag.

And that, of course, is the point. It is always hard to get to the inside and see who is really there. Almost without exception, the faces on the inside of the bag are angry faces, faces with tears rolling down their cheeks. When the patient writes about this part of herself, it is a very different self from the happy face on the outside of the bag.

As we discussed in an earlier chapter, this splitting occurs in anorexics and bulimics. They see themselves as either all good or all bad. This exercise is part of their learning to integrate the two and to recognize the extreme neediness within them.

This neediness must be addressed. Patients must learn to express their needs, which is part of therapy. Patients at the hospital must ask to have their needs met. For instance, anything sharp or harmful is taken from them upon entering the hospital. If they need to use their hair curler or makeup, they must ask for that. No Makeup Day, when patients are not allowed to wear makeup but must face everyone "just like they are," is another part of the treatment. Patients learn that others can like them as they are rather than because of a mask they wear to please or cope.

All of these methods are used to help anorexics and bulimics understand how to relate in a healthy assertive fashion. The goal is to help them believe and act according to the message: "I count and you count." Most anorexics and bulimics have previously been relating in one of three unhealthy ways: aggressiveness, which is based on the belief: "I count and you don't count"; passiveness, which springs from: "You count and I don't count"; or passive/aggressive, which sounds like: "Although I'm angry with you, I can't tell you because I don't count, but I'll get even with you later." This last method is usually carried out through silent treatments or procrastination.

Whatever mask the anorexic or bulimic wears, it must come off if healthy relationships are to be achieved. It is impossible to relate to someone else in an honest manner when we are not aware of who we are ourselves. But as feelings are acknowledged and masks removed, healing begins, relationships are cultivated and established, and the self-destructive lifestyles of the past are left behind. Most exciting of all, we find that the person who has emerged from behind the mask is someone we can like and respect.

TAKING INVENTORY OF RELATIONSHIPS

The behaviors associated with eating disorders have a profound effect on the anorexic's and bulimic's interpersonal relationships. As we review these relationships, why not take inventory of some of your relationships and see if you recognize yourself in any of the examples?

Opposite Sex

Rose, a bulimic, had very low self-esteem. Her identity centered on her current boyfriend—or lack of one. She felt she must have a boyfriend at all times or she was worthless. Because of her extreme neediness, she was never able to keep a boyfriend for long. Juliana, on the other hand, was anorexic. She believed that all men are bad and that they wanted only to hurt or control her. She purposely stayed painfully thin so men would not be attracted to her. Do you recognize yourself in either Rose or Juliana? Has your eating disorder distorted your views of men and their importance in your life? Let's find out.

How About You?

During my junior high years, three of my close friends of the opposite sex were:

1. _____
2. _____
3. _____

These relationships were enjoyable in the following ways (e.g., I *felt safe and secure*):

_____
_____
_____

These relationships were painful in the following ways (e.g., I *caught on very early that somehow I had to barter my sexuality to prove it*):

_____
_____
_____

During my high school years, three of my close friends of the opposite sex were:

1. _____
2. _____
3. _____

These relationships were enjoyable in the following ways (e.g., I *felt comfortable to say either yes or no to the control boundaries and sexual boundaries in this relationship*):

_____
_____
_____

These relationships were painful in the following ways (e.g., *as a girl I had to have intercourse with my boyfriend,* or *as a boy I had to score with a girl to prove my maleness*):

_____
_____
_____

During my college and later years, four of my close friends of the opposite sex were:

1. _____
2. _____
3. _____
4. _____

These relationships were enjoyable in the following ways (e.g., I *felt that my identity was respected by these persons; I did not have to prove myself by being the superscholar or the athletic champion*):

_____
_____
_____

These relationships were painful in the following ways (e.g., I *was never sure of my own identity, and I found myself always trying to fit into a group to prove myself to the opposite sex*):

_____
_____
_____

I was a
_____ people pleaser
_____ OPD
_____ actress
in these relationships.

Marriage

Lydia's anorexia had its onset during her early adolescence. Throughout high school and college, her weight remained below normal, usually hovering around eighty pounds. Extremely dependent on her family, she sensed that she was becoming a burden to them because of her anorexia. When she met Keith, she saw him as a way to relieve her family of that burden. Because Keith was patient and understanding with her, never pushing her for any more than she was able to give, she made the adjustment from dependent daughter to dependent wife. The anorexic behavior, however, followed her into her marriage. In essence, she was relating to her husband in the same way she had related to her parents. Sound familiar?

How About You?

Do you find yourself repeating the same behavioral patterns with your husband or dating partner that you did with your family of origin?

Yes _____   No _____

This relationship is enjoyable in the following ways (e.g., *we seem to have good skills in sharing money and authority in the marriage; the needs of both of us are reasonably well met*):

_____
_____
_____

This relationship is painful in the following ways (e.g., *My husband maintains almost dictatorial control over all my spending and investing and doles out an embarrassingly small allowance to me:*

_____
_____
_____

I am a
_____ people pleaser
_____ OPD
_____ actress
in these relationships.

After taking a relationships inventory, one male patient at the Minirth-Meier Clinic was amazed to see his pattern regarding women. "Look at that!" He pointed to his inventory. "In the past seven years I've walked out on every woman I cared for when I feared losing her. I walked out on her before she had a chance to walk out on me." Although the event had occurred at least five times, the patient had no idea of the pattern until he saw it in black and white and in his own handwriting.

The results of Marian Grier's inventory were equally revealing. Those very results helped her see the tie-in between her perfectionistic, people-pleasing relationship with her parents and the relationship she had developed with her husband, Bob. More demanding than Marian's parents and with much less tolerance for error, Bob lost his patience with Marian if she so much as spilled a glass of water at the dinner table. His rebukes were swift and demeaning, but Marian took them as her due, resolving to try harder next time—the same resolutions she had made time and again as a child.

Remember, the key is finding the pattern.

The pattern I've repeated over and over again in my relationships is:

_____ people pleaser

_____ OPD

_____ actress

Authority Figures

Diane has been in therapy for a short time but is having trouble relating honestly to her therapist, whom she views as an authority figure. She feels she must please her therapist, as she has other authority figures in her life. This feeling prevents her from being honest during her sessions. It also prevents healing. Have you been taught to please authority figures at all costs? Do you understand the difference between respecting authority figures and pleasing them? Do you find yourself shaking with fear at the thought of displeasing an authority figure?

How About You?

I liked these people because:

_____ They spent time with me.

_____ I sensed that they saw my special talents and attributes.

_____ They encouraged me to "be all I could be."

_____ They gave me new values and taught me important principles.

_____ Other _____

_____

I disliked them because:

_____ I could never live up to their expectations.

_____ One of them abused me verbally in front of my peers.

_____ One of them made fun of my values and morals.

_____ One of them abused me physically.

_____ One of them abused me sexually.

_____ Other _____

_____

Three authority figures in my present are (e.g., *my boss; my pastor; my doctor*):

1. _____

2. _____

3. _____

My feelings toward these people are much the same as my feelings about the authority figures in my childhood in the following ways (e.g., *my coach pushed me so hard in athletics that it compromised my grades; he exploited me and took advantage of me. Now my boss is doing the same thing.*):

_____

_____

_____

This causes me to respond to them in the following ways (e.g., *I can't stand for them to criticize me*, or *I'm always docile and submissive with any and all of the authority figures in my life*):

_____

_____

_____

I am a

_____ people pleaser

_____ OPD

_____ actress

in these relationships.

God

Helena became bulimarexic following a rape incident. Not only did she feel could no longer trust men, she also believed she could no longer trust God. Even though she had prayed during the rape, God had not stopped it. She was angry with God for letting her down. Five years later, after sporadic therapy, she still has a deep resentment toward God for not being there when she needed Him. At the same time, she wonders if she is now unacceptable and unloved by God because of her disease. She wonders if that is why He hasn't healed her of her eating disorder. She wonders if He ever will.

How About You?

Have you ever had these thoughts toward God? Has your eating disorder driven you further from God rather than closer to Him?

How were you taught about God as a child (e.g., *in Sunday school or by what your parents and relatives said*):

_____

_____

_____

I was taught that God was (e.g., *demanding; a scorekeeper; harsh*):

_____

I just don't enjoy going to church anymore because (e.g., *services are boring or irrelevant; I feel guilty and unworthy; I think people don't approve of me*):

_____

_____

I find it difficult to pray or read the Bible because (e.g., *I feel like a hypocrite; I don't understand it; I don't think God hears me*):

_____

_____

_____

Have you ever become disillusioned about God? If so, when? Why?

_____

_____

Do you ever feel that the faith of your childhood has failed you?
_____ Yes   _____ No
I feel as if my faith has failed me because:

_____

_____

_____

Sometimes our patients say to us, "God allowed me to become addicted to food," or "God allowed me to become addicted to work, and my life has spiraled downward ever since. I want nothing to do with God."

When patients feel this way, we often remind them that God did not create us as puppets under His full control; instead, we can make decisions throughout our lives. "God did not cause you to become addicted," we tell them. "He gave us free will, and sometimes the inappropriate exercise of our will by us or our parents has planted the seeds of addiction."

How do you feel about God now? *(Do you consider Him an invisible Parent who judges everything you do? Do you think that He loves you? Do you think of Him as a Friend?)*
I think of God as _____

_____

_____

_____

Laying aside your past bitterness against God and the church is paramount for your spiritual and emotional recovery. As the *Big Book of Alcoholics Anonymous* says, "We, who have traveled this dubious path, beg you to lay aside prejudice, even against organized religion. We have learned that whatever the human frailties of various faiths may be, those faiths have given purpose and direction to millions."

OPEN COMMUNICATIONS AND HEALTHY RELATIONSHIPS

Our friendships are initiated and developed by the communication we have with one another. If our communication patterns are destructive or unhealthy, our relationships will suffer. However, if our interactions are positive and constructive, our relationships will be enhanced.

Here are some guidelines for interaction that Marian and many others have found helpful in building healthy relationships.

Do Not Be Afraid to Say No

As the head nurse on a very active hospital floor, Carolyn was under constant stress from the demands of others. Whenever her nurses needed anything, she jumped. Whenever doctors made unreasonable demands, she smiled sweetly and said, "Sure, I'll be able to do that for you." But underneath she was unhappy and insecure.

To feel that she had some control over her life, she adhered to a routine of self-starvation. During a therapy session, Carolyn began to uncover the fact that she was using self-starvation to try to regain the control she had given to others. From that point forward, she started forming constructive patterns in her relationships. She began to say no when unreasonable requests were made.

When Carolyn risked saying her first no, she felt clumsy and awkward. She was out of her comfort zone. During those stretching times, she reminded herself that if she kept saying yes to everyone's demands, she would snap and end up institutionalized. To be an efficient head nurse, she had to say no to some things so that she could keep her priorities in order and be competent in her more important duties.

Paul's counsel in Ephesians 4:15 is wise. He doesn't say to speak the truth. He says to speak "the truth *in love*" (italics added). In other words, be careful and responsible in the ways you make honest statements so that those you're talking to won't be demeaned. Later on in the same chapter, he drives home the need to be loving in honesty: "Do not let any unwholesome talk come out of your mouths, but only what is helpful for building others up according to their needs, that it may benefit those who listen."[1]

Learning to say no is an essential part of responsible living. As you act on this truth, you will reap rewards and so will those around you. But remember, always couch your noes in loving explanations that will "benefit those who listen."

Take the Risk of Sharing Your Opinions and Feelings

For many families, keeping short accounts among themselves is an effective policy. They stay in touch with their feelings and find ways of reporting them as they occur. It has been said that relationships, particularly within the family, are only as good as the communication among those in the relationships.

Sharing negative feelings is sometimes an extra challenge, and the thought of expressing weakness can be uncomfortable. People often sell themselves short by believing that negative feelings are bad, and that strong people don't feel the pangs of deep sadness or anger. But we must remember that as humans we are made in God's image, according to His likeness.[2] We will experience all kinds of emotions because emotions, both pleasant and unpleasant, are part of God's character.

Does that statement surprise you? It surprises many people, those who view God as all-loving and merciful as well as those who view God as a dictatorial tyrant, waiting to mete out judgment on an unsuspecting world. Although God is love,[3] He is also a righteous God who punishes rebellion. The Old Testament especially is full of stories of God's punishment falling on disobedient people. The eighth chapter of Deuteronomy is a perfect example. The first ten verses of this chapter describe the multitude of blessings that come upon those who love God and walk according to His Word. The last ten verses, however, discuss the effects of disobedience and show the other side of God's nature, ending with the statement, "So you shall perish, because you would not be obedient to the voice of the LORD your God."[4]

It is evident, therefore, that God freely loves and forgives and blesses, but He also displays other emotions, including anger, grief, and sympathy. For instance, Hosea 11:8 declares;

> How can I give you up, Ephraim?
> How can I hand you over, Israel?
> How can I make you like Admah?
> How can I set you like Zeboiim?
> My heart churns within Me;
> My sympathy is stirred.

Even when His chosen people turned from Him, God's heart cried out for them, longing to restore them to Himself. Without a doubt, God experiences emotions.

As you take the risk of sharing your perspectives and feelings, you will enrich the lives of others. Don't rob people of the joy of knowing the real you. You may discover a wonderful boomerang effect. Psychological research shows that as one person discloses himself to another, the chances are very high that others will reciprocate that openness and honesty. Your transparency can actually refresh others and build bridges rather than walls.

Expect Conflict and Use It Constructively

Marian was fearful that if she expressed disagreement, others wouldn't like her. Her perspective was limited. She didn't realize that she ran the risk of others not liking her because she did not speak up for what she believed.

Can you imagine how predictable life would be if God had made all of us the same? We would exist as a bunch of clones, talking the same talk, looking the same look, walking the same walk—life would be a genuine, unadulterated bore.

No two people on earth are exactly the same. We will have differences of opinion and disagreements with others. Disagreements are as much a part of life as death and taxes. God knew what He was doing when He made each of us unique, according to His perfect plan. We must understand that uniqueness necessitates difference. Difference isn't bad. It's a built-in part of God's plan. As you share your opinions and feelings with others, sometimes you will run into disagreement. That's okay. Relax with those differences.

Conflict can actually bring out the best in you and your friends. According to Proverbs 27:17 (NIV), "As iron sharpens iron, so one man sharpens another." Through the process of rubbing up against another person's unique character qualities, our lives are sharpened. In conflict we have the privilege of learning new insights and gaining understanding. Don't run from conflict. Don't fear it. Don't short-circuit it. Conflict can work for you when you learn to work with it constructively.

In *Caring Enough to Confront,* David Augsburger explains some ingredients of constructive conflict. He says that working through differences by giving clear messages of both caring and confronting is most helpful. Below he lists the various ingredients of constructive conflict. In healthy relationships both caring and confronting hold equal importance. The persons interacting must relate in such a way that both ingredients are obvious in the way they communicate.

CARING (and at the same time) CONFRONTING

I care about our relationship . . .
(and at the same time)
. . . I feel deeply about the issue at stake.
I want to hear your view . . .
(and at the same time)
. . . I want to clearly express mine.
I want to respect your insights . . .
(and at the same time)

. . . I want respect for mine.
I trust you to handle my honest feelings . . .
(and at the same time)
. . . I want you to trust me with yours.
I promise to stay with the discussion until we've
reached an understanding . . .
(and at the same time)
. . . I want you to keep working with me until we've
reached an understanding.
I will not trick, pressure, manipulate, or distort the
differences . . .
(and at the same time)
. . . I want your unpressured, honest view of our
differences.
I give you my loving, honest respect . . .
(and at the same time)
. . . I want your caring, confronting response.[5]

Difficulties with Confrontation

Mary worked as an office manager of six executive secretaries. Multiple conflicts occurred daily. They came with the territory. She was forever having to settle clashes over scheduling, petty hassles between secretaries, and untimely outbursts by an explosive vice president.

Mary was a people pleaser who had a rough time handling conflict constructively. For years she had equated negative emotion with weakness. She had virtually cut off one-half of her emotional spectrum and refused to allow any negative feelings to surface. She had put on her people-pleasing mask and learned a pattern of denying and burying anything unpleasant. After three weeks of working at her job, bingeing and purging became a tool to avoid hassles and to relieve bottled anxiety.

At first the binges happened once a week. But they became more frequent the longer she worked at the office. When she began therapy, she was hooked into bingeing and purging eight to ten times a day.

Mary was caught in a vicious cycle. When inevitable conflicts arose, her usual response was to sweetly offer polite platitudes, while anger and frustration seethed beneath the surface. She didn't realize that the negative emotions she was hiding behind her mask were coming back to haunt her in a slow form of suicide—bulimia.

In therapy, Mary talked about her work during several sessions and, with the help of her therapist, established some guidelines for handling her conflicts constructively. To begin, she called a meeting with the six secretaries she supervised and gave each a copy of the caring/confronting list mentioned earlier. She told them that it was important to her that they all work effectively together and that they enjoy cooperative working relationships with one another. Each secretary was instructed to post the caring/confronting list on her desk and to read it twice *before* engaging in confrontation.

Rules for Differences

Mary also gave them another list of practical communication rules to follow whenever disagreements or differences arose. Maybe situations in your life lend themselves to recurring conflicts. Look to Mary's list of rules as you experience those challenges.

1. *Decide on a time and private place to discuss your conflict.* Mary offered the use of their small coffee room. It was slightly removed from the workplace, relaxed, and private during non-break times. Time is critical. Don't go into a heavy time of weeding out differences when you are ill or emotionally or physically exhausted. Logic is a rare commodity when you are run down. ("How good is a *timely* word.")[6]

2. *Think before you speak.* When emotions are boiling in the heat of conflict, it's easy to blurt out all kinds of tactless remarks, which is harmful to you and others. Before discussing a conflict, take a few minutes to collect your thoughts. Write them down; seeing things on paper can help you be more objective and ra-

tional. June, one of the secretaries in Mary's office, followed this advice. "I've always had a short fuse," June explained. "But when I take the time to write things down before spouting off, I usually find I've cooled down and can think and speak more rationally. Most of all, I'm not as apt to say things I'll regret later." ("Whoever guards his mouth and tongue / Keeps his soul from troubles.")[7]

3. *Set your mind to listen to a different point of view.* It takes two to have a difference of opinion. One of the best things you can do to resolve conflict is to be a good listener. Tune in to what the other person is saying. Mentally put yourself in the other's position to discover the reason for the strong feelings. As you listen well, you earn the right to be heard. When Cecelia, another of Mary's secretaries, took the time to really listen to others' opinions before jumping to conclusions, the situation often resolved itself then and there. ("He who answers a matter before he hears it, / It is folly and shame to him.")[8]

4. *State your opinion clearly and concisely.* Don't use loaded words or exaggerated points for persuasion. Speak the truth in a kind, loving way. Mary had to work on this area. Having always been a people pleaser, she tended to guard her words so carefully to keep from offending others that she ended up being unclear in what she said. ("Speaking the truth in love.")[9]

5. *Focus on the present problem.* Remain on the topic of disagreement. It's easy to bring up the past and a whole barrage of outdated information when you want to make a point, but you will get nowhere. Stay in the present and stick to the issue at hand to ensure better relationships for today and tomorrow. Again, June benefited from this suggestion. Because of her hot temper, she often spoke without thinking, and inevitably during the course of her tirade, she dragged in incidents from the past. Taking time before she said anything helped her focus on the real problem instead of getting off on a tangent. ("Forgetting those things which are behind and reaching forward to those things which are ahead.")[10]

6. *Do not allow yourself to quarrel and bicker over trivia.* Some people have a knack for bickering. They have a natural way of hooking you into a fight and seem to gain a sense of power by manipulating you into an argument. These interactions are not worth your time or energy. Politely excuse yourself rather than fall prey to power-hungry tactics. Because Trish was extremely sensitive, she always tended to react quickly to others' remarks. When one of the other secretaries was out of sorts and feeling argumentative, Trish was easy bait—until she realized what was happening and learned to deal with the situation accordingly. ("Stop contention before a quarrel starts.")[11]

7. *Relinquish your rights to change others.* Your calling in life is not to agree with everyone or to try to make others agree with you. Remember, uniqueness necessitates difference. Appreciate the uniqueness of others and give them space to differ from you. Work at forming relationships with a mixture of different types of people. Variety is the spice of life. Realizing that she did not have to agree with others to please them released Mary to stop feeling so frustrated over the differences of those around her. ("Love . . . is ever ready to believe the best of every person"—even when there are strong differences of opinions.)[12]

8. *When someone wrongs you, don't hold a grudge.* As human beings, we are imperfect. We all make mistakes. During the next few months of your life, somebody will likely say something that will hurt your feelings. The same is probably true of everyone. When hurtful remarks fly in your direction, don't allow them to become a cancer of bitterness in your heart. That will only magnify your anguish and pain. Forgiveness will get rid of bitterness and will allow your emotions to heal. As forgiveness began to flow between the women in Mary's office, a sense of closeness and unity developed, eventually spreading beyond their workplace and spilling over into their other relationships. ("Be kind to one another, tenderhearted, forgiving one another, just as God in Christ also forgave you.")[13]

9. *Tell others, "It's okay to disagree."* There will be times

when you will hold a completely different opinion from someone else, regardless of lengthy discussions and debate. That's fine. Simply tell your friend you realize that you both feel strongly about the issue, that you respect her position, and that it's okay for the two of you to disagree. Then part company peacefully. Sometimes, no matter how hard they tried, the women in Mary's office simply couldn't agree on certain issues. But recognizing that "it's okay to disagree" allowed them to move on with their work in harmony. ("Be completely humble and gentle; be patient, bearing with one another in love. Make every effort to keep the unity of the Spirit through the bond of peace.")[14]

Trying to live by the motto "peace at all costs" is destructive. People pleasing taken to the extreme leaves a person exhausted, empty, and floundering in identity confusion. You cannot possibly please all the people in your life all the time. It's irrational to think that you can even come close.

Recognizing this truth made such a profound impact on the work performance in Mary's department that she was awarded a substantial pay raise. But the benefits didn't stop there. Mary was learning a new way of life. She was expressing both negative and positive feelings and handling conflicts constructively; her binges were diminishing in frequency and duration.

God has made you a very special individual. Celebrate your individuality. Take the risk of openly sharing the real you with others. You are God's gift to your friends and family, and they are God's gift to you. Lavishly enjoy your similarities and deeply appreciate your differences. Both aspects are important parts of God's plan for your life—and for your relationships with others.

As you begin to celebrate your individuality, you must develop realistic expectations for yourself. You cannot please other people all of the time, nor can you please yourself all of the time. We'll discuss in the next chapter how to become free from placing perfectionistic demands on yourself.

8

THE PAIN OF PERFECTIONISM

For ten years Nancy Conway had flip-flopped between weeks of self-starvation and days of bingeing and vomiting or swallowing fifty to one hundred laxatives. She was a bulimarexic. At age thirty-two, she was convinced she was losing her mind. As a housewife and mother of two children, she felt like a marble on a roulette wheel tossed about by life's frantic whirls. Stability was gone.

One afternoon in therapy with Pam Vredevelt, Nancy cried, "My kids are driving me crazy with their constant demands. I'm beginning to hate being in the same house with them. I just can't cope. When I wake up in the morning, my arms and legs feel like lead. All I want to do is turn over, bury my head in a pillow, and escape. Steve tries to help with the kids, but he has a lot of demands at work. I hate myself for not being the perfect wife he needs or the good mother my kids deserve. But I can't even handle myself, let alone them.

"I feel pressured to never make mistakes. I can't stand being just average or good. I have to be the best at whatever I do. When I mess things up, I feel like a worthless idiot. At least when I binge, I can forget life and bury my frustrations.

"If I could just be a size three, everything would be fine. I know I could handle things and be a better mother and wife if I could lose another ten pounds. My goal is to weigh one hundred pounds. Once I reach it, I'll eat normally and have some peace of mind."

Nancy's entire life revolved around eating and exercising. She ran fifteen miles every morning from 4:00 A.M. to 6:00 A.M. while the rest of the family slept. After Steve left for work, she carted the kids to the baby sitter and exercised another three hours at the athletic club.

Nancy was plagued by what is often called the tyranny of the shoulds. She continuously told herself, I *should do this better;* I *should do more;* I *should not have eaten that.* These mental tapes played constantly. When she exercised, she drove herself to do more, thinking, I *should run two more miles; I should ride twenty more minutes on the bike; I should do another set of repetitions on the weights.* I should, I should, I should!

If Nancy ate one small apple—even after five hours of exercise—she felt guilty: If *only I hadn't eaten that apple, then more fat would be burned.* She was always pushing herself for what she thought was the best, but she could never quite make it because she felt she should do more.

What happened when Nancy "never quite made it"? She fell prey to the lie that she was an incurable, hopeless mass of mistakes. Her thoughts persuaded her that she was an ugly, unlovable misfit. If she couldn't accept herself, how could anyone else? She didn't feel that God could accept her either. He seemed far away. How could He possibly want to be involved with someone who failed so often? She was certain God was displeased with her.

At the close of one session, Pam Vredevelt asked Nancy to bring back a list of her "I shoulds." Pam anticipated a one-page list with about a dozen items. When Nancy returned, she was carrying four typed pages of rules and regulations for "living right." Actually, it was a set of externally imposed standards that she developed over the years to measure up to the expectations of others. Whenever she picked up a cue about how to please another person, she added it to her list. Her list would be adjusted for one friend and then readjusted for another. Every sermon at church gave her more do's and don'ts to add in order to please God.

Here are some of Nancy's beliefs:

- I must be happy all the time. People don't like grumps.
- I need to wear the latest styles wherever I go so people don't think I'm backward.
- I can't go out of the house without makeup. People don't like "plain Janes."
- I can't gain one pound. No one likes fat women.
- If I'm upset, I need to hide it. Spiritual Christians don't show negative emotions.
- I have to be better than my friends in exercising. Being #1 is the only way to be.
- I have to go to church every Sunday morning and night to please God.
- My house must be spotless. This is a sign of a virtuous woman.
- My kids cannot go out of the house in unmatched clothes. They must have washed hair every day and never be dirty.
- Meals must always be on time and be nutritious.
- I cannot allow my children to fight. Other people don't like it.
- I should have the house peaceful for Steve when he comes home from work.

These rules and regulations are only one-fourth of the ideas on the first page of Nancy's list. It went on and on. Just reading the list was an exhausting project. And that's exactly how Nancy felt—defeated and spent. She had no more fight power. Her do's and don'ts had done her in, and she was breaking under the load of perfectionistic thinking.

Nancy learned in the course of growing up that if she behaved in certain ways, she would be loved. If she did what was acceptable in the eyes of others, they would like her. This idea also filtered into her relationship with God. If she performed well, He would love her. If not, He would reject her. A theology of works and conditional love seeped into all of her relationships.

THE PERFECTIONISM SCALE

How much perfectionistic thinking do you experience in your life? Is your mental vocabulary saturated with "I shoulds" and "I musts"? If you're not sure whether or not you struggle with perfectionistic thinking, you might want to test yourself with the following scale. This inventory lists a number of attitudes or beliefs that people sometimes hold.

Decide how frequently each statement reflects your thinking. Fill in the blank with the number that best describes how you think most of the time. Be sure to choose only one answer for each attitude. There are no right or wrong answers, so try to respond honestly.

1. _____ If I don't set the highest standards for myself, I am likely to end up a second-rate person.
   1) never   2) rarely   3) sometimes   4) often

2. _____ People will probably think less of me if I make a mistake.
   1) never   2) rarely   3) sometimes   4) often

3. _____ If I cannot do something really well, there is little point in doing it at all.
   1) never   2) rarely   3) sometimes   4) often

4. _____ I should be upset if I make a mistake.
   1) never   2) rarely   3) sometimes   4) often

5. _____ If I try hard enough, I should be able to excel at anything I attempt.
   1) never   2) rarely   3) sometimes   4) often

6. _____ It is shameful for me to display weaknesses or foolish behavior.
   1) never   2) rarely   3) sometimes   4) often
7. _____ I shouldn't have to repeat the same mistake many times.
   1) never   2) rarely   3) sometimes   4) often
8. _____ An average performance is bound to be unsatisfying to me.
   1) never   2) rarely   3) sometimes   4) often
9. _____ Failing at something important means I'm less of a person.
   1) never   2) rarely   3) sometimes   4) often
10. _____ If I scold myself for failing to live up to my expectations, it will help me to do better in the future.
    1) never   2) rarely   3) sometimes   4) often

Scoring: Add up your scores. The total may generally be interpreted as follows:
   10–20—nonperfectionistic
   21–30—average tendencies toward perfectionism
   31–40—very perfectionistic

If you scored in the high range, go back and analyze each statement. To which did you respond with *often?* Those statements are your irrational beliefs, which need to be challenged.[1]

Marian Grier chose *often* for statement 4 ("I should be upset if I make a mistake") and several other statements. She obviously suffered from extreme perfectionistic tendencies. Voted most likely to succeed in college, Marian had married Bob soon after graduation. Bob also was a high achiever. He was an accomplished corporate business manager, with high standards for himself and others. More than once he had commented how his attractive wife was an asset to his career.

As their marriage progressed and the children were born, the pressure to be a perfect wife, a perfect mother, a perfect career-woman, and a perfect asset to Bob's career escalated to unbearable proportions. It was then that Marian first approached Pam Vredevelt after the seminar.

After several months of therapy, Pam asked her to challenge her perfectionistic tendencies and to get rid of the word *should* from her vocabulary. Marian needed to know there are no "shoulds," only options. Marian reached a healing point as she thought about this statement and recognized the value of imperfections. It came shortly after a shopping trip in which she had purchased a wallet for Bob's birthday.

"You wouldn't believe it," she told Pam. "I had just bought him this leather wallet for $50 at one of my favorite department stores. I'd had it wrapped and was on my way home with it when I passed by a leather shop and, there in the window, was an almost identical wallet for $350. I just stood there for a moment, congratulating myself on my good deal, until I noticed that the wallet in the window had some imperfections. The more I looked at it, the more I had to find out how an imperfect wallet could possibly cost seven times more than a perfect one. So I went in and asked.

"The owner just smiled and asked me where I had bought the $50 wallet. I felt a little foolish, as if he were chastising me for buying a cheaper item, but I told him anyway. That's when he explained that the department store can sell them so much cheaper because the store buys them from a factory. That, of course, explains why they have no imperfections. He, on the other hand, buys his materials from individuals who handcraft each item. Hence, the imperfections—and the added cost."

Marian's bright blue eyes shone with the excitement of discovery. "It's the first time in my life that I realized there could actually be value in imperfection! I don't have to believe that I should be upset if I make a mistake."

She had begun to weed out the "I shoulds" from her thinking.

WEEDING OUT "I SHOULDS"

That's what we suggested Nancy Conway do. She was depressed because she always fell short of the unrealistic expectations on her four-page list of "I shoulds." Piece by piece, she examined those expectations and looked for healthy and realistic alternatives.

Pam Vredevelt encouraged her to practice a technique called thought recording. In the Bible, God tells us to "take captive every thought."[2] We are to be aware of what we are thinking and align our thoughts with Scripture's perspectives. One way to do this is to use a Thought Record. It will help you see on paper some of the ways your unhealthy thoughts are tied to unpleasant emotions.

Research indicates that changing beliefs, in and of itself, can often lead to emotional healing. An irrational belief that occurs most frequently is that all undertakings must be done with perfection.[3] By keeping a Thought Record, Nancy discovered perfectionistic beliefs that were contributing to her eating disorder and depression. Once she became aware of those thoughts, she began to replace them with healthy perspectives, and her depression lifted.

On page 129 is a copy of Nancy's record. A blank chart has been included in Appendix 4. Feel free to make several copies to put in your Personal Growth Notebook so you can monitor your moods and thoughts. Nancy's automatic "I should" thoughts had locked her into black-and-white thinking.

The Black-and-White Mind-Set

A major characteristic of perfectionism is an all-or-nothing mind-set in which life is viewed in extremes. Everything is either black or white; there are no gray areas. Something is either a total success or a total failure. One is either a glowing saint or a diabolical sinner. There are no in-betweens.

In the person with an eating disorder, this black-and-white thinking appears in the areas of food, body image, and performance. It is a specific type of irrational thinking characteristic of perfectionists. Here are some examples of black-and-white thinking patterns common to anorexics and bulimics along with the rational alternatives we suggested to Nancy and others.

1. **Black/White Thinking:** "I have a list in my mind of safe foods and forbidden foods. I should never touch the forbidden foods, or I'll get fat."

One of Nancy Conway's taboo foods was crackers. Anytime she ate a few crackers she would go into an immediate binge-purge cycle. After she ate six crackers, her perfectionistic thoughts were, "These crackers will make me fat if I keep them down. I might as well binge and then vomit everything."

Rational Thinking: Nancy began to challenge those thoughts with rational ideas like, "I had six crackers, which equals seventy-five calories. There is no possible way a person can get fat or gain weight on seventy-five calories. So don't worry about the crackers. Enjoy them and get on with the rest of the day."

2. **Black/White Thinking:** "I can't eat anything," Nancy Conway told Pam in one counseling session, "or I'll get fat. Even water is bad because it makes me bloated."

Rational Thinking: Nancy began to make recovery when she fought these perfectionistic thoughts with statements like, "It's a good idea to eat something small when I'm hungry. If I keep the calories low, I can have energy without getting fat. I want more pep and strength, so it's okay to eat and feel full for a little while. The full feeling will pass, and having more energy is worth it."

3. **Black/White Thinking:** "When I binge and purge, I am a terrible failure and sinner."

Rational Thinking: Nancy Conway was constantly depressed by

THOUGHT RECORD

Date	Situation	Feeling(s)	Automatic Thoughts	Realistic Answers	Outcome
	What were you doing or thinking about when you started to feel like bingeing?	What symptom(s) did you notice (e.g., anger, apathy)? How bad did you feel? (On a scale from 0–100 with zero as "terrible" and 100 as "fine.")	What was going through your mind immediately before you started to feel like bingeing?	How can you answer the negative thoughts realistically and constructively? Is there anything you can do to test out the thoughts or handle the situation differently in the future?	How did you feel now that you have tried to answer the thoughts? (On a scale from 0–100 with zero as "terrible" and 100 as "fine.")
	Sitting on couch in living room after kids left for school, & Steve left for work.	Lonely, depressed, hopeless, sad, anxious (80%).	—7 loads of laundry —3 beds to make —toys all over the family room —I want to eat —I want pancakes, bacon, peanut butter, ice cream, Twinkies®, . . . —windows are filthy with fingerprints —the bathroom is dirty with scum on the tub.	I don't have to do all the housework all at once. I can set a goal to make the beds and do two loads of laundry. Then I will reward myself with a walk around the block and get some fresh air.	Still anxious and lonely (50%).

her inability to do things perfectly. She began making progress in therapy when she stopped punishing herself after a setback of bingeing. She fought her black/white thinking with: "I'm not a total failure. Yes, I did have a temporary setback, but that doesn't mean everything else in my life is a flop. Everyone makes mistakes. It's part of being human. Would God send His Son to die for me on the cross if He thought I was worthless or a piece of junk? No, God sees my weaknesses and yet has promised to walk with me in the healing process."

4. **Black/White Thinking:** "I should be liked by everyone."
Rational Thinking: Nancy realized through therapy that she had an insatiable desire to be loved by everyone. Her recognition of this perfectionistic impossibility freed her to be herself.

Thoughts like these helped her: "I know now that everyone won't like me no matter how nice a person I am. I can't please everyone all the time. It's ridiculous to try. The most fun and fulfilling way to live is just to be myself. I'll focus on loving others rather than on being loved."

5. **Black/White Thinking:** "I can't stand to have things happen that are different from what I expected. Frustrations are intolerable and should not happen."

Nancy hated kinks in her schedule. When things happened beyond her control, anger soared.
Rational Thinking: A breakthrough came when Nancy began to think: "I don't like it when unpredictable things pop up, but I can't control everything. Even the best laid plans are often defeated. If I can't change things to improve the situation, I'd better accept it and get on with life."

We often suggest that patients like Nancy repeat the Serenity Prayer each day as part of their morning meditation time: "God, grant me the serenity to accept the things I cannot change, the courage to change the things I can, and the wisdom to know the difference." Then we suggest that they apply this philosophy through the rest of the day.

6. **Black/White Thinking:** "I should always be competent, intelligent, and achieving."

Raylene was a lawyer who felt pressed by her profession to perform with constant excellence. She used self-starvation and binge-purge cycles to keep her weight down.

Rational Thinking: Raylene found freedom when she began to tell herself: "My worth as a human being isn't based on my IQ or whether I won my last court case. I have value because God loves me, and I am His valuable and precious child in spite of my abilities to perform. I don't always have to achieve. I don't always have to be competent. It's okay to have a nonproductive day once in a while. I have human limitations and fallibilities just like everyone else in the human race."

7. **Black/White Thinking:** "I can't have any fat on my body. I must have a perfect figure."

Cari was a marathon runner and extremely conscientious about her percentage of body fat and muscular tone. She drove herself with abusive exercise to rid her body of any possible fat.

Rational Thinking: Cari saw great progress in her recovery when she substituted black/white thoughts with, "There's no such thing as a perfect figure. What's perfect, anyway? Not to have any fat on my body would mean death. My body has to have some portion of fat to function properly. Get back to reality!"

Perfectionistic thinking can bring tremendous pain. It causes us to feel that we're never good enough and always on the brink of one more failure. It paralyzes us and stifles our creativity.

Black-and-white thinking doesn't just happen. It is learned. And anything that is learned can be unlearned and replaced in time. All that is required is a choice that says, "I'm going to take personal responsibility to discover my perfectionistic thoughts and then to argue with those destructive ideas, replacing them with healthy, rational ones."

Nancy's depression didn't leave all at once. It left in small increments, a little at a time. But it did leave after several weeks and eventually was not a part of her day-to-day life.

As you become aware of your perfectionistic thoughts, you'll be in a good position to take charge of them. Awareness is the first step toward change, so take the risk of becoming aware.

ADMITTING PERFECTIONISM

Admitting perfectionism is a scary thing, but it is also freeing. Tina Morgan began to recognize that truth one day while she was in therapy with Debi.

They were discussing Tina's need for appearing perfect in all areas of her life. Debi discovered that Tina's need for perfectionism seemed to be rooted in her perceptions of her place within her family. The Morgans were a slightly lower-than-middle-class family. The father worked for many years as a lineman for the power company, while the mother stayed home to care for the six children. Countless times, Tina heard her parents comment on how she was the most attractive one in the family, how she got the best grades at school, what a pleasant personality she had. Somewhere along the line, Tina picked up the message that, although the rest of the family probably wouldn't rise above their current financial status, they expected more of her. Instead of bringing her satisfaction, however, her achievements only convinced her to set her goals a notch or two higher.

It is easy to see how all of this carried over to her appearance. The more compliments Tina received on her looks, the harder she tried to look better. By the time she reached her teens, she was obsessed with fashion magazines, staring for hours at what she considered to be the perfect, sexy bodies of the models displayed on the glossy pages. For Tina, it wasn't enough to be thin. She had to look like the models—thin, sexy, and perfect. Nothing less would do.

Anyone who knew Tina would think she had achieved her goal. She was indeed a strikingly attractive young lady with a slim, trim figure. Unfortunately, Tina couldn't see it that way.

"I'm so fat," she moaned as she sat on the edge of her hospital bed, talking to Debi. "If I could just get my stomach to go completely flat like those models in the magazines. If I could just get my thighs to be as thin as theirs!" She sighed and shook her head, her long black hair shimmering under the overhead light. Suddenly, her green eyes filled with tears. "It's not just the fat," she said, dropping her eyes to the floor. "It's . . . it's my . . . deformity."

Debi hesitated, puzzled. That was the first she had heard about any deformity. "What do you mean?" she asked gently. "I wasn't aware that you had a deformity."

Tina's head nodded slightly, but she didn't look up. "Yes, when I was fourteen, I had a bad stomach ache. Mom was so preoccupied with everyone else she didn't pay much attention. By the time I got to the hospital, my appendix had ruptured. Because of complications after the surgery, I had to be opened up down my entire stomach. I have a horrible scar and don't have a belly button." Tina was sobbing by this time.

For years the surgical scar which Tina saw as a "gross deformity," had fueled her need to be perfect, somehow hoping to compensate for what she was sure was an extremely repulsive physical feature. For this reason, she had forgone the pleasures of going to camp, slumber parties, or other situations where she would not have complete privacy for dressing. She had taken great pains to learn how to get dressed for gym, so no one ever saw her scar.

Just admitting the scar was a start for Tina. The healing of Tina's perfectionism would take time—a lot of time, but for now, it had begun.

UNCONDITIONAL LOVE AND ACCEPTANCE

If they are to truly be healed, anorexics and bulimics desperately need to understand that God loves them just like they are, as we mentioned in Chapter 5. People who have eating disorders often carry their concept of the need to be perfect in order to gain acceptance over into their relationship with God. They read their Bible, ignoring all the verses about love and acceptance and forgiveness while dwelling on Scriptures such as Matthew 5:48 (NIV): "Be perfect, therefore, as your heavenly Father is perfect"; or they give up on their relationship with God entirely. Either method is self-defeating.

God doesn't want you to try to be perfect before you come to Him. He wants you to come just as you are and then let Him help you make the changes. His heart-cry to you is, "Come to Me, all you who labor and are heavy laden, and I will give you rest."[4]

Let God love you. Let Him help you as you choose to work with Him in transforming your destructive thought patterns. Ask God to help you learn to think in new ways. He will be faithful to hear your cry and to answer your prayer: "The eyes of the LORD are on the righteous, / And His ears are open to their cry."[5]

Nancy Conway spent over a year and a half in therapy. Step by step, she learned to deal with her perfectionism and reprogram her ideas about herself and others. It had taken her years to establish destructive thought patterns, and it took time for her to build a new mind-set. The healing needed for perfectionism happens in a deep, gradual, but thorough way.

9

FEELING
FREE

By the time someone with an eating disorder has reached the stage of exploring areas underlying the compulsion to binge and purge or starve, emotions are beginning to surface. Particularly in the controlled setting of a hospital, these emotions must be faced and dealt with because the use of food as an anesthetic—an alternative to coping with emotions—is no longer an option. This period of time is referred to as experiencing emotional feelings or getting back in touch with internal cues.

Persons with eating disorders have been out of touch with their feelings so long that this part of therapy represents a foreign concept to them. More than that, it can be terrifying.

RELIVING THE EXPERIENCE

Cindy Briscoe came to terms with this frightening experience during a therapy session with Harry Beverly. As they discussed her family, Cindy mentioned an incident between her older brother, Bill, and her father. Although Cindy had made some progress in relaxing and opening up to Harry prior to this point, she seemed to become tense and somewhat agitated as she related what happened in her home a couple of years earlier.

"Bill was about nineteen then," she recalled, twisting her hair loosely about her finger. "Dad wanted us all to go to dinner at my aunt and uncle's house. It was my aunt's birthday, and they were having sort of a family get-together thing, you know?"

Harry nodded as Cindy continued.

"Bill didn't want to go because he already had plans to go to a ball game with his friends. But Dad . . . he insisted." Her eyes narrowed. She began to twist her hair more tightly, but her voice remained steady. "They got into an argument—a loud one. And then . . . the next thing I knew, they were fighting. Dad was hitting Bill and . . . I couldn't believe it! He just kept hitting him and yelling at him. I could tell Bill wanted to hit him back, but he was trying real hard not to. I started screaming at my father to stop, but he wouldn't. Mom wasn't home, so I started for the front door to get help. My dad must have realized what I was doing because he quit hitting Bill and told me that everything was going to be all right."

"And was it?" Harry asked.

Cindy shrugged. "I guess so," she said. "I mean, we all went to my aunt's as soon as my mom got home."

"I see," said Harry. "And how did that make you feel?"

Cindy looked puzzled. "What do you mean?" she asked. "How did what make me feel?"

"All of it," Harry answered. "The fight between your dad and brother, the way your dad wouldn't stop when you asked him to, the fact that your mom wasn't there—all of it. Let's talk through all of it again and see if we can identify some of your feelings while all that was going on."

Cindy's face went from puzzled to frightened. "I don't know," she said. "Maybe I . . . I shouldn't have brought this up. I really don't like to talk about it, you know. It was so long ago and all. It doesn't matter much anymore, does it?"

"I believe it does," Harry said. "I believe that's why you

brought it up. I know it's a little scary to try to remember how you felt when these things were happening, but it's necessary if you're going to get past it in your healing."

Cindy swallowed and nodded. "All right," she said. "I'll try."

She related the incident again, slowly this time, and the feelings began to surface. By the time she was telling Harry about the fight and her futile attempts to stop it, she was pounding the side of her chair in rage.

"He made me so mad!" she declared. "Didn't he know I was scared? Couldn't he hear me begging him to stop hitting my brother? But he just kept on and on. I couldn't understand. He never got angry with my mom when she treated me bad. It seemed like he never got angry at all. He was so calm and quiet, and yet there he was, beating on Bill over something stupid like maintaining our perfect family image on my aunt's birthday!" She pounded the chair one final time. Then the tears came, and her thin shoulders began to heave. "Oh," she sobbed, "it makes me furious just to think about it!"

After a long cry, during which Cindy expressed her anger toward her father, her fear for her brother, and her frustration at her inability to stop what was happening, she was exhausted. The next day, however, she announced that she felt good about "getting rid of all that stuff inside." It was an exciting turning point in her therapy.

FROM ANGER TO FORGIVENESS

Although forgiveness is, without a doubt, the key to emotional healing, it cannot come until the underlying anger has been acknowledged and expressed. Cindy had acknowledged her anger, so it was time for her to process it and move on in her healing. It was time for her to write a letter to her parents.

Harry had to convince Cindy that it was safe and acceptable for her to write this letter, that it wasn't to be mailed, that she could write everything she was feeling and not betray her family. Getting started was difficult for her, but as she progressed, she picked up momentum. By the time she finished, she was amazed with the results. She filled almost twenty pages of paper with feelings and memories she had almost forgotten she had. Even more amazing to Cindy was the fact that she seemed to have uncovered more anger directed toward her father than her mother.

"I thought this letter was going to be to my mom," she said. "And some of it is. But an awful lot of it is to my dad, not just for what he did to my brother, but for all the times he didn't protect me from Mom."

After they discussed her letter, Harry suggested another exercise. Cindy would sit opposite two empty chairs. She would imagine that her parents were sitting there in these chairs, and then she would read the letter out loud to them.

The first time through, Cindy's voice had little emotion. She read the letter mechanically, almost as if in fear of her absent parents' reactions. But when Harry urged her to read it through again as if she really meant it, she did so with conviction. Pouring out all the anger and hurt buried in her heart for so long, she began to experience a sense of emotional freedom for the very first time.

Harry smiled inwardly as he watched Cindy. Although he knew that she had a long way to go, and that it could get worse before it got better, he also knew she had just taken an important step in the forgiveness process.

IDENTIFYING EMOTIONS

All of us experience countless emotions on a regular basis, as you can see from the emotion chart on page 140. Let's review some of the more disquieting emotions for anorexics and bulimics.

Anger/Rage

Many young girls, particularly from Christian homes, grow up believing that anger is not an acceptable emotion. They haven't been taught that it is normal to feel anger and absolutely essential for good mental health to identify and acknowledge it. The expression of anger must be controlled, as confirmed in the Scripture: "Be angry, and do not sin."[1] It is as if the psalmist is telling us to feel our anger but to deal with it appropriately so as not to sin.

An eating disorder is *not* a sin. Yet anorexics and bulimics may get caught up in the cycle of confessing what they consider their "sin" to God, promising never to do it again, and then lapsing into despair and condemnation when they repeat their familiar patterns of bingeing and purging or starving. Anorexics and bulimics must understand that the real sin is not the eating disorder but the fact that they are relying on the eating disorder to get them through their pain rather than turning to God for the help He longs to give them. In essence, they have made the eating disorder their god.

One reason anorexics and bulimics are so prone to make the eating disorder their god is that, deep down, they are angry with God and feel they cannot trust Him. However, because they are so used to turning their anger inward, they are usually unaware of their anger toward God. Often, when they get into recovery and realize that anger, they don't know what to do with it.

Sue Ann had been making bargains with God all her life. When it seemed He had failed to keep His end of the bargain, she rationalized that, if only she had behaved better, God would have come through for her. And so she would try harder.

For instance, after her parents separated during her childhood, she made a bargain with God that if He would bring her father back, she would dedicate her life to being a missionary in a for-

HOW DO I FEEL TODAY?

daring	childish	edgy	quiet
spiritual	tender	regretful	popular
vulnerable	worthless	zealous	unloved
fearless	jolly	independent	harrassed
generous	kind	listless	mixed-up
nervous	optimistic	opinionated	miserable
hateful	hurt	grumpy	helpless
hopeful	fearful	frightened	liked
meek	overcommitted	negative	mad
erotic	comfortable	appealing	impatient
contented	bored	indifferent	glad
inhibited	loved	brave	at ease
appreciated	dissatisfied	homeless	joyful
excited	dependent	angry	shy
envious	addicted	lethargic	bothered
moody	confused	esteemed	eager
indignant	hated	bewildered	infuriated
courageous	proud	apprehensive	gloomy
dismayed	brilliant	gratified	concerned
patient	anxious	dejected	enthusiastic
funky	consoled	frustrated	stubborn
suspicious	paranoid	important	elated
determined	guilty	annoyed	fed up
humiliated	lonely	depressed	capable
dscounted	provoked	respected	snobby
good	abandoned	intelligent	relieved
apathetic	degraded	amused	lustful
reluctant	pitied	contemptuous	disappointed
inadequate	friendly	dumb	admired
delighted	abused	prayerful	cynical
alienated	disgusted	affectionate	puzzled
inspired	controlling	forlorn	ineffectual
fatigued	horrified	bad	hopeless
immature	ashamed	compelled	embarrassed
alive	indecisive	dishonest	dreadful
baffled	controlled	empathic	peaceful
antagonistic	bashful	bitter	exhausted
driven	happy	honest	detested
pleased	vibrant	worn out	useless
unsure	unimportant	venturesome	worried
rejected	unhappy	tempted	vengeful
trapped	weak	upset	people-pleasing
wanted	unwanted	wise	strong
relaxed	terrified	superior	wishful
understood	valuable	torn	secure
sure	sympathetic	smart	threatened
reflective	scared	timid	sick
silly	tense	resentful	rebellious
resigned	understanding	tired	troubled
uncomfortable	self-conscious	sad	unpopular

eign country. Her father did not return, and her unacknowledged anger toward God increased.

The legalistic teachings of the church that Sue Ann and her mother attended deepened her feelings of moral failure before God, and she was sure that was the reason for her heartaches. She expended enormous amounts of energy trying to do everything right but never seemed to achieve the approval or help from God that she so desired. She had no real relationship with God, only a fear of Him and a perfectionistic need to please Him.

In therapy, Sue Ann finally realized that she could do nothing to please God; she could never be good enough to earn His acceptance. As she faced herself more honestly, she was able to acknowledge her anger toward God. Why had He allowed her father to leave? Why hadn't He brought him back? Why hadn't He kept His end of the many bargains Sue Ann had made with Him? Never before did she have the freedom to ask all these questions. As she did, her therapist encouraged her to write a letter to God, telling Him how she felt. When she finished, the therapist explained to her that her anger toward God was legitimate, but it was not justified. She also explained that God is big enough and loves her enough to meet her right where she is. And so, at last, Sue Ann experienced the deep and satisfying relationship with God that had been suppressed so long by anger.

Guilt

Guilt is a valid emotion. But there are two types of guilt—true guilt and false guilt. We feel true guilt when we have done something wrong. False guilt is what we have allowed to be placed on us because of irrational beliefs and/or unrealistic expectations. For example, it is irrational and unrealistic to expect to please everyone all the time; many persons with eating disorders, however, feel false guilt for that very reason—no matter how hard they try, they are not able to please everyone all the time. This thinking is fueled by their perfectionistic mind-sets and can be resolved only when it is recognized for what it is—false guilt. We are imperfect beings living in an imperfect world, and if we strive to be perfect, we will be frustrated.

True guilt, on the other hand, also needs to be recognized. We must acknowledge our guilt before God and then ask for and receive His forgiveness. Romans 4:7–8 (NIV) asserts, "Blessed are they whose transgressions are forgiven, whose sins are covered. / Blessed is the man whose sin the Lord will never count against him."

Tina Morgan had no awareness of her true guilt. She was, however, overwhelmed by false guilt. She felt guilty because she did not make straight *A*'s; she felt guilty because she had not yet met "Mr. Right"; she felt guilty because she had not been able to "rescue" the rest of her family from what she considered their low-achiever mentality. Tina was so overwhelmed by false guilt that she did not feel true guilt. She didn't feel guilty about not accepting God's love and forgiveness because she reasoned that she was too terrible for God to love and forgive. She didn't feel guilty that her life centered on becoming a "respectable citizen" rather than on becoming more Christlike.

When Debi Newman asked Tina to write down all the issues about which she felt guilty, Tina resisted. She had tried for so long to hide from guilt that the exercise seemed extremely uncomfortable. Finally, she agreed, and she returned a week later with an extensive list. After reading over the list, Debi crossed off everything that was not a sin and explained to Tina that God did not hold her morally accountable for those things. The only thing left on her list were stealing her roomates' food, calling in sick at work when she wasn't, and cheating on her reading log for her history class.

Debi then discussed with Tina the meaning of 1 John 1:9: "If we confess our sins, He is faithful and just to forgive us our sins and to cleanse us from all unrighteousness." They also discussed King David's reaction to sin. The Bible describes David as a man after God's own heart, even though he committed the sins of adultery and murder. The Bible can say that about David because he so well understood God's willingness to forgive and restore.

Debi challenged Tina to daily read Psalm 51, which tells of David's acknowledgment of his sin before God and God's subsequent forgiveness and restoration, keeping in mind her crossed-off guilt list as she did so. Although Tina agreed, her concern was that she would just sin again. But as Debi pointed out, that, too, is part of the confession-and-forgiveness process. Tina soon discovered that this concept was the key to maintaining a loving relationship with God and ongoing freedom from both true and false guilt.

Shame

Although both true and false shame are possible, shame is different from guilt. Guilt concerns something we have done, whereas shame concerns who we are. The most common example of false shame in bulimics is their revulsion toward their disease, which they consider disgusting. They berate themselves with questions: What kind of person would steal food or laxatives?; How can I be so gross that I actually purge my food?; What would people think if they knew what kind of person I really am? Only as we begin to realize that God's love truly is unconditional, that He loves us even when we are purging, can healing come to these areas of false shame.

The issue of true shame is a serious one—but one with a solution. Without shame, we would never acknowledge our need for God or for His forgiveness. Only as we see ourselves for the sinners that we are, realizing that we can do nothing in and of ourselves, can we throw ourselves on God's mercy and receive the forgiveness He provided for us through His Son's death at Calvary. Jesus took all our shame and our sins when He went to the cross. He did it to free us of those sins and shame, and that is exactly what He did. John 8:36 declares, "Therefore if the Son makes you free, you shall be free indeed." And free you are when you have received His forgiveness! If you have never experienced the freedom that comes with God's forgiveness, we urge you to consider doing that right now—and then let the healing begin!

Della refused to consider herself a victim of sexual abuse. When asked about it, she declared, "I'm a virgin, and I plan to stay that way until I'm married." Still, she showed many signs of having sexual shame. (Sexual abuse, perhaps because it involves our most intimate body parts, produces a devastating amount of false shame; we will discuss sexuality and shame in chapter 10.)

One day, during therapy, Della blurted out, "I really don't think I'm a virgin." She then told about a night during high school when she went out with a guy she hadn't known too well. She was physically attracted to him and allowed herself to get involved in a petting session. When he took it too far, she tried to stop him, but he forced himself on her. In the act of trying to penetrate her, he became so disgusted with her fighting that he gave up and left. Although he had not ejaculated inside her, she had some bleeding. Because of that, she no longer considered herself a virgin.

In therapy, she came to understand that she was not responsible for his actions, that he had forced himself on her against her will, and that her shame over that act was false. She did acknowledge her responsibility in getting involved in the petting episode in the first place but was finally able to break free of the false shame over what had happened to her physically. Although technically she might no longer be a virgin physically, she came to accept herself as a virgin emotionally.

Shame begets shame. The whole binge-purge cycle evokes tremendous shame. As explained earlier, the trauma is the beginning point of the cycle. Usually, this trauma is somehow affected by shame. Eventually, the pain and shame of the trauma are buried beneath the pain and shame of the binge-purge cycle or, for the anorexic, the shame of wanting to eat.

Dan Allender, in his book *The Wounded Heart,* says that false shame breeds in abusive or dysfunctional homes because, as children, we look to our parents to teach us about the world. Our parents are like God to us. When they mistreat us, even as children, we are aware of it. We experience false shame because we believe that we are the reason our parents abuse us.

After Adam ate the fruit of the tree of the knowledge of good and evil, he and Eve experienced their first pangs of shame. Their response was to try to hide. God gives us shame for His purposes. We cannot understand or accept our need for Him unless we feel our shame—our utter worthlessness before Him. Fortunately, God has an answer to our shame. It is the blood of Jesus. Sadly, we often do not turn to Him in our shame, choosing instead, like Adam and Eve, to try to hide from Him. Shame is such an excruciating and humiliating experience, we do just about anything to escape it. We hide from God; we hide from ourselves; we hide from others. The only solution to shame—true or false—is to come out of hiding and stand before God.

Worry/Anxiety

Almost all anorexics and bulimics experience chronic anxiety or worry. The sense of never being good enough, or of being the one to cause problems as a result of shortcomings, fuels this anxiety or worry. They must identify and confront these concerns.

What is the worst thing that could possibly happen if you discuss your family realistically rather than idealistically? Will the family disintegrate? Will your parents get divorced? Will one of them die of a heart attack? Will they disown you and write you out of the family? Although one or more of these situations could possibly occur, it is highly unlikely. What is much more likely is that you will finally begin to receive healing.

Split-Off Feelings

Do you have split-off feelings from growing up in a family where you were not allowed to acknowledge feelings and not allowed to know your needs?

In healthy families, everyone has permission to experience and express feelings and needs. Certain feelings, such as anger, sadness, or sexual feelings, are not viewed as bad. In dysfunctional families, however, people try to deny all such awarenesses. These now become split off or disowned. They are dangerous, like a loose cannon on the lower deck of a ship. Those needs will try to assert themselves, and they may come out in damaging ways. For example, a child (particularly a girl) from a family where anger was denied may develop an eating disorder. All three patients—Marian, Tina, and Cindy—grew up in homes where they were taught that it was inappropriate to express anger. Keeping that anger bottled up inside them all those years turned it to rage, and eventually that rage spilled out in the form of eating disorders. When they split off feelings, they lost control of them.

Were any feelings forbidden in your family? Check the ones that apply:

_____ Anger

_____ Sensitivity *(Our family demanded that members—particularly male members—consistently present a tough-guy facade.)*

_____ Sexuality *(Any expressions or feelings of sexuality generated embarrassment or shame.)*

_____ Vulnerability *(Family members did not have permission to acknowledge their pain or neediness.)*

_____ Negative emotions *(Our family demanded that we act optimistic and congenial at all costs.)*

_____ Sadness

_____ Worry

_____ Fear

_____ Other _____

Were certain feelings abused in your family? *(For instance, every time someone was angry, that anger was expressed in a damaging or dehumanizing way.)* Check the ones that apply:

_____ Explosive or projected anger

_____ Sexual acting out *(The only sexual expressions in the family were those that violated the boundaries of other family members, such as extramarital affairs or sexual abuse.)*

_____ Other _____

Could you have split off these feelings? (*For instance, did you ever think,* I want no part of anger if that's the way it's expressed; I will binge [or starve myself] to suppress the pain of stuffing down the anger?) Check the ones that you split off:

_____ Anger

_____ Tenderness

_____ Sexuality

_____ Vulnerability

_____ Sadness or grief

_____ Fear

_____ Worry

_____ Other _____

How has this caused you to deal with this emotion in a destructive way? (*For instance, I have become depressed because I stuff my anger. Or I am too passive and allow others to dominate me.*)

For most people this look back into childhood is a gradual and progressive discovery. It's like going through layer after layer of denial. But you must recognize your need to feel your emotions. If you come from a family where feeling certain emotions was unacceptable, you have become expert at burying your feelings rather than expressing them. When you realize that other people experience a multitude of emotions every day and that it is perfectly acceptable to do so, you will begin to get in touch with your feelings and to find positive, constructive ways to handle them.

For instance, when loneliness strikes, you can call a friend. Suffering in silence only intensifies the pain. Or if you anticipate a situation that could trigger anxiety or depression, you can plan ahead. While they are in certain stages of counseling, many anorexics and bulimics find visits from their families upsetting. They may be agitated during the visit and depressed afterward.

Having a planned activity following the visit can lessen the depression.

Another effective means of alleviating depression is realizing that much depression stems from repressed anger. As that anger is released during therapy, the depression usually dissipates.

JOURNALING

Marian Grier did not check into a hospital for treatment of her bulimia. Instead, she saw Pam Vredevelt in individual counseling and participated in group therapy. At Pam's suggestion, Marian kept a journal of her emotions, especially at the times she felt tempted to binge and purge or immediately after a binge-purge session.

"It's amazing," she told Pam, sitting across from her in one of their sessions. "By forcing myself to write down my feelings at the times when I'm tempted to binge and purge, I think I'm beginning to see a pattern. My worst times seem to be when everyone's pulling on me, demanding my time and attention, and I'm trying so hard to meet all their needs, to be a good wife and mother. And . . . well, it wasn't until I started writing things down that I realized I actually felt angry with them for demanding so much from me!" Admitting anger toward her husband and children was a big step for Marian. She, too, had been raised to believe that anger was an unacceptable emotion.

Journaling is an unusual experience for those who have been out of touch with their feelings for the majority of their lives. But by starting with simple physical feelings (such as, "I feel hot," "I feel tired," "I feel tense"), they can eventually move beyond the physical to the emotional. Most of them are expressing for the first time, "I am feeling angry," "I am feeling hurt," "I am feeling lonely," "I am feeling rejected." As they put these feelings down on paper, they can begin to understand that their emotions are their friends rather than their enemies. At this point the anesthesia in the addiction cycle—food—wanes in importance, even if slightly. Now that they know it's okay to *feel,* they don't have to be numb anymore!

A CRUCIAL PLACE

Although this is one of the most beautiful times in therapy, it can also be one of the scariest. Defenses are coming down, feelings are being acknowledged, relationships are being put into proper perspective—and all of this territory is unfamiliar to the anorexic and bulimic. It is a time when they have to say to themselves, "Okay, bingeing and purging or starving is no longer an option. I must choose to do something else to soothe my anxiety. It is possible to 'feel' my way through these situations and find freedom on the other side."

The individual with the eating disorder is finally becoming a "real" person. Love and support are crucial at this stage. If the family members react positively to the patient's therapy and treatment, their interaction is encouraged. The therapist will often call in the family at this time, encouraging the patient to confront her family in a loving way with what she has discovered. Some patients choose to read their letters, such as the one Cindy wrote to her parents. Others sit and talk with them. If the family reacts negatively and defensively, then further contact may be discouraged for a time. If, however, they react positively, then further interaction is encouraged.

Cindy Briscoe's family was well aware of her anorexia, but Marian Grier and Tina Morgan never said a word about their bulimia to their families, even when they decided to seek treatment.

Because Tina was supporting herself while she worked her way through college, sharing an apartment with two other girls, it was easy for her to hide her bulimia from her parents. Even when she eventually told them about it during the course of her therapy, they weren't supportive. As usual, they depended on Tina to take care of herself. Her support came primarily from her roommates, who helped her learn healthy relationship principles.

Marian was in a different situation. Pam suggested to Marian that she involve her husband, Bob, in their therapy sessions since the probability of success is higher for a husband and wife working through therapy together than for a married woman trying to do it alone. Marian was horrified.

"Oh, I couldn't!" she exclaimed the first time Pam mentioned the possibility of Bob's joining them. "He'd never understand! Why, he thinks I'm the perfect wife. If he knew how really disgusting I am, he wouldn't love me anymore. He'd leave me. I'm sure of it!"

Eventually, though, Marian mustered the courage to bring Bob to a session. He did not know what to expect. Marian had told him only that she had "seen a therapist a couple of times for a little counseling, and she thinks you should come too."

As Marian's story unfolded, Bob was shocked. How could she have been involved in such behavior throughout their entire marriage without his knowing it? And yet, in spite of his initial reaction, he announced his desire to help.

Pam explained to Bob that Marian's emotions would be volatile and unpredictable for a while. Because expressing her feelings was new to her, Marian might not always do so appropriately. The best support he could give her would be to show patience and understanding as she worked her way from one end of the emotional expression pendulum to the other, eventually settling into a healthy place near the middle.

Pam reflected on the session as Marian and Bob walked out the door. Marian was relieved to know that her husband wanted to help her rather than leave her. Bob was still sorting through his feelings from the new revelation of his wife's lifestyle. Pam knew they would have a long, tough road ahead, but they were committed to making the journey together—and Pam felt confident they would succeed.

10

SEXUALITY AND SHAME

When Harry Beverly first asked Cindy about possible incidences of sexual abuse in her past, she repeatedly denied any. Even when Harry described the different levels of sexual abuse, Cindy continued in her denial. She had been in therapy for some time before she made a statement on the subject that caught Harry's attention, a statement that began to shed some light on her past experiences.

Harry and Cindy had been discussing her progression from young childhood into adolescence. Cindy described how she had been raised in church, and that she had felt loved and secure in her younger years. But things had changed as she approached her teens. She remembered a lot of friction between her parents. She also remembered how her mother vented anger on her while her father withdrew from Cindy emotionally.

"Things were never the same after that," she said. "I guess maybe that's why I started spending so much time with the Boltons."

"The Boltons?" Harry asked. "I don't remember your mentioning them before. Were they friends of your family?"

Cindy bit her lip for a moment as if she regretted having mentioned the name. She began to twist her hair around her finger. "Um, not exactly," she said, looking away from Harry. "Well, in a way, yes. I mean, Jonathan—Mr. Bolton—he was my piano teacher. He'd been coming to the house to give me lessons since I was about seven, so I guess we'd known him for a long time . . . sort of."

Knowing that the vast majority of persons with eating disorders have, at some time in their lives, been sexually abused, Harry felt they might have stumbled onto something.

"You said you spent a lot of time with the Boltons," Harry commented. "Does that mean you knew the whole family?"

Cindy nodded, turning her eyes back toward Harry. "Yes. Sarah, Jonathan's wife, was really nice. I loved going over to visit her. We used to make cookies together, and I loved to watch her paint. She was really good. Sometimes she let me help with the baby."

"They had a baby," Harry commented. "Did they have any other children?"

"No," answered Cindy, smiling slightly. "Just Mikey. He was really cute."

"So you liked spending time at their place," said Harry.

Cindy nodded again. "Mostly," she said. "I mean, yeah, I did. Except . . ." She dropped her eyes.

"Except what?" Harry asked gently.

Cindy shrugged her thin shoulders. She spoke so softly Harry had to strain to hear her answer.

"Except when . . . when he looked at me or . . . said stuff."

Harry paused a moment, knowing how difficult this discussion was for her. "What kind of stuff, Cindy?" he asked.

There were tears in her huge dark eyes as she looked up at Harry. "Stuff like . . . like how beautiful I was, what a nice body I had, how . . . how sexy I was." Her jawline twitched as she gritted her teeth. "Sometimes he'd put his arm around me or try to hold my hand. I hated it," she said, tears spilling down onto her cheeks. "I really hated it."

WHAT IS SEXUAL ABUSE?

Although Cindy's piano teacher never had sexual relations with her, he was guilty of sexual abuse. At a time when Cindy was feeling rejected and unloved at home, Jonathan Bolton took advantage of her neediness by inviting her into his home and encouraging her to feel like a part of his family. Even as she soaked up this much-needed love and attention, his suggestive actions made her feel dirty and ashamed. She was torn between her need for a surrogate family and her desire to escape Jonathan's abuse. But at thirteen, she was too young and immature to understand how to deal with it. And so, since she saw her maturing body as the cause of all her problems, she began to starve herself in an effort to stave off approaching womanhood.

How common is Cindy's story? More common than most people would like to believe. It is uncommon to find an anorexic or a bulimic who has not, in some way, experienced sexual abuse. Most people with eating disorders deny they have been sexually abused because they are not aware of what constitutes sexual abuse.

Several terms can be used to describe sexual abuse, but we will concentrate on three: *incest, sexual molestation,* and *sexual misuse.* In *Surviving the Secret: Healing the Hurts of Sexual Abuse,* authors Pamela Vredevelt and Kathryn Rodriguez explain these terms this way:

Incest describes any sexual approach, including exposure, genital fondling, oral-genital contact, and vaginal or anal intercourse between relatives by blood, marriage or adoption.

Sexual molestation refers to the inappropriate sexual stimulation of a child, when no family relationship exists.

The *sexual misuse* of a child refers to situations in which a child is exposed to any type of sexual stimulation considered inappropriate for his or her age, level of development, or role in the family. Showing a child a pornographic magazine, touching a child's body inappropriately, or allowing a child to view an X-rated movie can be considered sexual misuse. Encouraging a child to be in bed with the opposite-sex parent, when the parent is naked, can also be considered sexual misuse if the child is old enough to understand that this is wrong.[1]

As you can see, sexual abuse covers a wide range of actions and includes both touching and nontouching offenses. Without a doubt, Cindy's experiences with her piano teacher qualify as sexual abuse.

Eva was sexually abused. From the time she was a little girl, whenever she went anywhere with her parents, her father would stare at other women, making remarks like, "Now that's what a woman's supposed to look like," and "I sure wish your mother looked half as good as that." When Eva witnessed lust in her father, she experienced a form of sexual abuse.

SEXUALITY AND FEMININITY

A young girl who has been sexually abused is bound to be confused about her sexuality and femininity as she grows older. In addition to Cindy's abuse by her piano teacher, she was confused by her parents' treatment of her compared to their treatment of her brothers. As often happens when girls reach adolescence, Cindy's father was uncomfortable with her emerging womanhood. Afraid of responding inappropriately to his maturing daughter, he withdrew his affection at a time she needed it most. Cindy read his reaction as a rejection of her because she was female. She also believed that being female was the reason her mother treated her with such hostility. Cindy began to hate her femininity, wishing with all her heart that she had been born a boy.

This belief is fairly prevalent among anorexics. The anorexic feels that if she can just look as unfeminine as possible, if she can shrink—even disappear—she won't be hurt anymore. All of her feelings of low self-esteem and unworthiness are tied up with her femininity; therefore, she wants no part of it. Of course, her feelings about sex in general are affected. Sex becomes disgusting and repulsive to her, and she wants to avoid it at all costs.

The bulimic, on the other hand, craves as much love and attention as she can get. She believes that the sexier she is, the more attention she will get from men, and the more easily she will be able to control them. Her self-worth is tied up in the amount of attention men give her. She is often promiscuous from an early age and uses sex to get what she wants. Deep down, she feels she has nothing else to offer.

One way we encourage patients to get in touch with their femininity is to send them out on a pass to shop for a lacy blouse, makeup, or perfume. These young ladies must identify with their femininity in a positive way without feeling the need to act out their sexuality through promiscuity.

Whether male or female, children should learn to validate their sexuality as early in life as possible. A young girl may sense rejection from her parents because they wanted a boy, or a boy may feel rejection because his parents wanted a girl. If that feeling is reinforced through the growing-up years, the child is going to feel uncomfortable with his or her sexuality.

God created us as sexual beings. Understanding that assists us in accepting our sexuality as well as the sexual dynamics in relationships. It also establishes acceptable borders and limits for acting out our sexuality. Without this understanding, a maturing child can easily get these messages: "Sex is evil"; "Being female is being second class"; "Sex is all anybody wants from me, so I might as well use it to my advantage"; "Sex is the only way I can feel loved and accepted."

As a teenager, Constance became promiscuous in an attempt to find love. When she was hurt and rejected by someone she deeply cared for, she decided she would never allow anyone to hurt her again. Not only did she choose not to be involved in any more sexual relationships, she chose not to be sexual at all. In writing a detailed description of herself during therapy, she told about every aspect of her life—her job, her friendships, her hobbies—but she never talked about herself as a woman. When her therapist pointed out this omission to her, Constance was surprised. She had not realized that she was denying her sexuality. By recognizing what had happened, she was able to rediscover her femininity and sexuality and to establish healthy relationships with both men and women.

Joanie was the baby in her family. She had one older sister, no brothers. While her mother was carrying Joanie, she and her husband hoped for a boy. Their disappointment upon having another daughter was compounded when the doctors told them that, because of the difficult delivery, they would probably not be able to have more children.

In Joanie's younger years, her father tried to mask his disappointment at not having a son by taking Joanie on fishing trips and to sporting events. She did her best to please her father. She became an active tomboy who tried very hard not to exhibit any feminine traits. When she began to develop in her early teens, however, neither she nor her father could deny her sexuality any longer. Their relationship became strained, and Joanie tried to numb her pain through a growing obsession with food.

Although eating disorders are much less common among males, young boys can lack sexual identity. Martin, for instance, was an only child. His father abandoned him and his mother before Martin was old enough to remember him. He grew up hearing his mother berate men, describing them as "the scum of the earth." She assured Martin that he was the exception to that rule, yet he was never able to believe her. He hated his masculinity and wished he had been born a girl. Food became his escape from himself.

Angie's older brother sexually abused her during her early adolescence. As she grew into womanhood, she carried the message that sex is dirty and that being a woman is disgusting and undesirable. She totally denied her sexuality and refused to see that there could be anything positive in being feminine.

In so many cases, it has been found that eating disorders start soon after the first incident of sexual abuse. That was true for Angie. Almost immediately after her brother first abused her, she began to starve herself. In the mind of the victim, sexual abuse and bodily abuse go hand in hand. When a girl is sexually abused, she often turns her rage inward and finds self-destructive ways to abuse her body. These bodily abuses can range from eating disorders to self-mutilation to excessive exercise to suicide. If you have experienced sexual abuse and find yourself trapped in self-destructive behaviors, particularly an eating disorder, the following sections can help you along in the healing process and assist you in forming a healthy view of your sexuality.

BREAKING OUT OF THE CYCLE

Eating disorders usually start with a trauma, often a form of sexual abuse. This trauma leads to faulty beliefs, for example, "If I weren't like I am, this wouldn't have happened; therefore, this is my fault." These beliefs lead to illegitimate shame and self-hate, which can be acted out in self-destructive ways.

The first step in breaking out of this self-destructive cycle is for the victim to face and work through past traumas; individual and/or group therapy is essential. Although the person will resist taking this first step on the pathway to recovery for obvious reasons, it must be done if healing is to come.

As the victim acknowledges past traumas, her therapist can help her understand that she is not at fault, that the perpetrator was to blame, and that any guilt she might feel over what happened to her is false guilt. Although she may experience an extreme amount of shame over having been sexually abused, that shame and its accompanying pain can be reduced, possibly even eliminated entirely.

THREE STAGES OF HEALING

Many persons with eating disorders choose to limit their therapy to individual sessions, but most therapists strongly recommend combining individual counseling with group therapy. Three stages of healing for sexual abuse victims can occur in therapy.

Kathleen had been in individual therapy for several months before she consented to begin group therapy. Because of her shame at having been sexually molested as a child, she resisted group interaction; she was sure no one would accept her or understand what she had been through. The *first stage* of healing came for Kathleen when she realized the group members did accept her, and they did understand what she had been through because their experiences were similar. She was then able to feel safe with the group. She knew she was among people who would not judge or criticize her. An alliance, based on mutual support and understanding, quickly formed between Kathleen and the other members of the group.

The *second stage* of healing came for Kathleen when she was able to face the need to revisit the memory of the trauma for the purpose of connecting feelings with facts. Most girls who have been sexually abused tend to block out all feelings related to the incident. Revisiting the memory forces them to get back in touch with those feelings, so they can deal with them honestly. One reason stated most often for not wanting to revisit the memory is that it is as if the incident is happening again. In group therapy, Kathleen learned that reenacting the incident did not mean it was happening again; it was simply getting back in touch with the feelings she had repressed since it happened.

The *third stage* of healing can occur when "men" issues are addressed. Those who have been sexually abused, particularly bulimics like Kathleen, hate men, yet exhibit a tendency to act seductively toward them. It becomes a game: they lead men on, then cut them off in a sort of power play, an attempt to allay their own anger and rage. This behavior can be dangerous if the woman encounters a man who is violent or aggressive. Fortunately for Kathleen, group therapy gave her an opportunity to work through her feelings toward men openly and honestly, and to move beyond her hatred to forgiveness, opening the door for healthy relationships in the future.

OVERCOMING

Although, at first, revisiting the memory of her trauma seemed like the worst thing Kathleen had ever been asked to do, once she did it, she found she had taken a step toward overcoming the aftereffects of her abuse—namely, her eating disorder. But not everyone who has been sexually abused can remember the incident. Sometimes the pain is so great that the memories are repressed and no amount of trying to remember can dredge them back up.

If you believe this might be true in your case, don't despair. Even if you can't recall a specific instance of sexual abuse, you can experience healing from your eating disorder. Try praying this simple prayer: "God, show me what I need to know to overcome my eating disorder." If, over a period of time, you recall an incident, consider discussing it with a therapist. If you never remember anything, assume that you know all you need to know for now to move on in the healing process.

The first emotions Kathleen felt as she recalled her trauma were guilt and shame, mixed with moments of numbness. But as she talked it out with her therapist and in group, she connected her anger and rage to the perpetrator of her abuse. When a victim begins to make that connection, it may be appropriate to get that anger and rage out through one of the exercises mentioned in Chapter 9, such as writing a letter or talking to an empty chair. For Kathleen, pouring her feelings out in a letter proved beneficial.

After a sexual abuse victim has acknowledged her emotions, she must allow herself to grieve and to express her feelings. Some victims may feel the need to confront the offender; others may feel more comfortable expressing their emotions to the members of their group, as Kathleen did. If a woman does want to confront her offender, we suggest that she do this after she is well on her way to recovery, and that she proceed with great caution. We have seen too many victims revictimized who hastily confronted their offenders before reaching a point of stability and health.

The next step for Kathleen was to confront the false ideas she had come to believe about herself: "I am worthless"; "My body is ugly and repulsive"; "I would never have had these problems if I had been a different kind of person."

The final and possibly the most challenging step for Kathleen in overcoming the effects of her sexual abuse was that of forgiveness. Even mentioning this step to a sexual abuse victim is difficult, especially if she has revisited the memory of her trauma and is in touch with the anger and rage that were buried for so long.

THE PROCESS OF FORGIVENESS AND RECONCILIATION

"Will it ever be possible for me to forgive my father for what he did to me? Can our relationship ever be reconciled?" Kathleen asked as tears filled her eyes.

"My friends at church tell me I have to forgive him. But I can't! He was wrong! All those years he offended me over and over and over again! He knew better. . . . He doesn't deserve to be forgiven!"

Many who were abused as children experience feelings similar to Kathleen's. Forgiveness and reconciliation seem impossible. And humanly speaking, we would agree that it is next to impossible. It requires supernatural help from God. And it doesn't happen overnight. It is a process. As therapists, we see the process happening in three phases.

Phase 1: Choosing to Forgive

Webster's New World Dictionary gives this definition for the word *forgiveness:* "to give up resentment against or the desire to punish." The first step toward forgiveness is honesty. You take a good hard look at your losses and allow yourself to feel the emotions attached to those losses. You fully acknowledge the offenses that require forgiveness. You vent your anger in constructive ways such as writing letters, talking, exercising, and crying. All the secrets come out of the closet, and feelings are fully expressed within safe limits.

You can make the intellectual decision to forgive anytime in life, but during this period of ventilation and grieving, you experientially give up, release, or let go of the bitterness in your heart. Feeling your pain and expressing it in constructive ways eventually lead to the release of your pain. When effective grief work is done in recovery, forgiveness moves beyond a choice of the intellect to an experience of the heart where you emotionally let go of your pain.

When Kathleen chose to forgive her offender, she did not say that what he did was right or condone his offenses. Neither did she have warm, tender feelings toward her father.

One night in her support group she talked about forgiving: "I've worked hard at getting the rage out of my heart. This group has helped me talk about my feelings. You have heard my anger toward my family and God. Prayer and journaling have helped too. When I started therapy, I never thought I'd be able to forgive. I knew God wanted me to forgive so that I might heal, and I wanted to obey Him, but I felt stuck. I just couldn't let my father off the hook. My therapist said that it would take time and that forgiveness was a process. After the first session I remember asking God to help me become willing to forgive. Many months later I see that He answered that prayer.

"A couple of months ago I knelt by my bed and began talking to God. I told Him that I forgave my father, myself, and Him because I refused to be chained to my pain and resentment any longer. I had been stuck in feelings of hatred and anger for twenty-three years, and it was time to move on. Forgiveness had nothing to do with whether or not my father deserved it. Of course he didn't deserve it! I forgave him because I deserved to get past my pain. The bitterness I was packing around wasn't hurting him in the slightest, but it was killing me. Forgiveness was a gift I gave myself. I believe God wants to heal me, and this is part of His prescription. And I think I finally understand that God and the manifestation of sin in this world are not the same thing."

For Kathleen, and for most victims of childhood abuse, forgiveness is a choice that involves a process. It begins with honesty. It continues through grief. And eventually feelings of the heart catch up with the intellectual decision. It takes time. It takes God's supernatural help.

If you are feeling stuck and unable to forgive, perhaps you can start where Kathleen started. Ask God to help you become willing to be willing. He will answer this prayer and make His power available to you. The God who forgave all humankind for all sin can help you forgive those who have sinned against you. May we encourage you to begin the process today? It can start with a simple prayer.

Phase 2: Choosing to Confront

After the forgiveness phase, some women desire to reconcile with their offenders. This is possible if the offender is still living, if his whereabouts are known, and if the risk of being reoffended is minimal.

After a year in therapy Kathleen chose to arrange a face-to-face confrontation with her offender to express her thoughts and feelings about his offenses. The purpose of the confrontation was strictly to inform her offender of his wrongs and to make him aware of how his behavior affected the victim. Before the confrontation Kathleen knew there were no guarantees that the confrontation would automatically lead to reconciliation.

Her father denied his offenses and chose not to right his wrongs. Reconciliation couldn't proceed due to his hardness of heart. The confrontation was very painful for Kathleen since he offered no validation for the losses she suffered. At the end of that meeting she chose to detach herself from further interactions with her father. She told him that whenever he was willing to admit his wrongs and work toward reconciliation, she would meet with him. She prays consistently for God's help to let go of trying to make the relationship work and to leave her father in God's hands.

Unfortunately, in many cases offenders do not responsibly admit their wrongs, and the relationship is never restored. However, in a small percentage of cases, confrontation does prove to be a positive step toward reconciliation. Terri was able to see the reconciliation process through to completion.

Phase 3: Choosing to Reconcile

Terri's father, Mark, responded differently from Kathleen's father when confronted. After two years of separation Terri scheduled a time to meet with her father. She told him that she had been counseling with a therapist for the past year and that she wanted him to come to a session with her. Although he was hesitant, he did agree to attend the session. During the hour, Terri confronted her father about sexually abusing her when she was in junior high school. She explained the pain that his offenses had created in her life.

Rather than deny his wrongs, Mark broke down with tears of repentance and admitted to hurting Terri. He acknowledged that he remembered the offenses she mentioned and wanted to know what he could do to make things right between them.

Terri told her father that one tangible way he could demonstrate his sincerity was to pay for her counseling expenses for the past year. She also requested that he commit to several months of counseling with her for the purpose of rebuilding their relationship. He agreed and followed through on both.

Reconciliation is possible only when both the offender and the victim are involved in an ongoing dialogue and are committed to rebuilding the relationship. The old dysfunctional family rules need to be broken and replaced with healthy ways of interacting. Former victims must risk setting new limits with their offenders. This is often scary and is best accomplished with professional support.

One final caution. When forgiveness occurs and reconciliation begins, we encourage victims to move ahead slowly and not to feel as if they need to give their former offenders carte blanche to their lives and children. Some offenders try to impose guilt by saying, "If you've truly forgiven me and put the past behind you, then why won't you let my grandchildren spend the night?"

Victims must trust their own judgment. There is nothing wrong with not providing what may cause the offenders to sin. In fact, Scripture tells us that we are to guard against making others stumble. Not allowing their children to spend the night may be best for both their children and their offenders. Victims who desire reconciliation must learn to firmly hold to their new boundaries. If offenders are not willing or able to honor these new limits, perhaps the option of reconciliation needs to be reevaluated.[2]

Many with eating disorders were sexually abused as children. Some were not. But whether or not sexual abuse was a part of your experience, sexuality confusion is usually tied in with an eating disorder.

For those on the pathway to recovery, the trek can seem long and hard. But healing is possible. Being pleased with who you are sexually is an option. Be patient. Trust that God is at work in you. With His help you'll see changes happen, and like Kathleen, you'll come to a point where you're able to say good-bye to the tyranny of the past once and for all.

11

SAYING GOOD-BYE TO THE LOSSES

T he day that Tina showed Debi Newman the scar on her stomach and her missing belly button was the day she began to grieve her loss. The loss, of course, happened many years earlier, but Tina never allowed herself to acknowledge the pain of that loss; therefore, she could not grieve.

Grieving a loss is one of the most natural and healing things a person can do. Granted, it hurts, but once grief has been allowed to run its natural course, the past loses its power and gives way to new beginnings.

In the first ten chapters of this book, you have identified and said hello to those issues having to do with your eating disorder. Now it is time to begin to say good-bye to them. Saying good-bye is the beginning of the grieving process.

NAMING THE LOSSES

Before examining the grieving process itself, let's review some issues that need to be grieved. We can do that by naming the losses.

Loss of Identity

The anorexic or bulimic has established her identity in her eating disorder. To let go of that eating disorder is to let go of her identity. But only through saying good-bye and grieving that loss can she move on to establish a new and healthy identity.

Physical Loss

Another loss that must be faced is possible permanent damage to the body. Anyone who has been anorexic or bulimic for an extended period of time must realize that irreversible damage may have been done to her body, such as infertility or weakening of bones and/or tissue. The important thing here is to forgive yourself for this damage, and thank God that He has spared you from anything worse.

Loss of Perfectionism

This loss encompasses many facets of the anorexic's or bulimic's life. The first and most obvious area is that of body image.

Every anorexic and bulimic struggles in this area; Tina Morgan was no exception. As an active, competitive college student, Tina was driven with the need to be perfect in every possible area—particularly the physical. She was involved in a bulimic lifestyle to achieve and maintain what she considered a perfect figure, and she went to great pains to keep others from knowing of her scar and missing belly button—the "gross deformity" that prevented her from being perfect.

In Chapter 13 we will discuss how to develop a healthy body image. For now, we need to concentrate on saying good-bye to that unrealistic image of a perfect body, which no one has achieved or will achieve.

The second area is that of the family of origin. After choosing to see your family through rose-colored glasses for years, saying good-bye to that picture-perfect facade and looking at them realistically for the first time will be like seeing them through shattered glass. But the truth is, you will be seeing them as they really area, as others have seen them all along.

Tina came face-to-face with this reality when she recognized that neither she nor her parents could be perfect. Seeing them as the imperfect couple that they were, she was able to forgive them for not taking her to the hospital sooner.

You will also have to face losses in relationships, both past and current. Although there is no such thing as a perfect relationship, this step can be painful, especially when you realize what could have been but wasn't because you weren't in touch with yourself enough to invest emotionally in those relationships. Saying good-bye to those relationships, however, can free you to say hello to some healthy new ones. Realizing that other families didn't have perfect relationships helped Tina accept the limitations on her relationship with her family as well as look for ways to improve that relationship in the future.

Saying good-bye to the years wasted on being obsessed with your eating disorder is much the same as saying good-bye to lost relationships. Although you could not have spent those years perfectly, you have to grieve the fact that you could have spent them much more constructively than you did. This loss can spur you on to using your future more wisely—which is exactly what Tina determined to do after she finally made the break with her bulimic past.

STAGES OF GRIEF

Now that we've reviewed the issues to be grieved as you move away from your past and into a more promising future, let's discuss the five progressive stages in the normal grief process:

- Denial
- Anger turned outward
- Anger turned inward

- Genuine sorrow
- Resolution and acceptance[1]

Denial

Even after years of counseling, therapists are amazed at some stories they hear from their clients describing extremely abusive situations, and yet the clients never realized that the occurrences were abnormal or abusive. The first thing the therapist must do is help the client move beyond this oppressive stage of denial.

Whether or not abuse has occurred, every anorexic or bulimic who wishes to get better must take this same step of moving beyond denial. Although Tina experienced no major forms of outward abuse, she was in deep denial when she first came to the Minirth-Meier Clinic for treatment.

After fourteen-year-old Tina learned she had lost her belly button, she went into denial. In fact, she became a master at it. As she grew older, she changed her sphere of friends, eliminating those who knew of her surgery. She was meticulously careful to prevent anyone from seeing her stomach. She avoided dressing and undressing in front of her girlfriends in the locker room at school or at slumber parties. Even at home, she turned away from anyone who might see her stomach. It seemed as though she had convinced herself that if no one ever saw her stomach, she really wasn't missing a belly button and she wasn't scarred. Therefore, she could still be perfect.

Anger

Anger turned outward and anger turned inward often cross over in the grief process. Anorexics and bulimics tend to deny anger toward others, so their anger is turned inward. They often get stuck here in the grieving process. Through therapy, they learn to connect their anger with their memories and discover their buried anger toward others. Thus, they move past both phases of anger, inward and outward.

Tina had dwelled on her anger turned inward for years. If only she had taken better care of herself, maybe she never would have needed the operation. But as she got in touch with her anger, she realized she had a lot of anger towards her parents about the surgery. She felt her mother should have listened to her when she first complained of her stomach ache. Her father should have been available earlier to drive her to the hospital. If only they had been doing their job, she would still be perfect! She was also surprised to discover the anger and resentment she felt toward them for not having more drive, ambition, and money, and a nicer home and car like those of the families of her friends at school.

Whether the anger is directed inward or outward, discuss it openly and honestly with God. God already knows your feelings—even if you're feeling anger toward Him—so why not tell Him how you feel?

The Bible offers countless examples of people who got angry and frustrated with God. Joshua was one of them. Soon after taking over leadership of the Israelites from Moses, Joshua led them in an attack on Jericho. God gave them a great victory. Unfortunately, an Israelite disobeyed God's orders not to take any of the spoil of Jericho for themselves. Because of the man's disobedience, the Israelites suffered a humiliating defeat the next time they went into battle.

Joshua couldn't understand it. He threw himself on the ground and poured out his anger and frustration to God. God, of course, already knew how Joshua felt. He also knew what the problem was and what Joshua had to do to remedy it. So He waited until Joshua finished throwing his tantrum and then told him to get up and take care of the problem concerning the man who had stolen the goods from Jericho.

Job, on the other hand, never got a direct answer from God about why everything seemed to be falling apart around him. But he presented his case to the Lord and eventually received peace in his heart and restoration of his health, family, and prosperity.

Nothing is too awful to tell God. We encourage you to allow

your anger and pain to drive you to God rather than away from Him. Perhaps you could start with a simple prayer.

Genuine Sorrow

Genuine sorrow is different from depression. Depression can suck you down into its dark depths and keep you there as long as you let it. Genuine sorrow, however, is a legitimate sadness over a loss. When you allow yourself to feel and express your sorrow, it will run its course and eventually pass away.

Once Janet began to grieve the loss of her toe, she went through a period of genuine sorrow for about a week. She had to say things to herself like, "I wish I had a toe, but I don't and there's nothing I can do to change that." During that time, she was able to forgive herself for incurring the accident and her parents for allowing it to happen.

Resolution and Acceptance

In this final stage of grief you accept your loss and make peace with the fact that what happened cannot be changed. Then you are free to move on with your life.

After getting past her time of genuine sorrow, Tina decided it was time to stop being so obsessive about her loss. Although it took all the nerve she could muster, she accepted an invitation to a pool party. She wore her bathing suit to the party but afterward was able to change from her suit into her shorts and shirt without hiding from the other girls as she dressed. When she realized that no one noticed her missing scar or missing belly button, she experienced freedom from her loss for the very first time.

PRESSING ON

As we stated at the beginning of the chapter, the grieving process is a turning point in each person's recovery. It is a time of leaving the old behind and moving on to the new. It is a time of telling yourself, "Okay, I didn't get the love I needed from Mom and Dad. I didn't get the attention I wanted. My needs weren't met, and it made me sad and angry. But I can't go back and change that. I can't change other people. And I can't fill the emptiness with food. It's time to say good-bye to all that and move on."

We therapists refer to this period of time as closure. It is a time when clients must learn to be assertive in letting go. It is not enough to let go emotionally. Sometimes a person may need to physically let go as well. For instance, simply declaring, "I'm letting go of Mom," is not going to work if you call her four times a week.

This stage of treatment may or may not require the involvement of family members, depending on the current relationship between the client and her family. If the family is supportive of the client's healing process, the therapist will probably encourage interaction with the family at this point. But even if the family does not cooperate, the client must seek closure so that she can move on.

Letting go requires concerted effort to keep from getting stuck in the grief process. The apostle Paul knew about letting go: "Forgetting what is behind and straining toward what is ahead, I press on toward the goal."[2]

We may never fully forget the past, but we still can press on toward wholeness in spite of the past. Saying good-bye can break us loose from the hold the past has had on us for so long. We can glance back at the past but need not stare. Staring gets us stuck and causes us to forfeit the present and the future. It's time now to heed Paul's counsel and press on toward the goal.

12

ESTABLISHING HEALTHY EATING PATTERNS

P art of Tina Morgan's therapy involved meeting with Laura Bertzyk, a registered dietitian at the Minirth-Meier unit at Westpark Hospital. Laura's eyes sparkled as she smiled across the desk at Tina. Her natural warmth and caring attitude were obvious in her demeanor. As is her practice, Laura reviewed with Tina some basic points relating to the history of Tina's bulimia, her weight history, and her previous and current eating patterns and behaviors.

Upon completing this general review, Laura pulled out a blank sheet of paper and handed it to Tina.

"So far I've been doing all the work," Laura explained with a smile. "Now it's your turn. What I'd like you to do for me is to divide this sheet of paper by a line down the middle. On one side of the line, I would like you to list what you consider to be your 'safe' foods; on the other side, list your 'nonsafe' foods."

Laura asked, "Do you understand what I mean by safe and non-safe foods, Tina?"

Tina's green eyes grew large as she looked up from the paper to Laura. "Oh, definitely," she exclaimed. "I've been dividing food into these two lists for a long time. The safe foods are the ones I can eat without worrying about getting fat. The unsafe foods are the ones that make me binge and purge, right?"

Laura smiled again. "Sounds like you know what to do," she said. "Why don't you go ahead and work on that while I spend some time going over the other information you gave me."

Tina nodded and picked up a pen from Laura's desk. It didn't take long for her to fill up both sides of her paper.

"How's this?" Tina handed the paper across the desk to Laura, who began to read through the lists:

Safe Foods

Coffee, tea	Oatmeal
Diet pop	Lettuce
Yogurt	Tomatoes
Celery	Cabbage
Carrots	Spinach
Strawberries	Green beans
Cottage cheese	Chicken, beef broth

Nonsafe Foods

Ding-dongs®	Potatoes
Twinkies®	All meats
Chips	Hard cheese
Pretzels	All cereal
Peanuts	Milk
Cookies	Fruit pies
Ice cream	Candy
Donuts	Sandwiches
Doritos®	Eggs
All bread	Butter, oils

The lists came as no surprise to Laura. She had seen similar versions countless times. As her work with Tina progressed,

Laura's goal would be to have Tina transfer one item a week from her nonsafe list to her safe list. Since her safe food diet was so obviously low in protein, the first item Laura encouraged Tina to add was a glass of skim milk. The next week Tina agreed to eat an egg for breakfast occasionally. The following week she added a piece of bread at lunch. Each week, she continued to add one more item to her safe food list.

After several months, Tina could handle going to a friend's home for a full-course meal without panicking. She learned that moderate amounts of any food wouldn't make her fat. By increasing her safe foods, she decreased her trigger foods (which caused her to crave a certain food and then binge) and heightened her peace of mind.

HELPFUL STEPS

We live in a food-oriented culture. In light of this fact, variety is a must in moving toward normalcy. Eventually, you are going to be stuck in a situation where you will have no control over the food being served. Someday you will have to face breads, steak, pastas, and even desserts. If all of these foods are nonsafe items on your list, you will probably panic, embarrassing yourself and offending others. However, if your acceptable food list is expanded, you're less likely to set yourself up for failure and more likely to stick with a normal eating program.

Why don't you take a moment and do the exercise Tina did with the dietitian? Take a sheet of paper, divide it down the middle, then list your safe foods and your nonsafe foods. Set a goal for this week. Pick one food from your nonsafe food list, and add it to your safe food list. For instance, this week you might add a potato or an ear of corn or a piece of bread. Remember, any food eaten in moderation will not make you fat. Give yourself *full permission* to eat it. Negative guilt feelings will not allow you to enjoy the food and could set you up for a binge-purge cycle. Take the risk and decide to move toward normal eating habits. You'll be glad you did!

Another helpful step in moving toward healthy eating habits is to create your meals using variety. When you forbid yourself certain foods, you may end up feeling psychologically deprived. The best way to avoid this feeling is to vary the foods you choose at each meal. Mix crunchy with mushy foods, chewy with soft foods, orange with green, red with yellow.

After you have planned those menus, stick to them, even if you panic at the thought of eating some of the foods on your menu. Your natural inclination may be to skip a meal entirely, but never set yourself up to binge by skipping scheduled meals. People who starve themselves all day set themselves up to binge in the late afternoon or evening. Psychologically, they feel cheated of the food they thought about throughout the day; physically, they are tired from the day's work and improper nutrition; emotionally, they have no fight power. The result? Usually a full-blown binge. Those with eating disorders must maintain their eating schedules—whether they feel like it or not. Learning a new pattern demands consistency.

Most anorexics or bulimics don't feel like eating according to a plan because they are conditioned to inconsistent eating patterns. But when they make the choice to stick with the plan, regardless of their feelings, they learn to eat normally. Yes, for a time it feels uncomfortable, but one or two months of discomfort are a small price to pay for a lifetime of increased control and normalcy.

A key step in establishing healthy eating patterns is to never restrict your food intake to less than 1,200 calories.

WHY 1,200 CALORIES?

Trying to get by on less than 1,200 calories will leave you feeling hungry most of the time, therefore setting yourself up for a binge. In addition, a diet of less than 1,200 calories per day cannot possibly meet all of your nutritional needs. Finally, a continued diet of less than 1,200 calories per day will alter your body chemistry, thus slowing down its metabolic rate. Your diet will then become a self-defeating effort, because as your metabolism slows down, so does your ability to lose weight.

As Laura, the dietitian at Minirth-Meier, often explains to her patients, you can eat normally, get adequate nutrition, and still lose weight. She compares this process to that of a car running in third gear. Then, as you reduce your caloric intake, it is as if the car downshifted into first gear—everything slows down to conserve energy.

If your ultimate goal is weight loss, you must maintain your caloric intake at a minimum of 1,200 calories daily—for your health's sake as well as your weight.

HOW DO I BALANCE MY CALORIC INTAKE?

So far we've talked about the need to balance your caloric intake, but we haven't really been specific. Let's do that now.

At the Minirth-Meier Clinic, meals are planned from Food Exchange Lists, which group different types of food. There are six lists, divided according to the nutrients found in food:

(1) Starch/Bread Exchanges; (2) Meat Exchanges; (3) Vegetable Exchanges; (4) Fruit Exchanges; (5) Milk Exchanges; and (6) Fat Exchanges.

Each food on a certain list has about the same amount of carbohydrate, protein, fat, and calories as the other foods on that list. They are called Food Exchange Lists because any food on the list can be exchanged for any other food on the same list.

For example, on the Fruit Exchange List, you can trade ⅓ cup of grape juice for one small pear; on the Starch/Bread Exchange List, you can trade three graham cracker squares for one slice of bread. But your trade or "exchange" must come from the same list. You may not trade an item on the Fruit Exchange List for one on the Starch/Bread Exchange List. These lists are invaluable for planning your meals to ensure proper nutrition.[1]

The calorie-controlled Food Exchange Lists for you to use in meal planning appear in Appendix 1. We have included the Milk Exchange List here so you can see how the process works.

List 5—Milk Exchanges
(Includes nonfat, low-fat, and whole milk)

If milk is used in food preparation, it must be included in the daily meal pattern.

Skim and very low-fat milk
One exchange of skim, very low-fat milk contains 12 grams of carbohydrate, 8 grams of protein, a trace of fat, and 90 calories.
*Buttermilk (made from skim milk) .... 1 cup
Evaporated skim milk .... 1/2 cup
Powdered milk (nonfat dry, before adding water) ...... 1/3 cup
Skim milk .... 1 cup
Yogurt (plain, nonfat) .... 1 cup
1/2% or 1% fat milk .... 1 cup

Low-fat milk
One exchange of low-fat milk contains 12 grams of carbohydrate, 8 grams of protein, 5 grams of fat, and 120 calories.
Canned, evaporated 2% milk .... 1 cup
Soy milk .... 1 cup
Yogurt (plain and unflavored made with 2% fortified milk) 1 cup
2% fat milk .... 1 cup

Whole milk
One exchange of whole milk contains 12 grams of carbohydrate, 8 grams of protein, 8 grams of fat, and 150 calories.
Evaporated whole milk .... 1/2 cup
Goat milk .... 1 cup
Whole milk .... 1 cup

Yogurt (plain made from whole milk) .... 1 cup

Not allowed: condensed milk, malted beverages, chocolate beverages, sweetened fruit-flavored yogurt.
*High in sodium.[2]

SAMPLE MEAL PLANNING FOR 1,200-CALORIE DIET

Now that you have the Food Exchange Lists to refer to, we will give you a suggested Seven-Day Meal Plan in Appendix 2 for a balanced 1,200-calorie-per-day diet. We have included Day One in this chapter so you can see a typical day. In Appendix 3, you will find a blank meal planner, like the one in this chapter, so you can come up with some variations of your own.

Day One

Breakfast
1 Fruit Exchange — List 4: 1 peach
1 Starch/Bread Exchange — List 1: ½ cup bran flakes
0 Meat Exchange — List 2:
0 Fat Exchange — List 6:
1 Milk Exchange — List 5: 4 oz. skim milk or ½ cup nonfat yogurt

Noon meal
2 Meat Exchanges — List 2: 2 1-oz. meatballs
2 Starch/Bread Exchanges — List 1: 1 cup cooked pasta
2 Vegetable Exchanges — List 3: ½ cup tomato sauce
1 cup salad veggies
free veggies
lemon/vinegar or
1 tbsp. fat-free dressing

0 Fruit Exchange — List 4:
0 Fat Exchange — List 6:
0 Milk Exchange — List 5:

Evening meal

3 Meat Exchanges	List 2: 3 oz. grilled chicken
1 Starch/Bread Exchange	List 1: 1 dinner roll
0 Vegetable Exchange	List 3: free dinner salad
2 Fruit Exchanges	List 4: 1 cup mixed fruit
0 Fat Exchange	List 6:
0 Milk Exchange	List 5:

Bedtime snack

1 Fruit Exchange	List 4: ½ banana
1 Starch/Bread and	List 1 and
1 Fat Exchange	List 6: 6 small vanilla wafers

Before beginning your meal planning based on the Food Exchange Lists in Appendix 1, you need to remember five basic things:

1. Eat all foods allowed on your meal plan each day at the specific mealtime.

2. With the assistance of your dietitian, establish specific, realistic goals for both weight loss and changes in eating behaviors. For instance, because Tina had so little weight to lose, she set a reasonable yet realistic goal of losing one to two pounds per month. As far as changing her eating behaviors, she agreed to work with Laura to move one item each week from her nonsafe foods list to her safe foods list. To try to do more than that all at once would have been self-defeating. By setting these realistic goals, Tina did not feel overwhelmed by her own expectations and was better able to achieve success with her new diet plan.

3. Try to reach your goal weight and maintain that weight within a three-pound range.

4. Follow your exchange plan. The exchanges are based on six food groups: starch/bread, meat, vegetable, fruit, milk, and fat.

Each contains foods with similar amounts of protein, carbohy-drate, fat, and calories, according to the portion size listed.

5. Avoid interchanging foods from one exchange group to an-other. Foods in one exchange list cannot be replaced by foods from another list.[3]

THE SET-POINT THEORY

One of Tina's main concerns about her future eating habits was that, unless she stayed on her 1,200-calorie diet indefinitely, she would begin to gain weight and never be able to stop. All anorex-ics and bulimics fear this uncontrolled weight gain. Laura, how-ever, was able to ease Tina's mind by explaining to her what is commonly called the set-point theory.

"I understand your concern," said Laura. "But you cannot stay on a 1,200-calorie diet indefinitely for the plain and simple reason that you don't need to lose much weight. Some people would say that you don't need to lose any at all. But to help you establish proper eating habits, we'll start you at 1,200 calories and then work your way up slowly, adding approximately 200 calories per week until you get to a point where your weight stabilizes."

Tina frowned. "But are you sure that will happen?" she asked. "I mean, what if I don't stabilize? What if I . . ."

"If you learn proper eating habits and stick to them," Laura interjected, "your weight will stabilize, I assure you. It's what's known as the set-point theory. Here, I have some literature on the subject. Let's go over it together."

Tina took the material anxiously and began to read it through as Laura discussed it.

"You see, Tina," she explained, "although some surveys sug-gest that as many as 90 percent of Americans consider themselves overweight, only 25 percent are, in fact, significantly obese. Cul-tural pressures tend to sway our thinking so that the majority of us look in the mirror and think we're overweight when, in reality, we aren't.

"The set-point theory is one of the latest theories in weight control studies. According to this theory, every person has a genetic point at which his or her weight is the healthiest and easiest to maintain. In an ideal world we would all reach our set-point weight at adulthood and stay there. Unfortunately, everyone knows that isn't how life works. But finding your set point and staying there can make lifetime weight control much more comfortable than trying to look like your favorite movie star or sports figure."

Laura paused for a moment to be sure that Tina was following along. It was obvious by her captivated expression that she was. "There are several ways to determine your set point," Laura went on. "Life insurance height and weight charts can be helpful, and you can determine your percentage of body fat, which for a man should probably be around 15 to 20 percent, while for a woman it should be around 20 to 27 percent. Doctors, health club therapists, and coaches are often trained to take such measurements.

"Here at the Minirth-Meier Clinic we have a very simple formula that Dr. Minirth has given us. Women should weigh 100 pounds, plus 5 pounds for every inch of height above five feet. For men, weight should be 106 pounds plus 6 pounds for every inch above five feet. Of course, this is not an absolute. It is simply a weight range, varying from plus or minus 10 percent, but it can be a useful guideline."

Laura could tell that Tina was doing some quick mental calculating. Suddenly, her eyes opened wide.

"If I went by the guideline you just gave me," Tina exclaimed, "that would mean I'm almost exactly where I need to be with my weight because I weigh 130 pounds. I . . . I may not have much weight to lose after all!"

"Not very much at all," Laura agreed. "But the important thing is to get you established in healthy eating habits so your body can find its set point and stay there naturally. You see, your set point is probably going to be slightly different from that of someone else of your same age and height because your set point is the weight at which you, as an individual, are most physiologically comfortable. Notice I said *physiologically,* not emotionally or psychologically comfortable according to societal standards. There can be a big difference between these comfort zones. For example, one woman five feet seven inches tall may have a set point of 125 pounds, while another may have an optimal weight of 135 pounds.

"Proponents of the set-point theory say that your metabolic rate speeds up or slows down to keep you at your set point. When you reduce your caloric intake to lose weight, your metabolism slows down. So everything equalizes. You eat less, burn less, and therefore remain the same. Many people become discouraged because they have set unrealistic weight loss goals for themselves instead of allowing the body to organize itself to balance energy intake and output to remain at its optimal weight or set point."[4]

Tina was nodding slowly as a smile crept across her face. "It makes sense," she mused, almost as if she were alone in the room. "It really makes sense. It's not going to be easy, but I'm going to work on getting my weight to my set point and then work on my attitude so I'll be satisfied to leave it there."

Special Tips for Successful Weight Control

By the time Laura got Tina started on meal planning according to the Food Exchange Lists, Tina was excited. But she was also apprehensive.

"I don't know," she said, glancing nervously back and forth from the lists in her lap to the dietitian sitting across the desk from her. "The variety is great, and the idea of being in control . . . I love it! But . . ." A flicker of fear flashed through her green eyes. "I don't know if I can do it," she said, her shoulders sagging slightly. "I mean, what about when I get tempted? Can you give me some ideas about what to do to keep from giving in to the urge to binge?"

Laura smiled. "Yes," she answered. "And please understand that your concern is perfectly normal. You will be tempted, Tina. Many times. And you may very well fall. The important thing is that you get right back up again and keep going. Prayer, of course, is your first line of defense."

Laura handed Tina another sheet of paper. "These tips will help you learn to control your weight successfully. Memorize them. Let them become a way of life, and the day will come when you'll find yourself maintaining your weight without any conscious effort. There's a lot of freedom in that."

Tina nodded, encouraged. Then she read slowly through the list:

1. Keep a record of everything you eat (you may want to note when and where you eat), your mood when you eat, and who you eat with. Recording the food before you eat may be helpful in controlling the amount you eat and making you aware of cues that trigger eating.

2. Before you eat, ask yourself, Am I really hungry? If the answer is no, do something else. Have a list of five to ten enjoyable activities to do instead of eating.

3. Delay eating. A ten to fifteen minute wait before eating will help in establishing control over eating habits.

4. When you eat, try not to do anything else. Don't watch television, read the paper, or write a letter.

5. While you are cooking, serving, or cleaning the table, try to avoid sampling the food.

6. Eat everything from dishes, not from the containers. Containers disguise how much you are really eating.

7. Use small plates to make your servings look more appealing. The same amount of food will look much more satisfying served on a small plate rather than on a large one.

8. Start your meal with a low-calorie beverage or soup. It will slow your eating and help you to feel full.

9. Remove serving platters from the table.

10. Slow your speed of eating. Put your fork down between

bites. Pause to talk and relax during the meal. Take sips of water throughout the meal.

11. Leave some food on your plate.

12. Leave the table immediately after you finish eating.

13. Grocery shop *after* you have eaten. It is too easy to make unnecessary purchases if you are hungry.

14. Keep low-calorie foods, like fruits and vegetables, for snacks in the most visual place in your refrigerator.

15. Shop from a detailed list. You will save both calories and money by eliminating impulse buying.

16. Buy food that requires preparation. If making a snack requires time and effort, you will give more thought to eating that snack.

17. Keep food well wrapped and out of sight. Keep much of your food frozen or in hard-to-reach places. A lock may not be a bad idea.[5]

18. Avoid finger foods; plan meals with foods that require the use of utensils.

19. Increase meal satiety by including warm foods rather than cold or room temperature foods.

20. Include vegetables, salad, and/or fruit at a meal to prolong the meal duration; choose whole grain and high-fiber breads and cereals.

21. Prescribe well-balanced diet and meals, both to increase satiety and to increase the variety of foods eaten.

22. Use foods that are naturally divided into portions, such as potatoes (rather than rice or pasta); 4- and 8-oz. containers of yogurt, ice cream, or cottage cheese; precut steak or chicken parts; and frozen dinners and entrees.

23. Include foods containing adequate amounts of complex carbohydrates (which promote meal satiety) and fat (which slow gastric emptying and further enhance the feeling of fullness).

24. Eat meals and snacks sitting down.

25. Plan meals and snacks, and keep a food diary by recording food prior to eating.[6]

THE REALITY CHALLENGE

Laura Bertzyk's meeting with Cindy Briscoe was much more of a challenge. Where Tina was eagerly anticipating learning to establish her new eating habits, Cindy was terrified of eating anything at all that hadn't been part of her strictly observed rituals during the past few years of her anorexia. When Laura showed her what a 1,000- to 1,200-calorie diet consisted of, Cindy was horrified. It was more food than she normally allowed herself over a period of several days. And Laura's explanation of the set-point theory fell on totally deaf ears. It wasn't until Laura brought Cindy a pair of shorts that belonged to an eight-year-old and convinced her to try them on that the first sliver of reality began to penetrate Cindy's denial. The eight-year-old's shorts were too big for her!

Soon, however, Cindy decided that she was being tricked. She was sure someone had switched the tags in the shorts, and they did not actually belong to an eight-year-old child. Obviously, it was going to take more than a sliver of reality to pierce Cindy's denial.

A patient works through four phases at the Minirth-Meier Clinic. During the first two phases, meals and snacks are planned for the patient, and she must eat all food. Cindy would require quite some time before reaching phase three where she would participate in her meal planning and where she would also be encouraged to transfer some of her nonsafe foods to her safe foods list.

For any patient as extremely anorexic as Cindy, a dietitian may decide to start her on a 1,000-calorie diet, gradually increasing her caloric intake by 200 to 250 calories per week. No matter how severely emaciated, the anorexic will insist that she is not hungry, that she absolutely cannot eat, and that if she eats so much as one full tray of food, she will immediately gain ten pounds. Cindy made this exaggerated statement one evening when Laura brought her dinner tray, so the dietitian used the opportunity to challenge Cindy with another sliver of reality.

"One pound is equal to 3,500 calories," Laura explained. "Do you remember how many calories I told you were in your entire three meals each day?"

Cindy twisted her hair nervously. "Around 1,000," she mumbled.

"That's right," Laura continued. "So you would have to eat three and a half times as much food as you do now to get enough calories to gain even one pound. Even then, you would burn some of those calories during the normal course of the day. Can you see that it is a physical impossibility to gain ten pounds by eating one meal?"

Cindy hesitated, then shrugged. "Maybe," she consented. "At least for most people, but for me . . . well, I'm just not sure. I . . . I don't want to take the chance."

It would be a long road to healing for Cindy, as it is for many anorexics and bulimics. But with God's help, along with trained, caring professionals on her side, she would eventually progress to the point of eating a normal, healthy diet each and every day of her life.

You can do the same. But you must start now—one step at a time. Establishing proper eating habits will be one of the biggest steps you will take on your road to recovery—but it is a step you will never regret.

13

I LIKE THE WAY I LOOK

Martha had been sick a lot as a young child. As a result, she had always been quite thin and frail. By the time she reached adolescence, however, her health had improved, and she began to fill out and develop normally.

Martha's mother had always been slightly overweight; "hippy" was the way Martha's father put it. One day when Martha was thirteen, her father walked by and slapped her lightly on the hip.

"Better watch out," he teased. "You keep gaining weight, you're going to end up as hippy as your mother."

Ten years later, no matter how skinny and emaciated Martha had managed to become, she saw only hips when she looked in the mirror. Because the anorexic's or bulimic's entire self-concept is so tied in with her body image, Martha felt like a total failure—not just at maintaining a slim appearance but at life in general.

WHAT IS A BODY IMAGE?

Although we are all three-part beings—body, soul, and spirit—anorexics and bulimics tend to think of themselves solely in terms of their bodies. If their bodies don't fit the image of what they consider perfect, they believe they have failed at life. They brand themselves failures because of a faulty body image.

Let's talk about body image for a moment. What exactly is meant by that term? In essence, *body image is what you think you look like on the outside*. It includes objective information such as eye and hair color, weight, height, and so on, but it goes beyond that to a less objective, imagined image. Because of that, this image may or may not be true. Yet in the mind of the anorexic or bulimic, it is the only truth—the truth that controls every aspect of life.

Most anorexics and bulimics do not realize that what they see when they look in the mirror is not necessarily the same image others see when they look at them. Even the image you see in the mirror today may not be the same image you see tomorrow. The point is, a body image is not just an objective image; it's subjective. And as the old saying goes, "Beauty is in the eye of the beholder."

WHAT IS BODY HATE?

Unfortunately, most anorexics and bulimics do not behold anything beautiful when they look in the mirror. Instead, they see an ugly failure, and they hate what they see.

Body hate, to some degree, is common, particularly among women. We all have certain things about our bodies that we would change if we could. Without a doubt, body hate has been fueled by a culture that emphasizes beauty and equates that beauty with thinness. Persons with eating disorders carry this body hate to an extreme, always striving for an impossible ideal, dwelling on their negative features, overlooking their positive ones.

Most women are concerned about the thighs and stomach. "I can't stand it if the insides of my legs touch," says Norma. "Or if I can't feel my bones against the chair when I sit down." And Pauline explains, "When I lie down, I don't just want my stomach to be flat. I want it to cave in—like the models in the magazines. That's how I want to look."

Breast size also troubles those with eating disorders. Elaine's anorexic behavior began as a result of what she considered her "flat chest." She was determined that, since she couldn't increase her breast size, she would reduce her hips accordingly.

Jackie and Patrick had been married eight years. In all that time, Patrick had never seen her without her bra on—even when they made love. She was just too ashamed to let him see what she referred to as her "nonexistent breasts."

Many persons with eating disorders, particularly bulimics, have established an impossible ideal for themselves. To them, the models in the magazines are "the perfect women." They figure that if the models can do it, why can't they?

They don't realize that most models achieve their extremely thin figures with constant dieting—in some cases, even starving and/or purging. But the pictures of these models, compounded by the "beautiful" people on television and in movies, put extreme pressure on people to measure up. And although women fall prey to this pressure more often than men, men are not immune.

Phil began weight lifting in his late teens. The more time he spent at the gym, the more obsessed he became with developing his body into what he considered the epitome of masculinity—a mass of highly toned muscles. Having been abandoned by his father as a baby, he was emotionally starved for male attention. His weight lifting fed that need until he became obsessed with his body image. Before long he measured his muscles and recorded the results daily. When he couldn't get his waist down to his desired measurement, he eventually began to purge to flatten his stomach.

CONFRONTING YOUR BODY IMAGE

To overcome a poor body image and develop a healthy one, you must confront your body image to discover where it came from. Ask yourself the following questions:

- What do I dislike about my appearance?
- What do I like about my appearance?
- Where did I learn these things?

When Pam Vredevelt first asked these questions during therapy, Marian Grier had no trouble coming up with a long list of things she disliked about her appearance. When asked what she did like, however, she was stumped.

"Nothing," she hesitated. "Nothing . . . except my fingernails. They've always been long and really strong."

Had anyone else been asked to list positive aspects of Marian's appearance, it would have been quite simple. Marian was athletically trim, dressed immaculately, and had thick blonde hair, blue eyes, and a smooth, creamy complexion. Hardly anything to complain about. But when Marian looked in the mirror, she saw two main things—a stomach that she was sure was too big, and breasts that weren't big enough.

When Pam asked Marian to try to remember where she developed these ideas, Marian recalled an incident with her father.

"I was about sixteen," she said. "I had always been thin as a little girl. But when I got to be about thirteen or so, my stomach started poking out. I hated it. What was even worse, my breasts never grew at all. All my friends had big breasts by then, but I had nothing. That's when my dad . . ." She took a deep breath before continuing. "My dad reached out and touched my chest one day. Then he laughed and said, 'There's nothing there.' I wanted to die."

Marian had good reason to be embarrassed. To an already insecure teenager, her father's insensitive action and remark were devastating. From that day forward, she refused to be seen in a bathing suit. She refused all invitations to pool or beach parties, terrified that someone would discover what she considered to be a major deformity.

As a result of a faulty body image, those with eating disorders abuse themselves in various ways. They may restrict their activities to hide their bodies. They become involved in starving and/or

bingeing and purging, not realizing that years of vomiting and laxative abuse will destroy the colon's ability to function naturally
and therefore will destroy their ability to have a flat stomach.

Whatever forms self-abuse takes, considering where faulty
body images come from is important. Although in today's society,
the perfect body is presented as the willowy model, looking back
at the Renaissance period, we can see from paintings done then
that thin was not in. Food was not as plentiful in those days as it is
now. Therefore, being slightly rotund was a social statement that
you were well-to-do enough to be able to buy sufficient food. The
point is, fads and fashions are fickle. If we base body image on
current trends, we are standing on shaky ground.

DEVELOPING A HEALTHY BODY IMAGE

Now that we've confronted several issues that can lead to a poor
body image, let's talk about some tools to develop a new, healthy
body image.

Using Group Therapy Methods

One exercise used in group therapy at the Minirth-Meier Clinic
involves having the patient lie down on a big sheet of paper. Another member of the group traces around her. Then the paper is
hung on the wall, and the patient labels all the areas of her body
that she dislikes. Or the patient looks in the mirror and describes
the parts of her body that she sees as too big or too fat. These
exercises are especially meaningful for anorexics. When they la-
bel certain areas of their bodies as big or fat, the other members of
the group immediately point out to them that this assessment is
untrue.

The anorexic or bulimic needs to recognize that her body image
is a distortion of the truth and often a delusion. Actual weight has
very little, if any, bearing on the anorexic's or bulimic's belief that

she is big and fat. The anorexic or bulimic believes her body is the issue, but in reality the issue is her fear of getting fat.

Dealing with Dishonesty

Anorexics and bulimics are not comfortable with honesty. They have been living their lies for so long, they assume that others want them to lie. For instance, if a bulimic's counselor asks her how she has done all week, rather than admit she binged and purged five times, she announces, "Great. No problem. Everything's wonderful."

An exercise used at the Minirth-Meier Clinic to encourage the anorexic or bulimic to deal with dishonesty is to have her draw a picture of herself. Being as honest and realistic as possible, the therapist then draws a picture of the patient. If the patient has a big nose, the therapist draws the picture accordingly, then explains, "I see how you see yourself. Now you can see how I see you. I've tried to be as objective as I can." Honest feedback puts the patient back in touch with the idea that honesty is a positive thing, and that other people relate much better to it than they do to lies.

Establishing Realistic Views

Helping those with eating disorders perceive that most people do not look like the models in magazines is a vital part of the treatment program. Patients are asked, What have you weighed for the past five years? What do you believe is your healthy weight? What do doctors consider your healthy weight? (See the suggested weight chart on page 18.) Can we come up with a realistic figure for your ideal weight?

Working out an ideal weight with a patient must take several factors into account, especially bone structure. As explained in an earlier chapter, there is also a set point at which weight will stabilize when a person eats normally. This set point varies with each individual but is usually a realistic goal for the ideal weight.

Recognizing Emotional Hurts

The anorexic or bulimic must recognize her emotional hurts and confront the resulting beliefs. Marian had to realize that what her father said, even though it hurt terribly, was probably not said maliciously. Being able to forgive him for that opened the door to resolving the issue and building a healthy body image.

Accepting Your Body

Although you may never like everything about your body, you can learn to accept it as it is as well as the way it will be in the future. Never give in to the concept that you will be acceptable only when you reach a certain weight. You are acceptable now. Your stomach is okay. Your thighs are okay. Your breasts are okay. You have worth and dignity.

Group therapy can be beneficial in this area. For instance, group members can encourage a slightly overweight bulimic to lose the extra weight for her own sake and at the same time affirm her worth whether she loses the weight or not.

Learning to Love Your Body

Your body is a gift from God, and He meant for you to enjoy it. We want you to learn to appreciate your sexuality. God created marriage; He also created sexual pleasure for married couples. If you're not married, you can still enjoy holding hands with and kissing your boyfriend. Learn to enjoy the way you are made!

The five senses—taste, touch, sight, hearing, and smell—can also bring pleasure. Take the time to experience these God-given gifts, and realize that your body is your friend.

Get in touch with your body cues. Is your stomach tense? Cue into that emotion. What's going on? Are you feeling tired or anxious? Why? Stop and let your body tell you what's wrong.

Enjoy the physical activity a healthy body affords. Don't restrict your activities because of a poor body image.

Accepting What You Cannot Change

Heed the words of the Serenity Prayer: "God, grant me the serenity to accept the things I cannot change, the courage to change the things I can, and the wisdom to know the difference."

There's a lot to that prayer, which asks God to help us accept those things we cannot change. Apart from cosmetic surgery, most of those areas of the body that we don't like simply cannot be changed. If we think our breasts are too small or our legs are too short, we have exactly two choices: we can allow these things to continue to control our lives, or we can accept them as they are and take back the control of our lives.

At Minirth-Meier, patients are often instructed to sit in a busy shopping mall or on a park bench and watch the people walk by. They are to ask themselves, Are all of these people perfect? Do all of them have completely beautiful bodies? This reality exercise teaches patients to view themselves more objectively.

Putting an End to Judging and Evaluating

The previous exercise teaches patients to look at others, as well as themselves, more objectively. We don't look at others and notice how fat they are to make ourselves feel better. Instead, we accept ourselves and others as we are, and we quit judging or evaluating altogether. If we are looking at all the beautiful models in a magazine, we are setting ourselves and others up for failure. Again, group therapy can be helpful as patients learn to relate to others who, like themselves, do not have perfect bodies. It is also a time of learning that a healthy self-concept is not based on outward appearance.

CAUSES AND CURES OF A POOR SELF-CONCEPT

As we stated earlier, persons with eating disorders have almost no identity or self-concept apart from body image; therefore, it follows that their self-concept is poor.

According to Ed Lucas, a therapist at the Minirth-Meier Clinic in Virginia, every human being comes into the world with four basic emotional needs, which he calls LAWS: the need for *l*ove, *a*cceptance, *w*orth, and *s*ecurity. If these four needs are met in infancy and childhood, we will have a good self-concept; if they are not, our self-concept will be poor.

For the vast majority of persons with eating disorders, some or all of these needs have not been met. That is why anorexics and bulimics are such deeply needy people. Many of them have come from dysfunctional families and have spent their childhoods trying to meet their parents' needs; as adults, they are trying desperately to meet their needs through their obsessions with food.

Anorexics and bulimics have usually decided, at some point, that since other people are not going to meet their needs, they must find something else that will—food. Food is the perfect love object. Anyone with an eating disorder feels she has total control over food, and that control can cause her to feel loved and accepted, and even allow her to find a sense of worth and security.

In therapy, the anorexic or bulimic learns that the four basic needs—love, acceptance, worth, and security—were God-given gifts to Adam and Eve in the Garden of Eden. Before the Fall, they felt total love, acceptance, worth, and security from God. After the Fall, when they were separated from God, Adam and Eve hid themselves; they felt a loss of the relationship they previously shared with God. Our basic emotional needs stem from that lost relationship with God. Through a renewed relationship with Him, we can once again have those needs truly met.

THE NEED TO BELONG

Besides the four basic needs (LAWS), every human being has the need to belong. Anorexics and bulimics struggle terrifically with this need. They grew up feeling as if they never belonged in the family of origin. Now, as adults, they feel they don't belong anywhere either.

For that very reason, Cindy Briscoe put up with her piano teacher's sexual harassment—she wanted so much to belong. Because she no longer felt that at home, she hoped to find it in another family, so she eagerly joined in when the Boltons invited her to spend time with them. Had she not been so needy inside, Cindy probably would not have put up with the abuse she endured.

When Ed Lucas introduced the concept of LAWS, he also explained that, although Adam fell, God sent a Second Adam—God's Son, Jesus Christ. Jesus did not fall. Instead, He died in our place, then rose again to give us new life and to restore our relationship with the Father.

As Cindy learned this concept in therapy, she also understood that she no longer had to feel as if she didn't belong. God wanted to restore her—just as He wants to restore all of us—to the relationship that Adam and Eve originally had with Him in the Garden of Eden. Cindy had to stop believing the lies that she had been living for so long and start believing that God "has made us accepted in the Beloved."[1] That particular Scripture quickly became one of Cindy's favorites.

Many anorexics and bulimics share the common misconception that God is strict and controlling, intent on inflicting punishment. Invariably, this misconception can be traced back to an individual's relationship with her parents, particularly her father. A child who regards her father as loving and forgiving and understanding will regard God in the same way. However, if the father is rigid and undemonstrative of his love, a child will have difficulty relating to God as loving and forgiving.

We spend a lot of time working through this area with our patients. Grace and forgiveness and unconditional love are foreign concepts to most of them. We explain that, although we may experience the results of our sins, we are not punished for them. We lead them through numerous scriptures about love and forgiveness and acceptance. This vital part of therapy focuses on the true nature of God.

A key to building a healthy self-concept for the anorexic or bulimic is getting involved in group therapy. A support system during the healing process is essential. Without the proper support, anorexics in particular tend to be drawn toward narcissistic people, takers rather than givers. They should be in a group where there are reciprocal relationships, where there is give-and-take among the members as well as love and acceptance for who they are.

In therapy a patient will learn to identify the negative messages she is telling herself and to challenge their truthfulness. As she learns that she does not have to be the receptacle of all the negative messages she received as a child, as she learns to release her perfectionism and to accept herself even when she fails, she will gain confidence in herself for the very first time.

A useful exercise is to pin a piece of paper to the patient's back. Then she walks around the room, and each member of the group writes on that paper something she likes about the patient. After the session, the patient puts the paper on her bedroom mirror where she can read it first thing every morning.

On page 200 is a Positive Image-Building Calendar Pam found at a seminar on self-image in 1974 (author unknown), which represents thirty positive statements. Try copying one each morning, and then reading it aloud to yourself several times throughout the day. That evening, when you've memorized the statement, stand in front of your mirror, look yourself in the eyes, and say it out loud. By the end of the month, you will view yourself in an entirely new way!

You might try doing the same thing with some favorite promises from the Bible. For example, Philippians 4:13 declares, "I can do all things through Christ who strengthens me." The Psalms are full of comforting promises from the Lord:

Because you have made the LORD, who is my refuge,
Even the Most High, your habitation,
No evil shall befall you,
Nor shall any plague come near your dwelling. . . .
Because he has set his love upon Me, therefore I will deliver him;
I will set him on high, because he has known My name.
He shall call upon Me, and I will answer him;
I will be with him in trouble;
I will deliver him and honor him.
With long life I will satisfy him,
And show him My salvation.[2]

Find some of your favorites and commit them to memory, then speak them out loud when you are feeling fearful or overwhelmed by your circumstances. When you make it a practice to speak God's Word aloud, you will soon realize that you truly believe everything you say! And don't forget Cindy's favorite: "He has made us [*that means you!*] accepted in the Beloved."[3]

POSITIVE IMAGE-BUILDING CALENDAR

I am a very unique person, worthy of respect.	I love each moment of my life.	I am optimistic about life.	I take pride in being a person of worth.	I am an action person.
I am at ease at all times because I accept my assets and liabilities.	I have unconditional warm regard for others always.	I am relaxed even in tumult.	Others believe in me because I keep my word.	I know I can reach goals I have set for myself.
I take pride in my ability to implement ideas and programs.	If I fall, I will get up smiling and keep on going.	I am 100% alive because I think, speak, and act with great enthusiasm.	I enjoy expressing loving concern for those about me.	My openness and candor endear me to others.
People like to talk to me because I keep their confidence.	My husband's/friend's uniqueness brings joy to my heart.	Each time my life touches others', I enhance the meaning of life for them.	I pride myself in accepting others as they are.	My coworkers like to be around me because I reinforce their strengths.
I like myself unconditionally.	I am at peace within myself.	I am kind, gentle, and compassionate with myself.	I allow myself to think positively about others.	I count my blessings and rejoice in my growing awareness.
I accept compliments easily.	I have a real positive expectancy of the future.	I am content to fulfill my commitments with enthusiasm.	People like to be around me because I esteem myself and others.	I am a valuable and important person.

14

SETTING UP A
SUPPORT SYSTEM

W hen a person reaches the point in therapy of being
ready to set up a support system, it is a real transition
time, a time often referred to as a coming out party or a time for
being repeopled. As the individual is repeopled, she establishes
new relationships and/or reestablishes old ones. During therapy,
she has had the support of a therapist and/or group counseling
sessions. Making the transition from therapy, she needs a support
system of healthy relationships so that she can continue to grow
and not lapse back into the old, familiar self-destructive patterns
of her eating disorder.

Being repeopled can be somewhat scary to those in recovery; it
can also be risky if they do not have proper guidance as they establish a support system. Learning to build relationships based on
mutual trust and respect is a new concept to most anorexics or
bulimics. They also need to understand that, although they will
cross paths with countless people in the course of a lifetime, only
a few will become close and trusted companions.

Even Jesus, during His time on earth, had certain friends who
were closer to Him than others. Take, for instance, the night before His crucifixion when He went to the Garden of Gethsemane

to pray. Although He had been in the Upper Room sharing the Last Supper with all twelve of His disciples, only Peter, John, and James went with Him to the Garden. They were the same men He took with Him to the Mount of Transfiguration. Very obviously, those three disciples made up the inner circle of Jesus' closest friends and confidants.

In the past, food has been the anorexic's or bulimic's best friend. Now she is going to cultivate best-friend relationships with other people, people she can trust and depend on to love and accept her as she is, people who will be honest and care enough to support her continued healing and to confront her if they see her slipping into her old lifestyle. These best-friend relationships must be with those of the same sex to prevent the possibility of violating sexual boundaries.

Boundaries is a basic word to consider in establishing a support system of healthy relationships. These boundaries apply to all areas of our lives—emotional, physical, sexual, spiritual, and mental. Simply speaking, boundaries are the limits we set on how far and how much we will allow things to happen to us. For the anorexic or bulimic, boundaries have been violated so many times in the past that setting and maintaining new boundaries is not an easy task. That's why a support system of a trusted network of friends is so essential in the recovery process.

TRUST IN RELATIONSHIPS

A hard, cold fact of life is that not everyone is trustworthy. This fact is especially difficult to accept when some of those people are family members. And no one has more trouble accepting it than the "good little girl" who has been programmed to trust everybody. But as the recovering anorexic or bulimic establishes trusted, healthy relationships, she must be aware of four basic areas:

1. *The person needs to have a sense of predictability*. To trust

someone, you have to be able to know that this person will come through for you. How's her track record? Is he the kind of person whose actions and words usually line up? If not, you may be setting yourself up for disappointment.

Tina had to consider this issue long and hard when it was time for her to set up a support system. Although she forgave her parents and made peace with her past, she knew realistically that her family was not going to be the reliable support system she needed. Her roommates, however, had rallied to her support from the time they learned of her illness. Tina was confident that they would be there for her during her repeopling process as long as she needed them.

2. *There needs to be an absence of fear of betrayal or abandonment.* You can never trust someone you fear will betray or abandon you when the chips are down. This obstacle is a formidable one to overcome when there has been previous betrayal in a marriage relationship. If a husband has betrayed his wife and they decide to try to put their marriage back together, the wife has difficulty trusting her husband again. The husband, on the other hand, feels that if she can't trust him, they can never work things out. They need to understand that trust is a process, and it must be earned.

This point, too, was a deciding factor in Tina's decision to choose her roommates rather than her parents as her primary support system. Although she believed that her family loved her in their own way, she also knew that she couldn't necessarily trust them to put her interests ahead of their own. Because they had always expected so much of Tina, her parents often pursued their own interests at the expense of their daughter's, assuming that she would manage without them. Tina was wise enough to realize that she definitely needed the love and support of others.

3. *The person needs to be reliable.* This characteristic is close to the need to be predictable. Yet reliability includes the sense that this person is a mature, responsible human being who is sensitive to your needs. Tina's parents were adults, but that didn't automat-

ically make them mature. Their immaturity was the primary cause of their preoccupation with themselves and their own needs rather than Tina's.

4. *There must be a sense of mutual loyalty and security.* The person will be loyal to your best interests, she will be there for you when you need her, and she will step in and do what's right for you in any given situation.

In this area, Tina was positive that her roommates would be much more help than her family. Her parents, after all, had been the ones primarily responsible for setting up a faulty system in their home, one in which the parents' needs were more important than the children's. On the other hand, Tina's roommates had shown their loyalty and concern for her by standing by her faithfully throughout her treatment period. They had also expressed their willingness and availability to intervene whenever they saw Tina returning to self-destructive patterns.

CHARACTERISTICS OF NEW RELATIONSHIPS

We talked about unhealthy relationships in a previous chapter. Now let's examine some characteristics of healthy relationships.

Mutuality

In a healthy relationship, there is a sense of mutuality, of giving and receiving, of sharing concerns and responsibilities and victories. In her family, Tina had shouldered the majority of responsibilities, getting little input or assistance from her parents. It was a new and exciting concept for her to realize that she could have mutual relationships where receiving was as important as giving.

Warmth and Affection

Because of the anorexics' and bulimics' distorted views of their bodies, they have seldom experienced the physical warmth and affection available in healthy relationships. Hugging, kissing, touching—all within the proper boundaries—are God-given gifts to be enjoyed in healthy, trusted relationships. Cindy Briscoe, who had been starved for affection at home, turned to her piano teacher and his family, hoping to receive that much-needed warmth and caring. Instead, she was subjected to sexual abuse and consequently pulled away from any further display of affection from anyone. Through extensive counseling and therapy, Cindy and her parents were able to make progress toward a more normal, loving family relationship.

Healthy Boundaries

Boundaries in a healthy relationship can be spoken or unspoken, but they are always respected. Most anorexics or bulimics experience enmeshment in the family of origin. Oftentimes, when a recovering anorexic or bulimic is leaving the hospital, she must establish boundaries with her mother, such as, "Please do not call me every evening to ask me what I've eaten that day. This subject is off limits. If you ask me, I'm going to remind you that I do not wish to discuss it with you."

It is okay to set these boundaries; it is important to do so. Although others' needs are significant, so are yours. Realize that you are an individual, and that you do not have to let others control you by violating your boundaries.

Establishing and maintaining boundaries in healthy relationships is explored in detail during therapy at Minirth-Meier. Most incoming patients are not aware that there are such things as boundaries, and they must learn proper relationship boundaries with parents, spouse, boyfriend/girlfriend, church—and soon.

If you're confused about whether or not you lack boundaries in your life, ask yourself the following questions: Are there people in my life who

- make unreasonable demands on me?
- blame me for their feelings?
- make me feel uncomfortable sexually?
- I cannot say no to?

- never listen to my feelings?
- make me anxious and fearful when I think of them?
- cause me to wonder what they will think about every decision I make?
- I feel I will upset if I do things for myself?

If you answered yes to most of these questions, name the people in this category, then go through the following steps for each of them:

- Pray for wisdom about how to handle the relationship, brainstorm possible boundaries you need, and decide on the reasonable ones.
- Speak the truth in love where appropriate.
- Live out your boundaries whether the other person cooperates or not.
- Be open to relationship with this person (i.e., be forgiving; don't hold on to bitterness).

Exposure

Exposure is the feeling that you are known to another person, that she has seen both good and bad sides of you and she loves you anyway. Of course, exposure must work both ways. If the other person is to know and accept you as you are, you must know and accept her also. You take off the mask of perfectionism, recognize you are human, and allow others to see this in you. Candy, who referred to herself as "the perfect Christian wife with the secret problem of throwing up," after three months finally admitted to her group members that she didn't think she loved her husband. The others in her group responded, "We had already figured that out. We were just wondering when you would admit it."

Balance of Power

In a healthy relationship, one person does not always control while the other surrenders. One member of the relationship is not more important than the other. Although there are areas of submission and give as well as take in every relationship, there is a healthy balance in understanding the scriptural admonition to "submit to one another out of reverence for Christ."[1]

Lynette felt she had to have the upper hand in all of her relationships. She didn't have many friends, so she pushed her power mostly on people at work. She made her coworkers cry at times because of the cruel things she said. Part of her recovery was to apologize to her coworkers and to confess this way of trying to control by intimidation. The women were frankly shocked by the changes in Lynette, and the atmosphere at work improved dramatically.

NEW GUIDELINES FOR OLD RELATIONSHIPS

Much of what we have discussed so far applies to setting up a support system by establishing new and healthy relationships during the recovery process. These guidelines also apply to former relationships. Although the majority of the anorexic's or bulimic's former relationships are unhealthy ones, that does not necessarily mean they all should be abandoned. However, if they are to survive and become healthy relationships, new boundaries and guidelines must be defined—and maintained.

If you are unsure of who to involve in your support system, discuss your dilemma with your counselor, or call one of the many twelve-step recovery groups listed in your phone book. Alcoholics Anonymous, Al-Anon, Overeaters Anonymous, and numerous others are ready and available to help you through your recovery process.

Many anorexics and bulimics who seek treatment are married. When the individual has been married for a number of years, some rather unhealthy patterns have been followed within the marriage relationship—patterns that must be broken so that new patterns can be created.

Bob and Marian Grier discovered this truth as they progressed through therapy with Pam Vredevelt. Once Bob adjusted to the initial shock of finding out about Marian's illness, they made a verbal contract in which Bob agreed to never bring up Marian's eating disorder outside therapy. If Marian mentioned the subject, Bob would listen and respond, but he would not initiate the conversation. Marian gained a sense of control, and she was able to take responsibility for her problem.

Another guideline that helped Marian in her recovery was Bob's agreement to stop and pray with her anytime she felt an urge to binge. Again, the request came from Marian for prayer. Many times, their shared prayers circumvented the binge-purge process. And Marian realized that she wasn't really craving the food. Other things down deep needed attention. This intimate, shared time with her husband and God helped her get in touch with her needs. As she gave herself permission to meet those needs, the desire to binge and purge continued losing its grip. Sometimes Bob and Marian took turns praying, which helped them feel like equals—partners seeking God's strength and wisdom together. Where dependence and control had been chipping away at their love for each other, interdependence and mutual respect began finding their way into the relationship, creating healthy bonds between them. They were in the process of recovery, and Pam, Bob, and Marian liked the changes they saw.

15

HEALTHY EATING FOR LIFE

In his book *Diets Don't Work,* Bob Schwartz cites some amazing statistics:

Do you know how many people actually get the results they want by dieting? One out of every two hundred! The failure rate of diets and weight loss programs is 99.5 percent. Out of every two hundred people who go on a diet, only ten lose all the weight they set out to lose. And of those ten, only one keeps it off for any reasonable length of time.[1]

Most professionals wholeheartedly agree with Bob—*diets don't work.* Yes, hundreds of diet books are on the market. New fad diets come out each month, and people buy the new releases, even though they already have twenty-five other diet books that didn't work. There is a desperate longing in the hearts of many to find a quick method for weight control.

Many anorexics and bulimics believe the misconception that crash dieting is an effective and fast way to lose weight. Anorexics practice crash dieting on a daily basis by fasting and avoiding most foods. Bulimics practice crash dieting tactics on a regular basis following bingeing. Most of those who struggle with eating disorders have tried every crash diet on the market and have experimented with a wide variety of diet pills and diet aids. However, a crucial factor concerning these rigid patterns must not be overlooked.

In their efforts to lose weight quickly, those with eating disorders rarely realize that the critical issue is not how many pounds they lose but what kind of pounds they lose. Decline in pounds can be due to fat loss, water loss, or lean muscle tissue loss.

The loss of muscle tissue is serious and dangerous:

Low calorie diets—less than eight hundred calories per day—can accelerate the rate of muscle loss by increasing loss of body cell mass along with fat loss. The loss of lean body mass occurs as soon as extreme dieting begins. The ability to repair the loss of lean body mass decreases as age increases.[2]

Crash dieting throws off the balance of lean body mass and body fat. When this happens, the health risk is significant. Not only is a person with low lean body mass more susceptible to colds, flu, and other infections, he or she may also be at a higher risk for heart attacks and/or other circulatory and blood pressure problems. And when the goal of dieting is long-term weight loss, that goal will become harder and harder to reach as the percentage of lean body mass declines.

Some medical professionals believe that continued starving, bingeing, and purging slow down body chemistry so that more fat is stored and less is burned. In short, the extreme weight loss patterns that accompany anorexia and bulimia are a setup for a failure in long-term weight control. Starving, bingeing, and purging are not the answers to keeping weight off for life. These techniques may work for a season, but the long-term effects can go in only two directions: a fatality or the yo-yo syndrome, which ultimately leads to further weight gain.

YOU CAN EAT NORMALLY

For some reason anorexics and bulimics often feel that the more restrictive or rigid they are with diet, the more successful they'll be controlling their weight. However, the opposite is true. The more restrictive the diet, the more likely they are to go off it and fail.

If you are struggling with an eating disorder, you have to make a choice. *You have to choose whether you want to continue to fight against seeing a certain number of pounds on the bathroom scale or whether you want to learn to eat normally and experience long-term weight control.*

If you choose to remain obsessed with weight loss, the destructive chain of food's grasp on your life will tighten. If you choose to channel your energy toward learning how to eat normally, several positive by-products will be yours: increased peace of mind, stabilized eating patterns, and a chance to begin effective and lasting weight control.

Debi explained to Tina that anorexia and bulimia were not effective forms of weight control.

"But I've had this eating disorder for years," Tina cried in despair. "Sometimes I don't think I'll ever be able to eat normally again."

Tina and many of her struggling counterparts feel doomed to a life of lettuce and celery or to vomiting and taking laxatives after eating sweets or fattening foods. Happily, Tina was able to prove her statement wrong, and for the first time in many years, she is eating normally.

Tina's recovery began the day she made that critical and all-important choice to learn to eat normally. She chose to hide her scale and set a goal to concentrate on normal eating habits—not weight loss—for one month. After she made that choice, she worked hard at abiding by basic guidelines that naturally thin people observe.

Dr. Richard Stuart, psychological director for Weight Watchers International, has developed some of the following guidelines, which have helped millions of people struggling with weight control.[3]

Schedule Three Meals a Day at Regular Times

You can train yourself to think about food only at certain times of the day. When you're out of control, structured meals can diminish that obsession because you have previously decided that you will eat only at mealtimes. You can limit what, when, and how much you eat. You might want to start the day by planning your meals so that you will have a sense of control and something objective to refer to if you start to feel panicky about your new eating behavior.

Many persons recovering from eating disorders have responded favorably to these suggestions:

- Eat your food only at the family meal table.
- Do not allow yourself to nibble before, during, or after meal preparation. Before you put your fingers in the food, mentally set a goal to eat only when the meal is fully prepared. Use self-talk to help: "I'll enjoy my meal so much because I'm not spoiling my appetite by snitching."
- Concentrate on really experiencing your food. Notice the textures and smells. This approach is much more satisfying than frantically shoveling into your mouth everything you can get your hands on.
- Eat slowly. Consciously make an effort to chew each bite. Put your fork down between bites.
- Drink an eight-ounce glass of water before every meal. You will get three of the eight prescribed glasses of water a day, and you will fill up so that you won't be easily tempted to stray from your eating plan.
- At some point during your meal, pause. Put your fork down. Listen to table conversation or to music in the background.

Then resume eating. This step will break the impulsiveness of eating.

- Tell yourself, "It's absolutely normal to feel full after a meal." Your belt or waistband will feel tighter after you've eaten. But don't panic—in a few hours you won't feel full anymore, and your body will be well nourished.
- If you are uncertain about what foods constitute healthy eating, consult a nutritionist.
- When shopping, buy only from your meal plan—no spontaneous foods. Buy only small portions, which you know you will eat before going shopping again.
- Don't maintain a mental list of "forbidden" foods. Your diet should include foods that you like, even desserts.

Schedule Your Snacks as Small Meals

You want to be free from being obsessed with food all day long. Large variations in your eating schedule will defeat your efforts to control your thoughts about food. Dr. Stuart says,

If freedom from persistent urges to eat is important to you, the effort to retrain yourself to think of food only at the times that you choose will be a small price to pay. Once you have reconditioned yourself to think of food at certain times only, you can go back to a more natural flexibility.[4]

Recent research has found that the human body functions better on smaller and more frequent meals than on the traditional three. If this system works better for you, plan your diet around four or five equally caloric meals. If you still feel the need to snack, remember these hints:

- When you snack, take the food to the meal table, sit down, and eat it slowly as you would a meal.
- Forbid yourself to eat in the car, on the bus, in the bedroom or bathroom, or on the run. You will condition your eating to mealtimes only.

Plan to Succeed

Those who fail to plan, plan to fail! A daily planner is an inexpensive way to bring order to your daily food consumption. A spiral notebook is a good place to keep a running record of your nutrition plan. Papers don't get lost, and you'll be able to look back over previous days to see your progress.

A Daily Plan

A daily plan basically consists of two charts. The first, Tomorrow's Battle Plan, on page 274, lists what you plan to eat for your meals and snacks the next day as well as the number of calories for each. Concentrating on a plan helps persons with eating disorders avoid temptation. The second chart, Today's Success Strategy, on page 273, is to be filled in as you follow through with your battle plan. With it, you can see yourself winning. Each chart will take one page per day.

If you feel as though making daily menus is too much work, you may want to incorporate the plans offered by Weight Watchers Programs or by professional dietitians. A nutritionist can explain a balanced approach to food combinations and offer assistance and resources on the caloric and fat content of food items.

A Plan for Vulnerable Times

When are your vulnerable times with food? If evenings are tough, perhaps you'll want to record your plans after dinner. "Evenings are hard for me," Tina admitted. "I'm busy at work and school all day and have no desire to binge, but when I get home, I'm keyed up, and food relaxes me and brings consolation. At least I used to think it did. Actually I ended up with more anxiety, hating myself after eating so much. Now I plan my evenings. Every morning I have a fifteen-minute break at work. That's my time to plan a strategy for the evening." Tina's list includes these activities:

• Take a bubble bath and read one of my favorite magazines.

- Watch TV with a project that will keep my hands busy, such as crafts, sewing, needlepoint, laundry, or ironing.
- Write letters.
- Clean closets, organize my desk, or redo files.
- See a movie with friends.
- Go shopping or browse in bookstores.
- Exercise at the health spa or with an aerobic video.
- Ask a friend to go out for coffee.
- Listen to my relaxation tape or other favorite tapes.
- Read a good book.
- Ride my exercise bike during the evening news.
- Take my dog for a leisurely walk in the park.
- Pamper myself with a facial or manicure.

Maybe the break time at work is a trial for you because everyone else is having coffee and donuts. Try writing your battle plans during your break. You'll be amazed how uninteresting those donuts will become.

"It sure worked for me!" exclaimed Corin. "By eliminating those mid-morning donut breaks, I lost two pounds the first week!"

Kathy told Pam Vredevelt that her vulnerable time was driving to and from work. She said, "I used to hit all of the fast-food restaurants in one area each trip. Now I have a specific plan for that weakness. Before I leave in the morning I eat a small but healthy breakfast. Then I tell myself, 'Your only goal for this next hour is to drive straight to work with no stops.' I leave the checkbook at home and take just enough change to buy a soda with my lunch. Then I pray and sing all the way to work."

Weekends were distressing for Toni. "They used to be my bummer days," she explained. "Now they're fun. I reward myself on Saturday for all the binges I passed up during the week. I use my calculator to determine how much money I've saved through the week when I turned down a binge in the heat of temptation. Then I buy a new pair of earrings or something special for myself. Sometimes Marty and I will use the money to go to the movies or to buy records. This reward system really keeps me motivated through the week, and it gives me something fun to do on weekends."

Eating out with friends can challenge anyone trying to maintain healthy eating habits. But with proper planning, restaurant dining can be a healthy and enjoyable experience. The key principles to remember when eating out are:

- Eat in moderation;
- If you drink alcohol, drink in moderation;
- Eat in restaurants willing to prepare foods without added fat, salt, sauces, and gravies;
- If you do not know what is in an item and how it is prepared—ask!
- Your waiter-waitress should readily know how your food is prepared;
- If on a calculated diet, remember to bring your meal plan so that substituting foods can be done at a glance;
- Watch your portions. If too large, do not eat all that you have been served. Do ask for a "doggie bag";
- Ask for low-fat dressings, low-fat milk, fresh fruits. More restaurants are carrying them;
- Ask for dressings, sauces, margarine, or butter to be served on the side, so you can control the portion;
- Avoid foods in which calorie, fat, or sodium content cannot be reasonably estimated;
- Most foods in restaurants are prepared with salt, so don't use extra at the table.[5]

Have healthy snacks available. Whatever time of day or night is your vulnerable time, you will be more likely to stick to healthy snacks if they are readily available. Health food stores and many grocery and variety stores carry an assortment of quick, easy snacks. Unbuttered microwavable popcorn is an excellent example of a quick, low-fat snack. Weight Watchers and other companies produce several packaged, ready-to-eat snacks, from dried fruits to mini rice cakes to unsalted pretzels. You will also find several low-calorie, low-fat snacks listed under Free Foods and Foods for Moderate Use in Appendix 1. And, of course, nothing beats a snack of fresh fruits or vegetables.

Arrange your schedule to avoid being overwhelmed. After Marian Grier tried planning her day, she told Pam about her frustration: "In the morning I get up and feel overwhelmed with everything that needs to be done. I panic, which leads me to the refrigerator. Now I have a plan of action and turn my mornings into an opportunity to win. I set my alarm fifteen minutes earlier and sit at the kitchen table with a cup of coffee and my daily planner. On the left side of the page I write down the things that need to be done in order of priority. Then on the right I try to plan exactly what jobs I'll do for the day and what can be left for another day. Writing out a planned list takes away the confusion in doing my responsibilities. As I get each job done, I take a big red marker and cross another accomplishment off the list. I gain great satisfaction from seeing my progress through the day."

Yes, it does take time and energy to plan. But the benefits of normal eating are worth it. Set a goal to invest yourself in planning to succeed. You really do have what it takes to say good-bye to your eating disorder. Remember, if you aim at nothing, you'll be sure to hit it! Normal eating habits won't happen overnight, but as you plan, set goals, and take it one day at a time, you will see success.

HELPFUL HINTS FOR WEIGHT CONTROL

As you work with your plans for freedom, try some methods advocated by many weight control programs. New behaviors are learned and developed. They don't happen automatically, and normal eating patterns will come easier if you utilize some of the following tips.

Set short-range goals and force yourself to think in the here and now. Many anorexics and bulimics give up trying to eat normally because they think they have to handle everything all at once. They look at the huge mountain of the overall goal rather than at the one step that needs to be taken at the present moment. Instead of being overwhelmed with thoughts of the entire week, concentrate on making it through the next hour or the next meal.

Reward yourself when you stick to your battle plan. Marian came up with a great reward system. She earned a credit for every meal she stuck to her battle plan. As the credits accumulated, she treated herself with rewards. Here are some of her ideas: renting a video; exercising an extra morning at the athletic club with the kids in the nursery; spending a day at the beach with a friend; signing up for an oil painting class; buying a new accessory for her wardrobe.

Do not use food as a reward. Some people use food such as candy bars or donuts as a present for accomplishing a difficult task. While you are trying to learn to eat normally, substitute other rewards, like a bubble bath or a favorite magazine or a new bottle of nail polish, in place of food.

Remove binge foods from your house, particularly trigger foods. (Bulimics especially love milky foods—large cartons of ice cream, for example—because they are so easy to purge.) You can't eat what you don't have.

If family members want sweets, and you know it would upset the household to deprive them of desserts, *keep these items out of sight* or in containers that are out of easy reach.

Don't go grocery shopping while you're hungry. Write out your shopping list according to your battle plans, and shop on a full stomach. You will be more likely to stay away from high-calorie "extras."

All of these ideas serve one purpose: they make it hard for you to fudge on your battle plans. Don't allow yourself to be surrounded by stimuli that will pull out the worst in you. Instead, surround yourself with stimuli that will help you toward your goals. As you make wise choices, you'll be able to stand tall with many others and confidently say, "I used to have an eating disorder, but that's a part of my past!"

What About Exercise?

Even as you practice these helpful hints for weight control through proper eating, you should get involved in a regular physical exercise program. Physicians working with patients in healthy weight control programs recommend that a regular exercise program be maintained three or four times a week because exercise increases metabolic rate, causing calories to be burned more efficiently. But remember, *your goal in exercise is moderation*. Abusive exercise or overdoing it causes lean body muscle loss, which is dangerous to your health.

Research from the Harvard Medical School laboratories shows weight loss can occur without a loss of lean body mass when a balanced exercise program is followed with a balanced diet. In a recent study, people were randomly assigned to exercise and nonexercise groups. Both groups received the same number of calories in a balanced diet each day. After seven weeks the nonexercise group lost eighteen pounds—eleven pounds of fat, but seven pounds of lean muscle tissue. The exercise group lost twenty-three pounds of fat but, at the same time, gained four pounds of lean muscle tissue, which led to an overall weight loss of nineteen pounds.[6]

Moderate exercise means restraint to anorexics and bulimics. For years they have operated with the win-lose mentality that "more is better." They reason, "If I ran 5 miles today, I should run 5.5 miles tomorrow." Even eating disorder patients at the Minirth-Meier Clinic have to be reminded constantly of the necessity for moderation in their exercise. Their daily outings, which are designed to be leisurely and relaxing strolls, quickly become a race to burn calories.

A safe rule of thumb regarding exercise is that, if you are exercising three to four times each week for approximately thirty minutes to an hour at a time, and if you are comfortable with having to miss an exercise session occasionally, you are exercising at a healthy rate. But if your exercise routine has become such an obsession that everything else seems to be an interruption, things have gotten out of control.

The most effective way to lower your body's set point is a balanced, sustained exercise program. Most fitness specialists agree that to maintain weight control and optimal fitness, a person should exercise at least three times a week. To improve one's fitness level and lose weight, an exercise regimen of four or more days a week is suggested. As you raise your metabolism through exercise, you also increase your amount of muscle tissue and lower your level of body fat. Muscle tissue burns more calories than fat does.

We have elaborated the set-point theory because so many men and women are constantly comparing themselves to other people and coming out unfavorably. Many times clients will say, "I have a friend who is the same height as I am, and she weighs ten pounds less and never works at it." Chances are, that friend has a lower optimal weight. A real source of encouragement is understanding that weight loss struggles are not necessarily caused by weaknesses in personality but by built-in body chemistry. Some people are born with a genetic makeup that lends itself to natural thinness all through life. But most people are just not built that way.

Again, we encourage you to work with a nutritionist and a counselor who can help you establish normal eating habits and find the optimal weight for your body. Part of your unique design may include a set point. It will no doubt be different from the ideal weight that television and fashion magazines give you. You may have to come to grips with the fact that you were not meant to wear a size five. This is part of the healing process. You will be miserable if you try to fight your original design the rest of your life. But as you learn and discover more about your body and accept the way you were created, you can move from a stance of apathetic existing to celebrated living!

THE IMPORTANCE OF A RELAPSE PLAN

By the time a person with an eating disorder has reached the maintenance stage of therapy, she has made a lot of progress and is taking more responsibility for herself, moving toward less dependence on her counselor. Without a doubt, this is a positive and encouraging place for the recovering person to be. However, it can also be a vulnerable place—where relapse can easily occur.

Overcoming an eating disorder is a process, and maintenance is just one phase of that process. Although you may be "over the hump," the battle is not over. Temptations will come. Weaknesses will assault you. At times you may feel you have failed. But by planning ahead for those times when you are facing a possible relapse, you can keep from falling back into the self-destructive patterns that were so much a part of you before you began reading this book.

Steps in the Plan

Let's review some basic steps in any relapse plan:

1. *Know your enemy*. List situations that trigger a binge. For instance, if a phone call from your mother usually results in a binge-purge session, write that down. Next to it, write alternative courses of action—go for a walk, read a good book, or soak in a bubble bath. Be ready for these situations before they happen.

2. *Delay the binge*. When you are tempted to binge, try to delay it as long as possible. Again, read a good book, go for a walk, call a friend, soak in a hot bath, listen to a favorite record or tape, or slide an exercise video into the VCR. Perhaps by the time you have finished, the urge to binge will have subsided.

3. *Stop bingeing as soon as possible*. Should you give in to the urge to binge, stop at the earliest possible moment. For in-

stance, if your usual bulimic behavior is to finish off the binge with as much food as you can hold before purging, try to stop. As soon as you are able to stop, start journaling your feelings. Ask yourself the following questions: What is going on here? Why do I want to do this to myself? What am I feeling right now?

4. *Don't punish yourself.* If you feel you have failed by bingeing and/or purging, choose to be honest with your therapist. Tell him or her exactly what has happened, and don't allow yourself to fall into shame and condemnation.

5. *Tell someone.* Whatever you do, don't return to your old patterns of secrecy. Tell your husband or a trusted friend—but don't keep it to yourself! Keep a Top Ten list beside your phone, consisting of ten people you can call for support during this time. You may want to get involved in a support group such as Al-Anon or Codependents Anonymous (CODA) or Adult Children of Alcoholics (ACOA) or Association for Anorexia and Associated Disorders (ANAD), particularly if there were problems other than the eating disorder in the family of origin.

Most important, don't get discouraged. After all, if you have taken three steps forward and one back, you're still two steps ahead of where you were before you started. And as the old saying goes, you never fail until you quit trying!

Release Creative Energies Outside the Kitchen

Another area where recovering anorexics and bulimics struggle with relapse is that of spending hours in the kitchen creating lavish gourmet meals and fancy desserts. In the past, the anorexic would cook and then watch everyone else eat; the bulimic would usually eat with the rest of the family and then purge. Either way, the activity reinforced the obsession with food.

But now that you're on the road to recovery from your eating disorder, does that mean you have to give up creative cooking for the rest of your life? Definitely not! Of course, if you're trying to get an eating disorder under control, it's best not to set yourself up for failure by focusing excess energies on food, especially your favorite types. As you gain coping skills and make steps in recovery, creative cooking will become less an anxious obsession and more a relaxing joy.

Flee the Scene of the Crime

Relapse becomes a real concern when the cravings start to churn and you feel like you're moving into five-speed overdrive toward the kitchen. That's the time to flee the scene of the crime! It may sound ridiculous, but sometimes the best way to handle a craving for food is to run in the other direction.

Before starting therapy, Mary Lou had been eating only one small meal a day for three years while at the same time purging and using laxatives. She shared this story with her therapist during one counseling session. "I had been doing well," she said. "I hadn't skipped a meal for four days. It was Saturday, and we finished lunch and were relaxing in the living room. Suddenly, I got the biggest urge to take a box of laxatives. I battled the thoughts back and forth in my mind for twenty minutes. Finally, I was sick of hassling it all and walked up the stairs to the main level of my home to get some food from the cupboard. I was angry and anxious; I hated myself for wanting to blow it, but I also hated feeling full and fat.

"I got to the top of the stairs, saw the front door, and made a mad dash outside. I ran around the neighborhood for the next twenty minutes. I'm not a jogger, so that was a major run for me. I ran and cried and prayed and ran and cried and prayed some more. The battle inside me was exasperating. When I walked back into the house, I was different. I had won the battle. I had no desire to take the laxatives and knew I would be able to face dinner. It helped to literally flee temptation. By leaving, I gave myself a chance to talk to God and to get His help. He gave me the added strength I needed to be a winner."

See Yourself Winning

When clients are struggling with relapse, therapists sometimes encourage them to use the imagination for condemnation-free living. Use of the imagination for weight control has been shown to be very effective in predicting the long-term maintenance of weight loss. Dieters who imagine themselves as successful are more likely to maintain their weight control.[7]

God in His wisdom tells us to use our imaginations for good, and He also tells us what to do with unhealthy imaginings. One verse mentions "destroying speculations and every lofty thing raised up against the knowledge of God."[8] In other words, God tells us to cancel out bad imaginings contrary to His truths. We are to do away with thoughts that defeat and condemn us because "as he thinks in his heart, so is he."[9] See yourself winning—after all, that's how God sees you!

Throw Out Your Scale

Many recovering anorexics and bulimics have thrown out their scale entirely because it had become one of the strongest forces influencing their continued obsession with food and weight—and one of their greatest temptations to relapse. That may be true for you too. When you step on a scale, it will show you have gained, maintained, or lost weight.

If the scale shows you have gained weight since the last time you weighed, you will probably feel defeated because your discipline doesn't seem to be paying off.

Marian recalled with exasperation her repeated attempts at weight loss before beginning therapy: "When I'd step on the scale, I couldn't believe it. One time I hadn't binged for three days. I was sure I'd weigh less, but the scale showed I had gained two pounds. I was so discouraged I said, 'Why try?' and spent the next two hours bingeing."

Cindy related a similar experience: "I had starved all day and decided to weigh before I went to bed. I had already planned to eat three small meals the next day, but that idea fell apart when I got on the scale. I had gained a pound. That really depressed me, so I didn't eat anything for the next two days. I was working at getting well and eating healthy foods, but when I saw the weight on the scale, I panicked."

If the scale shows you weigh the same as the last time you weighed, you'll be disappointed.

Tina said, "For five days I ate small amounts three times a day. I didn't skip one meal. Doing that helped me not want to binge. I made it all week. I stepped on the scale and couldn't believe my weight didn't drop—not even one pound! It makes me wonder if all this healthy eating is really worth it."

Even when the scale shows you have lost weight, it can work against you.

"It had been four months since I was released from the hospital," Josephine, a recovering anorexic, explained. "When I got home, I promised myself I wouldn't use the scale I had hidden under my bed. Last week I got curious about my weight and decided to weigh just once. The scale read one hundred pounds. Then I got to thinking, *I'll bet I can make it read ninety-nine tomorrow.* So I skipped two meals. When I got on the scale in the morning, I weighed ninety-nine pounds. That started the ball rolling—I was 'high' on losing weight again." Two weeks later, Josephine's doctor placed her back in the hospital for tube feedings. Her scale was her enemy, luring her into relapse.

Starving, bingeing, and purging are learned behaviors. Learned behavior can be changed and another behavior—such as lifelong healthy eating—substituted for it. Your behavior can change as you take personal responsibility to learn how to change. In this chapter we've discussed some of the tools others have successfully used to bring about change. Be encouraged to use these tools for yourself. Take a risk toward good health. Yes, you will make mistakes, but so does everyone else. Try to view a mistake as an opportunity to learn. It's from blunders that we grow and develop and become all God wants us to be. Don't limit yourself from reaching your full potential: "Be strong and of good courage, do not fear nor be afraid . . . for the LORD your God . . . goes with you. He will not leave you nor forsake you."[10]

16

A WORD TO LOVED ONES

As the small groups at the seminar began interacting, Cindy Briscoe and her parents drew the seminar leader's attention. Cindy, who sat between her parents, was obviously being put on the spot. The seven members of the group were peering at her while her mom and dad commented about her in exasperation. Jack and Christine Briscoe seemed angry and confused. Cindy was on edge, defensive, and becoming more and more withdrawn as she blocked out the complaints and frustrations they voiced. The family, which in the beginning had experienced love and closeness, was being destroyed because of Cindy's anorexia.

Unfortunately, anorexia nervosa and bulimia affect more people than the individuals obsessed with food. When the grip of an eating disorder clamps onto a person's lifestyle, loved ones suffer too. Because the anorexic or bulimic feels isolated or rejected, communication can be difficult. Since many anorexics and bulimics refuse to admit they have a problem, those who care often feel shoved aside and confused.

In this chapter we will discuss how you can help someone with an eating disorder. The guidelines offered are those often shared in family therapy. If you are feeling helpless and overwhelmed by what is happening, we pray that you will receive encouragement and wisdom from the following pages. Let's first discuss a few things you should not do.

RESPONSES TO AVOID

Don't Get into Power Struggles Over Food

The anorexic or bulimic is an expert at controlling her food intake. When you interfere and try to take control, beware. Don't attempt to cram food into the anorexic—you'll simply anger her. Don't try to forcefully stop the bulimic from bingeing and purging—unless you have been asked to do so. Some bulimics ask family members to physically remove them from the binge site if they feel they are going to lose control. This is fine, but only when it is agreed upon beforehand.

Leave advice about meal and food planning in a counselor's hands. Any competent professional will not let these issues slide. Many counselors work closely with nutrition experts who can help your friend or loved one learn exactly what his or her body needs to lose, gain, or maintain weight.

If the patient is in recovery, ask her how you can best support her. Many times, we ask spouses, friends, or family not to address eating issues. This decision is based on the fact that the patient is being monitored and followed by the therapist or treatment team. The patient herself must take responsibility for her weight and eating habits. Concerned family and friends can be negative influences in her recovery if they focus on food and eating habits.

If the anorexic or bulimic is not in recovery, express concern over what you see her doing to her body. Ask her to seek counseling, but do not try to control her food for her.

Don't Offer Pat Answers

Anorexics and bulimics often complain that family members tend to offer pat answers. The following list of common platitudes only drives away those who are struggling:

- "Just start eating and be normal like everyone else."
- "I've never had a weight problem. I've eaten three meals a day all my life. Why don't you do what I do?"
- "Just pray about it and trust the Lord."
- "Can't you see what you're doing to yourself? You've got to stop this and stop it now!"
- "If your friends are making it hard for you to recover from your eating disorder, go find some new ones."
- "You should read your Bible more."
- "Pull yourself together and get on with life!"
- "Once you get right with God, you'll be fine."

The writer of the Book of Proverbs declared, "A man finds joy in giving an apt reply— / and how good is a timely word!"[1] Pat answers are rarely timely words. But as you ask God for insight, He will help you find words to bring encouragement to your loved one or friend.

Don't Impose Guilt

The writer of the Book of Proverbs observed, "Reckless words pierce like a sword, / but the tongue of the wise brings healing."[2] When you are worn out from helping, it's easy to make offhand remarks. Usually, they involve blaming the anorexic or bulimic for the misery of the rest of the family. Frequent comments are, "You're ruining our family!" or "Nothing is the same since you started this crazy behavior!" or "It sure would be nice to have things at home the way they used to be." These remarks do not motivate the anorexic or bulimic to change her behavior. They may drive her into deeper isolation and despair.

Don't Blame Yourself

Parents—mothers especially—often are convinced that their daughter's eating disorder is entirely their fault. They become guilt-ridden and continually blame themselves for everything they didn't do to be better parents.

One point stressed in family therapy is that an eating disorder is not any one person's fault. Moms and dads do not cause eating disorders. Spouses and loved ones cannot make anyone anorexic or bulimic. Depending on how they choose to relate to the anorexic or bulimic, family members can enhance or inhibit the recovery process, but they cannot be the sole cause of the problem.

Treat yourself with dignity, even when it seems that things in your family aren't going well. Don't neglect your marriage, your friends, or your other children. You will have ups and downs. In the midst of your hardships, try not to be hard on yourself. Try to realize you are doing the best you can.

WHAT SHOULD YOU DO?

Lovingly Confront an Anorexic or a Bulimic with Her Symptoms

Left untreated, an eating disorder can become deeply ingrained in a person's lifestyle. It may be fatal. If you detect the symptoms of anorexia or bulimia in a loved one, loving confrontation is a must.

Many anorexics and bulimics have admitted to desperately wanting someone to notice their peculiar patterns. Some go so far as to leave vomit in the toilet or diet pills on the counter. Be aware of ways your loved one may be crying out for your help. She may want you to intervene.

Even if you feel your loved one has attempted to hide all the evidence of her disorder, talk to her about it. Take the risk of mentioning that you have noticed specific signs and symptoms in behavior that are characteristic of anorexia or bulimia. You will be throwing her a lifeline—whether she realizes it or not. A negative reaction from your loved one may be uncomfortable for you, but it won't be harmful. Avoiding confrontation, however, can ruin a relationship and a life.

Not long after Bob Grier joined his wife, Marian, in therapy with Pam Vredevelt, he realized how many obvious signs of Marian's illness he had overlooked. Of course, he had not previously recognized them because he was not familiar with bulimic behavior. He wished he could have intervened and encouraged Marian to get help years earlier.

Get Professional Help for Family Members Under Legal Age

Parents are responsible for the welfare of their children prior to the legal age of adulthood. Your child may kick, scream, and threaten to hate you for life when you first mention the idea of counseling, but you will be doing her a great disservice if you don't require her to get help. It's never too early to confront the issue, but it can be too late.

If the person with the eating disorder is already of legal age, the same holds true. Do whatever you have to do to get help for your loved one. Acting quickly can save a life.

We also encourage you to do all you can to get your family member into a support group in addition to professional one-on-one counseling. Research shows that the most vital feature of a support group is the experience of sharing fears and misery and positive progress with others who "really know what it's all about."[3]

Get Support for Yourself

You are not the only person seeking to encourage and care for someone with an eating disorder. And there is no reason for you to meet this challenge alone. Many family members have received support from their pastors, Bible study groups, Overeaters Anonymous organizations, professional counselors, and close friends in whom they can confide. Remember, we are built with a need to be interdependent with others. Paul tells us that as Christian individuals, we are to see ourselves collectively as Christ's body. He exhorts believers, saying, "There should be no schism in the body, but that the members should have the same care for one another.

And if one member suffers, all the members suffer with it; or if one member is honored, all the members rejoice with it."[4] A support system can buffer the storms and heighten the joy of victories.

In recent years numerous organizations have been formed to offer support to persons with eating disorders and their loved ones. The organizations listed in Appendix 5 of this book can supply more information about the growth and support groups in your city. Many also produce a regular newsletter with information about eating disorders and how to relate to those who struggle with them.

Learn about Eating Disorders

Anxiety can be reduced when you gather facts and understand the behavioral and emotional patterns of these illnesses. Read books and articles; attend seminars on anorexia and bulimia; find out what current research is uncovering. The more you understand what contributes to your loved one's eating disorder, the easier it will be for you to detect the dynamics of your strained relationship.

Bob and Marian Grier discovered this in their recovery experience. Bob, having been a domineering and controlling husband for many years, at first expected Marian to "shape up" and get over her illness. But as he spent more time in therapy with her, learning about the many facets of eating disorders and the healing process, he realized that he, too, would have to make changes if Marian's eating disorder and their marriage were to be healed.

Through ongoing family therapy, Cindy Briscoe's mother learned that common family dynamics are sometimes found among those with eating disorders. By recognizing her overprotectiveness through her research of the problem, she was in a position to begin to change. In the following months, she devised ways to allow Cindy to express more independence and autonomy. One primary way was to encourage her daughter by telling her that, with help, she would be able to take care of her eating disorder.

The exciting by-product was that their relationship was less strained and much happier. Christine's research paid off.

Bob and Marian became aware of how they hooked each other into dysfunctional ways of relating. Bob's control hooked Marian's dependency. His pressure hooked her resistance. His explosions increased her isolation. As they focused on changing themselves, they were better able to love each other, which resulted in greater intimacy.

Require the Anorexic or Bulimic to Take Responsibility for Her Actions

In other words, make your loved one accountable for her behavior. Put a lock on the refrigerator, take the lock off the bathroom door, hide the scale, or require her to buy her own ritual foods. The last thing you want to do is to reinforce her destructive behavior by allowing her to shirk her responsibility to the rest of the family. Some bulimics have put their families in debt while spending over three hundred dollars a week on binge food. Other families have been restricted from enjoying certain restaurants because a salad bar wasn't available for their anorexic child. Don't allow one person to manipulate the activities of your family.

Get in Touch with Your Feelings

Very often family members ignore, deny, or swallow their anger, frustration, and fears. They hope that in time everything will pass and be all right again. Denial and avoidance are detrimental to everyone involved. You can pretend you don't have cancer, but that cancer will eat away at you if left untreated. The best thing to do is to acknowledge that you have strong feelings and deal with them openly and honestly.

You may want to keep a record of your emotions by jotting them down in a journal. Sometimes by seeing what you feel in black and white, you can clarify your feelings. Seek to understand yourself and the ways you respond emotionally. This growth process can benefit you and your family members too.

Recognize the Lies You Have Come to Believe

Before you can grapple with a problem, you must first recognize the lies you have come to believe in relation to it. Some common ones in this situation are:

- I must control my child/spouse.
- My child/spouse must be happy.
- I must do something to help my child/spouse get over his/her eating disorder.
- It is my responsibility to make my child/spouse well.
- I am responsible for my child's/spouse's problem.
- It is disgusting and shameful to have a child/spouse who acts this way.

Talk Openly and Honestly about Your Feelings

People with eating disorders are highly perceptive of the non-verbal cues people give them. That is why transparency on your part is significant. Talk about your feelings openly. If you are feeling guilt over ways you think you have failed as a parent, admit that and allow your child to respond. Your loved one will know where you stand, and you will get rid of any unhealthy guessing games.

Those in bondage to an eating disorder often alienate the people who love them most. Anorexics and bulimics need people surrounding them who will remain open, even in the heat of a struggle. Work hard at expressing yourself truthfully and showing honest care and concern. In doing so you'll provide a healing arena in which your loved one can experience new dimensions of wholeness.

Be Honest with an Anorexic or a Bulimic about Her Appearance

If she has gained weight, an anorexic needs to hear the reality that she is becoming more beautiful. On the other hand, the ninety-nine pound anorexic who looks like she's just stepped out of a concentration camp needs to hear that she looks emaciated. To her, thinness is beautiful, and if her perception of reality isn't challenged, she may starve herself into the grave. Bulimics need to hear that their swollen glands or puffy, bloodshot eyes are not attractive.

Attitude, tone of voice, and timing are critical factors in confrontation. Remember, the Bible says to speak "the truth in love," not just speak "the truth."[5] If you can't say something in a loving way, it's best not to say anything at all.

Talk about Issues Other Than Food

Those with eating disorders are obsessed with thoughts of food. Frequent discussions among family members about dieting, thinness, and physical appearances add to your loved one's obsession. You can help her by avoiding comments about your own weight, such as, "I just have to take off five pounds!" or "My thighs are too fat." Instead, focus your discussions on internal character qualities. Let her hear that you appreciate her kindness, patience, or enthusiasm. Tell her what you like about the person she is on the inside.

Take special care in giving attention to your loved one's personal interests. If computers, music, Bible study, or mystery books appeal to her, do what you can to cultivate and support development in these areas. Any time devoted to these interests means less time obsessed by food.

Listen

One of the greatest gifts you can give your loved one is a listening ear. Listening communicates genuine caring and will gain trust. It has been said that the average time parents listen to and actively communicate with their children is three minutes a day. Most of us are quick to give opinions and advice. The anorexic or bulimic is likely to know more about her problem than you do.

She really needs someone with whom she can feel safe to share transparently.

Show Love and Affection

Many times in the recovery process the anorexic or bulimic in your family will seem unlovely. Fits of rage aren't pretty. Depression is unbecoming. When we see these reactions, we naturally withdraw love and affection. But love and affection continue to be needed at these rough points. Rage, anger, and isolation are catalyzed by deep hurts and confusion. Those hurts need to be healed, and the best healing balm is unconditional love.

Hang in There!

No doubt you have wanted to throw in the towel. You are not alone. Healing takes time, and growth toward wholeness is a process of advances and setbacks. Sometimes you will feel you don't care and want to give up. When a setback occurs, don't be devastated by thinking that all is lost. It's not. It's just part of the growth process.

A few times as counselors we have felt like giving up on certain clients. We're not proud to say that, but it is the truth. When we get to that last strained point and our inner resources for giving are drained, we know that it is time to go to the Source of all strength and healing. During those times, we cry out for discernment and wisdom. We ask God for renewed strength and energy so that we can give beyond our reserves.

God has not called you to give only out of your own strength. He will use your strength and at the same time provide resources beyond your abilities. He has promised to give you all the love and energy you need to keep going: "And my God shall supply all your need according to His riches in glory [not your limited resources] by Christ Jesus."[6] When you feel like giving up, remember to heed the words of Jesus: "Come to Me, all you who labor and are heavy laden, and I will give you rest."[7]

COMMON QUESTIONS

You may feel alone and isolated, as if no one could possibly understand what you're going through. Yet we have found that almost everyone in this situation asks the same questions time and again. The following questions, along with our answers, pertain to the obvious problems arising out of an anorexic or a bulimic situation in the family. We hope they will give you hope and encouragement as you help your loved one along the pathway to recovery.

What Can I Do to Help My Daughter?

The family with an anorexic or a bulimic daughter needs to become educated about her eating disorder. Ask a professional about referrals in the community. Support groups are beneficial for families also. Learn about eating disorders through reading books and magazines and seeking counsel. Understand that your child considers her eating disorder the only way to cope; help her develop alternative coping skills to relieve her stress.

Let your daughter know that you accept her unconditionally. You are not giving her permission to continue her behavior, but you are reassuring her that she is loved and cared for as part of the family.

Be willing to participate in family therapy. Your daughter needs more support than lip service. Families will sometimes say they are willing to help, but when it comes to getting involved in therapy, they back down, becoming disinterested or defensive. The purpose of family therapy is not to place blame but to point out to the family the unhealthy patterns of interaction so that they can be replaced with healthy patterns.

The family must also look beyond the eating disorder. Refocus your energy from trying to make her eat to meeting her emotional and personal needs. Try to find out what is bothering your daughter and help her acknowledge these issues. Talking about food every time you are with her can make things worse rather than better.

The anorexic or bulimic is looking for active, physical changes on the part of others, especially family members. Therefore, if you promise to do something, do it. Words and promises mean little if they are not followed with action.

Get your child to a professional who understands eating disorders. Anorexics and bulimics need to talk with someone who can help them face the underlying issues. Family members often make poor counselors. Your daughter needs to be confronted by a professional to begin the process of recovery.

Above all, your daughter needs support and structure. Boredom is often a stress factor that anorexics and bulimics do not know how to handle. They need a degree of structure in their lives. Suggest ways your child can be more active in church and community activities, and encourage her to become involved in support groups.

What Can I Do to Help My Wife?

Most of the information in the previous answer applies here. In addition, *understanding* is probably a key word. Husbands are often puzzled about why their wives would do such a thing. A husband may take a passive role, leaving his wife feeling as if he doesn't care. If the husband is too aggressive, trying to take over and "fix" his wife's eating disorder, she may feel as if she is being treated like a child. Balance compassionate care along with permission for your wife to deal with the food issue on her own.

Another key word is *respect*. A husband may have great difficulty respecting his wife because of her eating disorder. Whether expressed overtly or covertly, this message will be picked up by the wife, causing her to react defensively. Remember, the anorexic or bulimic is more than an eating disorder; the person and her behavior must be separated to maintain her identity.

Finally, love her unconditionally. Ask her what she needs. She is capable of telling you. Listen to her, and follow through with her directions.

What Can I Do to Help My Friend?

Again, almost everything in the first two answers applies here. Remember not to treat your friend as a "freak" because of the eating disorder. Offer as much support as possible. Encourage your friend to fight his or her battles when necessary, if he or she is able.

Why Does My Daughter Say She Was Abused?

Some friends and family members are concerned about the memories of abuse an anorexic or a bulimic might express. Recognizing the degrees of abuse is important. What one parent may think was normal behavior in the family (based on what happened in his or her family of origin) may be considered abusive. The therapy centers on the feelings that have been denied as a result of the abuse. The parent may never agree that there has been abuse, but the daughter must come to terms with her memories as they occur and then forgive the parties and go on.

How Should I, as Her Husband, Treat Her Abusive Parents?

The marriage relationship is unique. As a marriage partner, you must work together with your spouse. Don't be a rescuer for her. She must deal with her parents herself, but she needs your support and viewpoints. You may be asked to talk to them also. Most important, allow your spouse to set the limits with her parents, and then be available to support those limits and step in when needed.

What Should I Tell the Children about Their Mother's Illness?

This answer depends on the ages of the children. Very young children need lots of reassurance. Tell them that Mommy is sick and that she is trying to do everything possible to get better. Assure them that Mommy is not going to leave forever if she needs to be hospitalized. "Transitional" toys are useful in this situation. For instance, buy the children new dolls or teddy bears and tell them to hug the toys every time they feel afraid that Mommy isn't coming back. A tape-recorded message from Mom can be comforting. Continue open communication with the children throughout Mom's hospitalization and recovery period.

Older children can understand what is going on, so be as honest as possible without scaring them. Talk to them about their fears and hopes. Reassure them that the situation is not their fault.

Many parents feel they are protecting the children by ignoring the problems in a family. In reality the children are left to come to their own conclusions. Naturally, they believe it is their fault that Mommy is sick. Be open with them. Don't concentrate on details they can't understand. Do tell them that Mommy has a problem and that she is getting help for it. Assure them that they can ask you any question.

What Should I Do if I Think She's Out of Control Again?

First, express your concerns to her. Then suggest that she call her therapist. If she does not do so, do it for her. Be assertive. Try to get as much evidence as possible without snooping. Present the evidence to her as fact and as the basis for your concern.

Having an eating disorder is like sliding down a slide. Once the person gets back into the anorexic or bulimic behavior, it quickly gets out of control; without intervention, the behavior will intensify until she hits bottom.

Be aware of the warning signals, especially the tendency to avoid others, feelings, or food. Enlist the help of others whom your wife listens to and trusts.

Why Does She Need Boundaries?

We all need boundaries. *Boundaries* is just another word for *limits*. Anorexics and bulimics have a problem setting boundaries and separating their identity from others because they are most often people pleasers. All healthy relationships must have boundaries. As your spouse establishes these boundaries during her recovery, respect and honor them.

Should I Repress All My Feelings Just Because She Is Sick?

No. That is what happens in unhealthy relationships. Your wife needs to hear and respond to your feelings, which you should express in love. You may find encouragement and guidance about how to do this in a support group.

We often hear that husbands feel like they have to walk on eggshells around their wives. They assume their wives are fragile and cannot handle confrontation. Communication needs to take place. It is okay to share your needs but not to demand or expect them to be met right away. Most anorexics and bulimics come from families or relationships where they felt—and have been—controlled. Your wife may be used to meeting needs for others but may never have learned to set boundaries or say no. Again, group counseling and support can prove vital.

17

ONE
FINAL WORD

As you have read through this book, we pray that the practical and spiritual insights we have shared have encouraged you. We also pray that you have realized the need for professional help. Our stories about Cindy, Tina, and Marian illustrated that individual and group counseling, God's help, and their determined effort to overcome their illnesses were the keys to achieving victory over their eating disorders.

CINDY

It had been two years since Cindy's release from the Minirth-Meier inpatient program. Although Harry Beverly continued to see Cindy on an outpatient basis for quite some time after her release, he was especially pleased when he arrived at work to find a postcard from his former patient.

Dear Mr. Beverly: Just wanted to write and remind you that today is my two-year anniversary—and I just finished eating a piece of cake to celebrate! Can you believe it? I never thought I'd see the day when I could eat a piece of cake and not worry about weighing a ton tomorrow. It's wonderful! Love, Cindy. P.S. Mom and Dad send their best—they had cake to celebrate too.

Harry smiled as he tacked the postcard to his bulletin board. Days like this made his job rewarding.

TINA

Debi Newman continued to see Tina on an outpatient basis for about a year after her release from the hospital. She still saw her occasionally and was really encouraged about the young woman's progress. The day Debi knew for sure that Tina was going to make it was the day she came to her counseling session to tell Debi about her latest grades.

Tina was a senior approaching graduation in May. "I'm proud of these grades," she boasted to Debi.

Debi looked at the grades—two A's and three B's. "I never would have believed it a couple years ago Tina, I'm so proud of you."

Someone overhearing the conversation might not have understood what Debi and Tina meant. Both were proud that Tina could do her best (given the multitude of pressures, full-time job, almost full-time school, social life, maintaining recovery) and be proud.

Debi commented "Your attitude today is like making A + + +'s in therapy."

"I can't believe I feel so good in spite of three B's." Tina responded. "If I had gotten these same grades last year, I know I would be bingeing right now instead of celebrating. I might even have gotten suicidal. It feels so good to be me. I know I'll never let myself get sucked back into that trap of trying to be perfect again."

MARIAN

Marian was in therapy with Pam Vredevelt for about a year and a half. Once a month she and Bob attended counseling to discuss their relationship and ways Bob could be supportive during her recovery.

Toward the close of therapy Bob said, "When I found out about Marian's eating disorder, I started blaming every conflict we had on her and the bulimia. I figured as soon as she got herself put back together, our marriage would be fine. Therapy helped me look at myself and my contributions to our relationship. Some of those contributions were good, others unhealthy. It has been a painfully tough year, but I wouldn't trade what we have now for anything."

For the first time in over twenty years, Marian is free of bingeing and purging. She and Bob continue to discover new levels of intimacy. With the added support of a marriage enrichment group at their church, they have learned to be more honest and patient with each other. The last time Pam saw them, they weren't sitting in her office. She spotted them at a local park giggling hilariously while playing leap frog with each other and their kids. The bottom line is, Marian is free to laugh and enjoy life more than ever before.

If you take away any message from this book, we hope it will be this: *recovery from your eating disorder is possible*. It will not be immediate, nor will it be easy—but hanging on to your eating disorder will not be easy either. In fact, it could be deadly.

Take steps to overcome your eating disorder. Admit your problem to yourself, to God, and to someone else. Seek professional and divine help. And then make the commitment to do whatever is necessary to walk the pathway to recovery into newness of life.

Take it from those who have walked the pathway before you. It's worth the risk. It's worth the investment. It's worth the work.

Remember, you won't be alone. Others will be there to guide and support you. God will be with you. His wisdom, strength, and healing power will be available to you each step of the way. Look to Him and the counselors He leads you to, to help you step out from behind your thin disguise.

APPENDICES

APPENDIX 1

FOOD EXCHANGE LISTS

List 1—Starch/Bread Exchanges

One exchange of bread contains 15 grams of carbohydrate, 3 grams of protein, a trace of fat, and 80 calories. Whole grain products contain about 2 grams of fiber per serving.

BREAD

Bagel 1/2
*Boston brown (with or without raisins) . . . . 3″ × 1/2″ slice
Bread crumbs (dried) . . . . 3 tbsp.
Bread crumbs (fresh) . . . . 1/2 cup
Croutons (low-fat) . . . . 1 cup
English muffin 1/2
Frankfurter bun 1/2
Hamburger bun 1/2
Low-calorie bread (40 calories/slice) . . . . 2 slices
Pita bread (6″ across) 1
Raisin (unfrosted) . . . . 1 slice
Roll (plain, small) 1
†Rye or Pumpernickel . . . . 1 slice
Tortilla (6″) 1

* High in sodium.
† Contains 3 grams or more of dietary fiber per serving.

White (including French and Italian) .... 1 slice
Whole wheat .... 1 slice

CRACKERS
Animal 8
Arrowroot 3
Bread sticks (4″ long × ¼″ diameter) 4
Bread sticks (crisp, 4″ long × ½″ diameter) 2
Graham (2½″ square) .... 3 each
Matzo (4″ × 6″) .... ½
Melba toast 5
*Oyster 24
*Pretzel (3″) .... 3 each
*Pretzel (3⅛″ long × ⅛″ diameter) 25
*Rye wafer crisp (2″ × 3½″) 4
*Saltines 6
*Soda (2½″) 4
*Wheatsworth 5
*Zwieback 3

CEREAL
†Bran flakes .... ½ cup
Bulgur (cooked) .... ½ cup
Cereal (cooked) .... ½ cup
Cornmeal (dry, whole ground) .... 2½ tbsp.
Cornstarch .... 2 tbsp.
Flour .... 2½ tbsp.
Grape-Nuts .... 3 tbsp.
Grits (cooked) .... ½ cup
Other ready-to-eat unsweetened cereals .... ¾ cup
Pasta (cooked spaghetti, noodles, macaroni) .... ½ cup
Popcorn (popped, no fat added) .... 3 cups
Puffed cereal (unfrosted) .... 1½ cups
Rice or barley (cooked) .... ⅓ cup
Shredded Wheat .... ½ cup
Tapioca (dry) .... 2 tbsp.
†Wheat germ .... 3 tbsp.

STARCHY VEGETABLES

Beans

　†*Baked (canned) .... ¼ cup

　†Black-eyed peas, or pinto, kidney, or white .... ⅓ cup

　　Garbanzo or chick-peas .... ½ cup

　†Lentils (dried and cooked) .... ⅓ cup

　†Lima .... ½ cup

†Corn .... ½ cup

†Corn on the cob (6″ long) 1

Mixed vegetables .... ½ cup

Parsnips .... ⅔ cup

†Peas, green (canned or frozen) .... ½ cup

Plantain .... ½ cup

Potato, white (baked) .... 1 small

Potato, white (mashed) .... ½ cup

Pumpkin .... ¾ cup

†Succotash (corn and lima) .... ½ cup

Winter squash, acorn or butternut .... ¾ cup

Yam or sweet potato .... ⅓ cup

COMBINATIONS

Count as 1 Starch/Bread Exchange plus 1 Fat Exchange.

*Biscuit (2½″ across) 1

Bread stuffing (prepared) .... ¼ cup

Chow mein noodles .... ½ cup

*Corn bread (2″ cube) 1

*Crackers, butter type 6

French fried potatoes (2″ to 3½″) 10

*Muffin (plain, small) 1

*Pancake (4″ across) 2

Popover (small) 1

Taco shell (6″ across) 2

Vanilla wafers 6

*Waffle (4½″ square) 1

*Whole wheat crackers (fat added) 4–6

Count as 1 Starch/Bread Exchange plus 2 Fat Exchanges.

Croissant (4″) 1

Pie crust (pastry type) .... 1/6 of a 9" shell
*Potato or corn chips 15

List 2—Meat Exchanges

Bake, boil, roast, or broil meats. Trim all excess fat off meats. Meats
should be weighed after cooking, allowing for bone and fat.

Lean meat
Meal patterns are calculated with 7 grams protein, 3 grams fat, and 55
calories for Meat Exchange.

Beef
   Baby beef (very lean), *chipped beef, flank steak, tenderloin, plate
   skirt steak, round (bottom top), all cuts rump, spare ribs, tripe 1 oz.

*Cheese
   *Any cottage cheese .... 1/4 cup
   *Diet cheeses (less than 55 calories per ounce) .... 1 oz.
   *Grated parmesan .... 2 tbsp.

Fish
   Any fresh or frozen fish .... 1 oz.
   Fresh crab, lobster, scallops, shrimp (*canned in water) .... 2 oz.
   *Herring (uncreamed or smoked) .... 1 oz.
   Oysters .... 6 medium
   *Sardines (canned) .... 2 medium
   *Tuna (canned in water) .... 1/4 cup

Other
   Egg substitute (less than 55 calories per 1/4 cup) .... 1/4 cup
   Egg whites .... 3 whites
   *Luncheon meat (95% fat-free) .... 1 oz.

Pork
   Lean pork, such as fresh ham; *canned, *cured, or boiled ham; *Canadian bacon; tenderloin .... 1 oz.

Poultry
   Chicken, turkey, Cornish hen, guinea hen, (all without skin) .. 1 oz.
   *Textured vegetable protein (1 Meat, 1/2 Starch/Bread Ex-
   change) .... 3/4 oz.

Veal

All cuts except veal cutlet (includes leg, loin, rib, shank, shoulder) .... 1 oz.

Wild game

Venison, rabbit, squirrel, pheasant, duck, goose (without skin) 1 oz.

Medium-fat meat

Meal patterns are calculated with 7 grams protein, 5 grams fat, and 75 calories for Meat Exchange. Most beef, pork, and lamb products are in this category.

Beef

All ground beef, roast (rib, chuck, rump), steak (cubed, porterhouse, T-bone), and meatloaf .... 1 oz.

*Cheese

Skim or part-skim milk cheeses, such as:

*Diet cheeses (56–80 calories per oz.) .... 1 oz.

*Mozzarella .... 1 oz.

*Ricotta .... ¼ cup

Fish

*Caviar, fish roe, eel, smelts .... 1 oz.

*Salmon (canned) .... ¼ cup

*Tuna (canned in oil and drained) .... ¼ cup

Lamb

Most lamb products (includes chops, leg, roast) .... 1 oz.

Other

Egg (high in cholesterol, limit to 3 per week) 1

Egg substitute (56–80 calories per ¼ cup) .... ¼ cup

Liver, heart, kidney, sweetbreads (all high in cholesterol) .... 1 oz.

*Luncheon meat (86% fat-free) .... 1 oz.

Tofu (2½″ × 2¾″ × 1″) .... 4 oz.

Pork

Most pork products (includes chops, loin roast, Boston butt, cutlets) .... 1 oz.

Poultry

Chicken (with skin), domestic duck or goose (well drained of fat), ground turkey .... 1 oz.

Veal

Cutlet (ground, cubed, unbreaded) .... 1 oz.

High-fat meat

Meal patterns are calculated with 7 grams protein, 8 grams fat, and 100 calories for Meat Exchange. Because these items are high in saturated fat, cholesterol, and calories, they should be used only three times per week.

Beef

Most USDA prime cuts of beef (ribs or club steak [often served in restaurants]), *corned beef, brisket . . . . 1 oz.

*Cheese

All regular cheeses, such as *American, *blue, *cheddar, *Monterey Jack, *Swiss . . . . 1 oz.

Fish

Any fried product . . . . 1 oz.

Lamb

Patties (ground) . . . . 1 oz.

Other

*Bratwurst . . . . 1 oz.

*Frankfurter (turkey or chicken @ 10 franks per pound) 1

*Knöckwurst (smoked) . . . . 1 oz.

*Luncheon meat (bologna, salami, pimento loaf) . . . . 1 oz.

*Peanut butter . . . . 1 tbsp.

*Sausage (Polish, Italian) . . . . 1 oz.

Pork

Spareribs, ground pork, *pork sausage (patty or link), *deviled ham . . . . 1 oz.

Count as 1 high-fat Meat plus 1 Fat Exchange.

*Frankfurter (beef, pork, or combination @ 10 franks per pound) . 1

Examples of 3 oz. servings, cooked (a 3 oz. serving compares in size to a deck of cards):

Half a breast, or leg and thigh, of 2½- or 3-pound chicken

Two slices roast beef or pot roast (3″ x 3″ x ¼″)

Two medium pork chops (½″ thick)

One hamburger patty (3″ across and ¾″ thick)

Examples of 1 oz. servings, cooked:

¼ cup canned tuna or salmon

¼ cup chicken meat, loosely packed

2 medium sardines
4 tbsp. (¹/₄ cup) cottage cheese

List 3—Vegetable Exchanges

One Vegetable Exchange is equal to 5 grams carbohydrate, 2 grams protein, and 25 calories. Unless otherwise noted, one exchange equals ¹/₂ cup cooked vegetables (or vegetable juice) or 1 cup raw vegetables. Generally, vegetables contain 2 to 3 grams of dietary fiber per serving. For sodium-restricted diets, do not use canned vegetables.

Artichoke (¹/₂ medium)
Asparagus
Beans (green, wax, Italian)
Bean sprouts
Beets
Broccoli
Brussels sprouts
Cabbage (cooked)
Carrots
Cauliflower
Eggplant
Greens
    Beet, chard, collards, dandelion, kale, mustard, poke, turnip
Kohlrabi
Lamb's-quarters
Leeks
Mushrooms (cooked)
Okra
Onions
Pea pods
Pepper (green, red)
*Pimento
Rutabaga
*Sauerkraut
Snow peas

Spinach (cooked)
Summer squash, crookneck
Tomatoes
*Tomato paste (2 tbsp.)
*Tomato puree (¼ cup)
*Tomato sauce (⅓ cup)
*Tomato/vegetable juice
Turnips
Water chestnuts (6 medium)
*Zucchini (cooked)

The following raw vegetables may be considered free foods when used as indicated:
1 cup raw
　　Cabbage, celery, †Chinese cabbage, cucumber, hot peppers, green onion, mushrooms, radishes, †zucchini
As desired
　　Alfalfa sprouts, chicory, endive, escarole, lettuce, parsley, romaine, spinach, watercress

Note: Starchy vegetables are found in the Starch/Bread Exchange List.

List 4—Fruit Exchanges

One Fruit Exchange contains 15 grams of carbohydrate and 60 calories.

Use fresh or unsweetened frozen fruits; unsweetened fruit juices; unsweetened canned fruits; or dried fruits. Fruits canned in unsweetened fruit juice are allowed in amounts listed.

Fresh, frozen, and dried fruits have 2 grams of dietary fiber per serving. Fruit juices contain little dietary fiber.

Apple (2″ across) . . . . 1 medium
Apple cider . . . . ½ cup
Apple juice . . . . ½ cup

†Apples (dried) .... 4 rings
Applesauce (unsweetened) .... ¹/₂ cup
Apricots (canned) .... 4 halves
†Apricots (dried) .... 7 halves
Apricots (fresh) .... 4 medium
Banana (9″ long) .... ¹/₂
Berries (raw)
  †Blackberries .... ³/₄ cup
  †Blueberries .... ³/₄ cup
  †Boysenberries .... ³/₄ cup
  †Gooseberries .... 1 cup
  †Raspberries .... 1 cup
  †Strawberries .... 1¹/₄ cups
Cherries (fresh) .... 12 large
Cherries (canned) .... ¹/₂ cup
Cranberry juice (low-calorie) .... 1 cup
Cranberry juice (sweetened) .... ¹/₃ cup
Currants .... 3 tbsp.
Dates 2¹/₂
†Figs (dried) 1¹/₂
Figs (fresh) 2
Fresh fruit cup .... ¹/₂ cup
Fruit cocktail (unsweetened) .... ¹/₂ cup
Grapefruit .... ¹/₂
Grapefruit juice .... ¹/₂ cup
Grapefruit sections .... ³/₄ cup
Grape juice .... ¹/₃ cup
Grapes (small) 15
Guava .... 1 small
Kiwi fruit .... 1 large
Kumquats .... 4 medium
Lemon .... 1 large
Lychees 7
Mandarin orange .... ³/₄ cup
Mango .... ¹/₂ small
Melon
  Cantaloupe (5″ across) .... ¹/₃
  Cantaloupe (cubes) .... 1 cup

Casaba .... 1 cup
Honeydew .... ¹/8 medium
Honeydew (cubes) .... 1 cup
Watermelon (cubes) .... 1¹/4 cups
†Nectarine (1¹/2″ across) 1
Nectars (apricot, peach, pear) .... ¹/3 cup
Orange (2¹/2″ across) 1
Orange-grapefruit juice .... ¹/2 cup
Orange juice .... ¹/2 cup
Papaya .... 1 cup
Peach (2³/4″ across) 1
Peach slices (canned) .... ¹/2 cup
Peach slices (fresh) .... ³/4 cup
Pear .... 1 small
Pear slices .... ¹/2 cup
Persimmon (native) .... 2 medium
Pineapple (canned) .... ¹/3 cup
Pineapple (fresh) .... ³/4 cup
Pineapple juice .... ¹/2 cup
Pineapple-orange juice .... ¹/2 cup
Plums (2″ across) 2
†Pomegranate ¹/2
Prune juice .... ¹/3 cup
†Prunes .... 3 medium
Raisins .... 2 tbsp.
Tangerines or tangelos .... 2 medium
Ugli fruit .... ¹/2 medium

List 5—Milk Exchanges
(Includes nonfat, low-fat, and whole milk)

If milk is used in food preparation, it must be included in the daily meal pattern.

Skim and very low-fat milk
One exchange of skim, very low-fat milk contains 12 grams of carbohydrate, 8 grams of protein, a trace of fat, and 90 calories.

*Buttermilk (made from skim milk) .... 1 cup
Evaporated skim milk .... ½ cup
Powdered milk (nonfat dry, before adding water) .... ⅓ cup
Skim milk .... 1 cup
Yogurt (plain, nonfat) .... 1 cup
½% or 1% fat milk .... 1 cup

Low-fat milk

One exchange of low-fat milk contains 12 grams of carbohydrate, 8 grams of protein, 5 grams of fat, and 120 calories.
Canned, evaporated 2% milk .... 1 cup
Soy milk .... 1 cup
Yogurt (plain and unflavored made with 2% fortified milk) .... 1 cup
2% fat milk .... 1 cup

Whole milk

One exchange of whole milk contains 12 grams of carbohydrate, 8 grams of protein, 8 grams of fat, and 150 calories.
Evaporated whole milk .... ½ cup
Goat milk .... 1 cup
Whole milk .... 1 cup
Yogurt (plain made from whole milk) .... 1 cup

Not allowed: condensed milk, malted beverages, chocolate beverages, sweetened fruit-flavored yogurt.

List 6—Fat Exchanges

One Fat Exchange contains 5 grams of fat and 45 calories.

To plan a diet low in saturated fat, select primarily those exchanges that appear in **bold type**. They are unsaturated.
*Almonds (dry roasted) .... 6 whole
Avocado (4″ diameter) .... ⅛
*Cashews (dry roasted) .... 1 tbsp.
*Margarine, diet .... 1 tbsp.
Margarine, soft tub .... 1 tsp.
*Nuts, other .... 1 tbsp.

Oil

Corn, cottonseed, peanut, safflower, soy, sunflower ...... 1 tsp.
*Olives .... 10 small or 5 large
*Peanuts
    Large .... 10 whole
    Small .... 20 whole
*Pecans .... 2 whole
*Pumpkin seeds .... 2 tsp.
*Seeds, pine nuts, sunflower without shells .... 1 tbsp.
*Walnuts .... 2 whole

Note: Nuts listed above are assumed to be salted. These are not allowed on sodium-restricted diets. However, unsalted nuts are permitted on sodium-restricted diets.

*Bacon (crisp) .... 1 strip
*Bacon fat .... 1 tsp.
Butter .... 1 tsp.
Chicken fat .... 1 tsp.
Chitterlings .... $1/2$ oz.
Coconut (shredded) .... 2 tbsp.
Coffee whitener (powder) .... 4 tsp.
Cream cheese .... 1 tbsp.
Cream, heavy .... 1 tbsp.
Cream, light .... 2 tbsp.
Cream, sour .... 2 tbsp.
*French dressing .... 1 tbsp.
*Gravy .... 2 tbsp.
*Italian dressing .... 1 tbsp.
Lard .... 1 tsp.
Margarine, regular stick .... 1 tsp.
Mayonnaise .... 1 tsp.
Nondairy cream substitute (liquid) .... 2 tbsp.
*Reduced calorie dressing
    Mayonnaise type .... 1 tbsp.
    Others .... 2 tbsp.
*Salad dressing (mayonnaise type) .... 2 tsp.
*Salt pork .... $1/4$ tsp.
*Tartar sauce .... 2 tsp.

Foods for Occasional Use

These foods can be worked into your meal plan. Check with your dietitian on frequency of use.

Food	Amount	Exchanges
Angel food cake	$^1/_{12}$ cake	2 Starch/Bread
Cake, no icing	$^1/_{12}$ cake or 3″ square	2 Starch/Bread, 2 Fat
Cookies	2 small (1³/₄″ across)	1 Starch/Bread, 1 Fat
Cookies, Lorna Doone	4	1 Starch/Bread, 1 Fat
Gingersnaps	3	1 Starch/Bread
Granola	$^1/_4$ cup	1 Starch/Bread, 1 Fat
Granola bar	1 small	1 Starch/Bread, 1 Fat
Ice cream, any flavor	$^1/_2$ cup	1 Starch/Bread, 2 Fat
Ice milk, any flavor	$^1/_2$ cup	1 Starch/Bread, 1 Fat
Sherbet, any flavor	$^1/_4$ cup	1 Starch/Bread
Snack chips, all varieties	1 oz.	1 Starch/Bread, 2 Fat
Vanilla wafers	6 small	1 Starch/Bread, 1 Fat
Yogurt, frozen low-fat	$^1/_3$ cup	1 Starch/Bread

APPENDIX 2

SEVEN-DAY MEAL PLAN

Day One

Breakfast

1 Fruit Exchange	List 4: 1 peach
1 Starch/Bread Exchange	List 1: ½ cup bran flakes
0 Meat Exchange	List 2:
0 Fat Exchange	List 6:
1 Milk Exchange	List 5: 8 oz. skim milk or
	1 cup nonfat yogurt

Noon meal

2 Meat Exchanges	List 2: 2 1-oz. meatballs
2 Starch/Bread Exchanges	List 1: 1 cup cooked pasta
2 Vegetable Exchanges	List 3: ½ cup sauce
	1 cup salad veggies
	free veggies
	lemon/vinegar or
	1 tbsp. fat-free dressing
0 Fruit Exchange	List 4:
0 Fat Exchange	List 6:
0 Milk Exchange	List 5:

Evening meal

3 Meat Exchanges	List 2: 3 oz. grilled chicken
1 Starch/Bread Exchange	List 1: 1 dinner roll

0 Vegetable Exchange — List 3: free dinner salad
2 Fruit Exchanges — List 4: 1 cup mixed fruit
0 Fat Exchange — List 6:
0 Milk Exchange — List 5:

Bedtime snack
1 Fruit Exchange — List 4: ½ banana
1 Starch/Bread and — List 1 and
   1 Fat Exchange — List 6: 6 small vanilla wafers

Day Two

Breakfast
2 Fruit Exchanges — List 4: 1 banana
1 Starch/Bread Exchange — List 1: 1 slice toast
1 Meat Exchange — List 2: 1 oz. Canadian bacon
1 Fat Exchange — List 6: 1 tbsp. diet margarine
½ Milk Exchange — List 5: ½ cup milk

Noon meal
2 Meat Exchanges — List 2: 2 oz. low-fat cheese
2 Starch/Bread Exchanges — List 1: 1 medium-large baked potato
1 Vegetable Exchange — List 3: ½ cup cooked broccoli
1 Fruit Exchange — List 4: 1¼ cups strawberries
0 Fat Exchange — List 6:
0 Milk Exchange — List 5:

Evening meal
2 Meat Exchanges — List 2: 2 oz. burger
1 Starch/Bread Exchange — List 1: ½ hamburger bun or 1 low-calorie bun
1 Vegetable Exchange — List 3: 1 cup tomatoes
1 Fruit Exchange — List 4: 1 orange
0 Fat Exchange — List 6:
0 Milk Exchange — List 5:

Bedtime snack
½ Milk Exchange — List 5: 4 oz. skim milk
1 Starch/Bread Exchange — List 1: 3 cups popcorn

Day Three

Breakfast

2 Fruit Exchanges	List 4: ¹/₂ cup orange juice
	¹/₂ banana
1 Starch/Bread Exchange	List 1: ¹/₂ cup Shredded Wheat®
0 Meat Exchange	List 2:
0 Fat Exchange	List 6:
¹/₂ Milk Exchange	List 5: 4 oz. skim milk

Noon meal

3 Meat Exchanges	List 2: 1 oz. low-fat cheese and
	2 oz. 95% fat-free luncheon
	meat
1 Starch/Bread Exchange	List 1: 2 slices diet bread =
	1 bread
1 Vegetable Exchange	List 3: 1 cup raw veggies
1 Fruit Exchange	List 4: 1 apple
1 Fat Exchange	List 6: 1 tbsp. diet mayonnaise
	free mustard, lettuce
0 Milk Exchange	List 5:

Evening meal (English muffin pizza)

2 Meat Exchanges	List 2: 2 oz. low-fat cheese
2 Starch/Bread Exchanges	List 1: 1 English muffin
1 Vegetable Exchange	List 3: ¹/₂ cup tomato sauce
	free veggies
1 Fruit Exchange	List 4: ¹/₂ cup fruit cocktail
0 Fat Exchange	List 6:
0 Milk Exchange	List 5:

Bedtime snack

¹/₂ Milk Exchange	List 5: 4 oz. skim milk
1 Starch/Bread Exchange	List 1: 1 baked 6″ pita bread
	(bake just until crisp, sprinkle
	with cinnamon)

Day Four

Breakfast

2 Fruit Exchanges	List 4: ¹/₂ cup orange juice and
	¹/₂ grapefruit

1 Starch/Bread Exchange	List 1: 1/2 cup cooked cereal
1 Meat Exchange	List 2: 1 scrambled egg (Pam® cooking spray or pop in microwave)
0 Fat Exchange	List 6:
1/2 Milk Exchange	List 5: 4 oz. skim milk

Noon meal

2 Meat Exchanges	List 2: 2 slices lean luncheon meat (1 oz. each)
2 Starch/Bread Exchanges	List 1: 2 slices bread
1 Vegetable Exchange	List 3: 1 cup raw carrots
1 Fruit Exchange	List 4: 1 apple
1 Fat Exchange	List 6: 1 tbsp. diet mayonnaise
0 Milk Exchange	List 5:

Evening meal

2 Meat Exchanges	List 2: 2 oz. meatloaf
1 Starch/Bread Exchange	List 1: 1 small potato
1 Vegetable Exchange	List 3: 1/2 cup cooked cauliflower free dinner salad
1 Fruit Exchange	List 4: 1/2 cup applesauce
0 Fat Exchange	List 6: 1 tbsp. fat-free dressing
0 Milk Exchange	List 5:

Bedtime snack

| 1/2 Milk Exchange | List 5: 4 oz. skim milk |
| 1 Starch/Bread Exchange | List 1: 3 graham crackers |

Day Five

Breakfast

1 Fruit Exchange	List 4: 1/2 banana
1 Starch/Bread Exchange	List 1: 1/2 English muffin
1 Meat Exchange	List 2: 1 tbsp. peanut butter
0 Fat Exchange	List 6:
1/2 Milk Exchange	List 5: 4 oz. nonfat yogurt (plain)

Noon meal (chef's salad)

2 Meat Exchanges	List 2: 1 oz. ham 1 oz. turkey
2 Starch/Bread Exchanges	List 1: 5 melba toast $1/2$ cup garbanzo beans
1 Vegetable Exchange	List 3: 1 cup veggies (broccoli, tomatoes, carrots) and free veggies for salad
2 Fruit Exchanges	List 4: 1 orange $1/2$ cup apple juice
0 Fat Exchange	List 6: 1 tbsp. low-calorie dressing or vinegar/lemon (free)
0 Milk Exchange	List 5:

Evening meal

2 Meat Exchanges	List 2: 2 oz. baked chicken breast
1 Starch/Bread Exchange	List 1: $1/2$ cup corn
1 Vegetable Exchange	List 3: $1/2$ cup cooked broccoli
1 Fruit Exchange	List 4: 1 pear
1 Fat Exchange	List 6: 1 tbsp. diet margarine on veggies

Bedtime snack

$1/2$ Milk Exchange	List 5: 4 oz. skim milk
1 Starch/Bread Exchange	List 1: 4 oz. nonfat frozen yogurt

Day Six

Breakfast

2 Fruit Exchanges	List 4: $1/2$ grapefruit and $1/2$ cup orange juice
2 Starch/Bread Exchanges	List 1: 1 bagel
0 Meat Exchange	List 2:
1 Fat Exchange	List 6: 1 tbsp. diet margarine or 1 tbsp. cream cheese
$1/2$ Milk Exchange	List 5: 4 oz. skim milk

Noon meal

2 Meat Exchanges	List 2: ½ cup cottage cheese
1 Starch/Bread Exchange	List 1: 8 animal crackers
1 Vegetable Exchange	List 3: 1 cup raw veggies and free veggies for salad
1 Fruit Exchange	List 4: ½ cup canned peaches
0 Fat Exchange	List 6:
0 Milk Exchange	List 5:

Evening meal

3 Meat Exchanges	List 2: 3 oz. grilled chicken or 2 oz. chicken and 1 oz. cheese
2 Starch/Bread Exchanges	List 1: 2 corn tortillas
1 Vegetable Exchange	List 3: ½ cup cooked green peppers/onions
0 Fruit Exchange	List 4:
0 Fat Exchange	List 6:
0 Milk Exchange	List 5:

Bedtime snack

1 Fruit Exchange	List 4: 1 apple
½ Milk Exchange	List 5: 4 oz. skim milk

Day Seven

Breakfast

2 Fruit Exchanges	List 4: ½ banana and ½ cup apple juice
1 Starch/Bread Exchange	List 1: ½ English muffin
1 Meat Exchange	List 2: 1 poached egg
1 Fat Exchange	List 6: 1 tbsp. diet margarine
½ Milk Exchange	List 5: 4 oz. skim milk

Noon meal

2 Meat Exchanges	List 2: 2 oz. 95% fat-free luncheon meat
2 Starch/Bread Exchanges	List 1: 2 slices whole wheat bread

1 Vegetable Exchange   List 3: 1 cup sliced tomatoes
1 Fruit Exchange   List 4: 1 apple
0 Fat Exchange   List 6:
0 Milk Exchange   List 5:

Evening meal
2 Meat Exchanges   List 2: 2 oz. baked chicken
1 Starch/Bread Exchange   List 1: 1 small baked potato
1 Vegetable Exchange   List 3: ½ cup cooked carrots
                                     free dinner salad
1 Fruit Exchange   List 4: ½ cup applesauce
0 Fat Exchange   List 6:
0 Milk Exchange   List 5:

Bedtime snack
1 Starch/Bread Exchange   List 1: 3 graham crackers
½ Milk Exchange   List 5: 4 oz. skim milk

APPENDIX 3

Exchange Lists for Meal Planning

You can use the Meal Planning List or the Daily Food Intake inventory to make a diary of what you eat each day. The Meal Planning List can be used for any daily caloric intake your doctor or nutritionist recommends. You can use the Seven-Day Meal Plan in Appendix 2 for a 1200-calorie a day diet. The Daily Food Intake inventory is set up for a 1200-calorie a day diet. The blank squares represent your allowance of exchanges from each food item for each day. Check a new box every time you eat an exchange from one of the groups. When you have checked all of the boxes, you will have eaten your allowance of food for the day.

NAME _____

Gm. CHO _____ Gm. PRO _____ Gm. FAT _____
TOTAL CALORIES _____

BREAKFAST   CHOOSE FROM   YOUR SAMPLE MENU

_____ Fruit Exchange   List 4 _____
_____ Starch/Bread Exchange   List 1 _____
_____ Meat Exchange   List 2 _____
_____ Fat Exchange   List 6 _____
_____ Milk Exchange   List 5 _____

NOON MEAL

_____ Meat Exchange	List 2 _____
_____ Starch/Bread Exchange	List 1 _____
_____ Vegetable Exchange	List 3 _____
_____ Fruit Exchange	List 4 _____
_____ Fat Exchange	List 6 _____
_____ Milk Exchange	List 5 _____

MID-AFTERNOON SNACK

_____
_____
_____

EVENING MEAL

_____ Meat Exchange	List 2 _____
_____ Starch/Bread Exchange	List 1 _____
_____ Vegetable Exchange	List 3 _____
_____ Fruit Exchange	List 4 _____
_____ Fat Exchange	List 6 _____
_____ Milk Exchange	List 5 _____

BEDTIME SNACK

_____
_____
_____

DAILY FOOD INTAKE

DAY _____

DATE _____

1,200-calorie Diet

Empty squares = daily food budget

MEAT	MILK	STARCH/ BREAD	FRUIT	VEG.	FAT	EXTRAS
☐	☐	☐	☐	☐	☐	☐
☐		☐	☐	☐		☐
☐		☐	☐			
☐		☐	☐			
☐		☐				

APPENDIX 4

THOUGHT RECORD

Date	Situation	Feeling(s)	Automatic Thoughts	Realistic Answers	Outcome

APPENDIX 5

DAILY FOOD PLANNERS

Today's Success Strategy

Date:

	Time	Place	Food Eaten	Calories	Thoughts & Feelings
Breakfast					
Lunch					
Dinner					
Snacks					
			TOTAL		

APPENDIX 5—Daily Food Planners (*Continued*)

Tomorrow's Battle Plan	Calories
Breakfast	
	subtotal:
Lunch	
	subtotal:
Dinner	
	subtotal:
Snacks	
	subtotal:
	TOTAL

APPENDIX 6

Organizations

For help or information on eating disorders, write to the address in your part of the country:

American Anorexia Nervosa Association, Inc.
418 East 76th Street
New York, New York 10021
(212) 734-1114

Anorexia Nervosa & Related Eating Disorders, Inc.
P.O. Box 5102
Eugene, Oregon 97405
(503) 344-1144

Anorexia Nervosa and Associated Disorders, Inc. (ANAD)
P.O. Box 7
Highland Park, IL 60035
(708) 831-3438

National Anorexic Aid Society, Inc.
1925 East Dublin Granville Rd.
Columbus, OH 43229
(614) 436-1112

Minirth-Meier Clinic
 National Headquarters
2100 N. Collins Blvd.
Richardson, Texas 75080
(214) 669-1733 or (800) 229-3000

For the Minirth-Meier Clinic nearest you, call toll-free (800) 545-1819.

NOTES

Chapter 1

1. George Bush, "Eating Disorders Awareness Week, 1990," *National Anorexic Aid Society, Inc.*, Jan.-Mar. 1991.
2. Dr. Myron Winick, "Nutrition in American Women," *Columbia University Journal of Nutrition and Health,* 2.
3. Raymond Vath, eating disorder symposium at Cedar Hills Hospital, Portland, Oregon, 7 Oct. 1983.
4. J. Allan Ryan, "Weight Reduction in Wrestling," *The Physician and Sports Medicine* 9 (Sept. 1981): 78–93.
5. Cathy Rigby McCoy, "A Onetime Olympic Gymnast Overcomes the Bulimia That Threatened Her Life," *People,* Aug. 1984.
6. Copyright 1982 by K. Kim Lampson. Used by permission.

Chapter 2

1. Marlene Boskind-White and William C. White, *Bulimarexia: The Binge-Purge Cycle* (New York: W. W. Norton, 1983), 45.

Chapter 3

1. Lawrence C. Kolb, *Modern Clinical Psychiatry* (Philadelphia: W. B. Saunders, 1975), 466.

Chapter 5

1. Regina Casper, "Bulimia: Its Incidence and Clinical Importance in Patients with Anorexia Nervosa," *Archives of General Psychiatry* 37 (Sept. 1980).
2. John 8:31–32 NIV.
3. Nehemiah 2:4–9
4. Ps. 73:23–24.

Chapter 7

1. Eph. 4:29 NIV.
2. See Gen. 1:26.
3. See 1 John 4:8.
4. Deut. 8:20.
5. Adapted from David Augsburger, *Caring Enough to Confront* (Ventura, Calif.: Regal Books, 1980), 15.
6. Prov. 15:23 NIV, italics added.
7. Prov. 21:23.
8. Prov. 18:13.
9. Eph. 4:15.
10. Phil. 3:13.
11. Prov. 17:14.
12. 1 Cor. 13:7 AMPLIFIED.
13. Eph. 4:32.
14. Eph. 4:2–3 NIV.

Chapter 8

1. David D. Burns, "The Perfectionism Scale," *Psychology Today,* Oct. 1980.
2. 2 Cor. 10:5 NIV.
3. "Controlling Depression through Cognitive Therapy," BMA Audio Cassette Publications, New York, 1982.
4. Matt. 11:28.
5. Ps. 34:15.

Chapter 9

1. Ps. 4:4.

Chapter 10

1. Adapted from Pamela Vredevelt and Kathryn Rodriguez, *Surviving the Secret: Healing the Hurts of Sexual Abuse,* rev. ed. (Tarrytown, NY: Gleneida Pub., 1992).
2. Ibid.

Chapter 11

1. Adapted from Vredevelt and Rodriguez, *Surviving the Secret* (Tarrytown, NY: Gleneida Pub., 1992).
2. Phil. 3:13–14 NIV.

Chapter 12
1. Nutritional Assessments and Counseling Center, Department of Nutrition and Food Sciences, Texas Woman's University, NACC 1/87 SS.
2. *Nutrition Concepts,* ARA Services, Inc.
3. Ibid.
4. Adapted from Irving Dardik and Denis Waitley, *Quantum Fitness* (New York: Pocket Books, 1984); and Dr. Frank Minirth, Dr. Paul Meier, Dr. Robert Hemfelt, and Dr. Sharon Sneed, *Love Hunger* (Nashville: Thomas Nelson, 1990).
5. *Nutrition Concepts,* ARA Services, Inc.
6. Adapted from C. L. Rock and J. Yager, "Nutrition and Eating Disorders: A Primer for Clinicians," *International Journal of Eating Disorders* 6 (1987): 276.

Chapter 13
1. Eph. 1:6.
2. Ps. 91:9–10, 14–16.
3. Eph. 1:6.

Chapter 14
1. Eph. 5:21 NIV.

Chapter 15
1. Bob Schwartz, *Diets Don't Work* (Galveston, Tex.: Breakthru Publishing, 1982).
2. Peter Nash, "A Matter of Fat," *Shape,* March 1985, 142.
3. Richard Stuart, *Act Thin, Stay Thin* (New York: W. W. Norton, 1979).
4. Ibid.
5. Nash, "A Matter of Fat."
6. Irving Dardik and Denis Waitley, *Quantum Fitness* (New York: Pocket Books, 1984), 56.
7. Richard Stuart, "Weight Loss and Beyond: Are They Taking It Off and Keeping It Off?" *Behavioral Medicine* (1980): 151–94.
8. 2 Cor. 10:5 NASB.
9. Prov. 23:7.
10. Deut. 31:6.

Chapter 16

1. Prov. 15:23 NIV
2. Prov. 12:18 NIV.
3. G. Lenihan and C. Sanders, "Guidelines for Group Therapy with Eating Disorder Victims," *Journal of Counseling and Development* 64 (Dec. 1984): 252–54.
4. 1 Cor. 12:25–26.
5. See Eph. 4:15.
6. Phil. 4:19.
7. Matt. 11:28.